Bruce Ansley has spent much of his life in the South Island. He was raised in New Brighton, Christchurch, and has lived in Dunedin, Christchurch, the Marlborough Sounds and Golden Bay. He has grown up with the south's people, its cities, towns, rivers, mountains, bush and plains. He has picked tobacco in Motueka, been a commercial fisherman in Fiordland and a deer farmer on Banks Peninsula. He has worked in radio, television and newspapers in the south too. For almost a quarter of a century he was the Christchurch-based writer for the *New Zealand Listener* magazine, until he became a full-time author. As a writer, tramper and traveller, and being professionally nosey, he has poked into many corners of the island, although nowhere near all of them: he finds the south and its people endlessly fascinating. He now lives on Waiheke Island to be close to his family, but his heart remains in the south. *Down South* is his eleventh book.

BRUCE ANSLEY

DOWN SOUTH

HarperCollins*Publishers*

HarperCollins_Publishers_
Australia • Brazil • Canada • France • Germany • Holland • India
Italy • Japan • Mexico • New Zealand • Poland • Spain • Sweden
Switzerland • United Kingdom • United States of America

First published in 2020
This edition published in 2023
by HarperCollins_Publishers_ (New Zealand) Limited
Unit D1, 63 Apollo Drive, Rosedale, Auckland 0632, New Zealand
harpercollins.co.nz

Copyright © Bruce Ansley 2020

Bruce Ansley asserts the moral right to be identified as the author of this work. This work is copyright. All rights reserved. No part of this publication may be reproduced, copied, scanned, stored in a retrieval system, recorded, or transmitted, in any form or by any means, without the prior written permission of the publisher.

A catalogue record for this book is available from the National Library of New Zealand.

ISBN 978 1 7755 4118 9 (pbk)
ISBN 978 1 7754 9148 4 (ebook)

Cover design and illustration by Julia Murray
Map illustrated by Julia Murray
Typeset in Sabon LT Std by Kirby Jones
Author photograph by Jane Ussher
Printed and bound in Australia by McPherson's Printing Group

For my sons,
Geoff, Sam and Simon

NEW ZEALAND
SOUTH ISLAND

KEY

GOLD/MINING

FARMING

TOURISM

EARTHQUAKES

CORNUCOPIA

TASMAN SEA

GAUNT CREEK
FRANZ JOSEF
FOX
MT COOK
TEKAPO
SOUTHERN
OMARAMA
MILFORD SOUND
WANAKA
MORVEN HILLS
GERTRUDE SADDLE
SKIPPERS CANYON
MAORI POINT
CAMPBELL PARK
QUEENSTOWN
CROMWELL
NEVIS
CLYDE/THE DUNSTAN
DOUBTFUL SOUND
MAVORA LAKES
SERPENTINE
MACRAES FLAT/ GOLDEN POINT
MIDDLEMARCH
WAIKOUAITI
GABRIELS GULLY /TUAPEKA
DUNEDIN
WOOLSHED /GLENORE
MILTON
MATAURA/TUTURAU
INVERCARGILL

CONTENTS

Prologue: The Quest   1

Chapter 1: City of Gold   9
Chapter 2: All That Glitters   53
Chapter 3: The Fleece   91
Chapter 4: The Gilded Life   142
Chapter 5: The New Argonauts   170
Chapter 6: A Silver Lining?   229
Chapter 7: The Place in the Sun   287
Chapter 8: The Bay at the End of the Rainbow   339

Acknowledgements   358

PROLOGUE

The Quest

Scarcely one hundred and fifty years ago the South Island had most of New Zealand's people and just about all of the money. It wasn't called the South Island then, for early European settlers were not romantic. The island was in the middle of the New Zealand mainland, so they named it Middle Island, and the southernmost island became South Island. The best I can say about all that is, at least they got the order right.

The first South Island soon shucked its sobriquet, preferring to be named after Stewart, an early sealer. Both names supplanted the original ones, the considerably more poetic Rakiura, meaning 'glowing skies', or the alternative Te Puka o Te Waka o Maui, 'the anchor stone of Maui's canoe'. Middle later became South, displacing the musical Te Wai Pounamu, 'waters of greenstone'. The settlers knew their sheep, but poetry was absent from their souls, and the original names were restored only in the twenty-first century.

Abel Tasman, a Dutch gent who in 1642 spent no more than the average annual vacation in the country and hastened away at the first sign of trouble, had mistaken the South Island for a rather grim extension of South America near Cape Horn, and dubbed it 'Staten Landt'. Back home in Holland, cartographers decided 'Nova Zeelandia' had a better ring to it. Evidently they did not think much of Tasman's discovery, for Zeeland was a Dutch province consisting of as much water as land and prone to flooding. Hardly anyone lived there.

Captain James Cook converted the name to 'New Zealand' and it, alas, took. But we cannot not blame Cook for 'Middle Island'. That was settler shorthand, stripped of all imagination and leaving only stark ambition, for those incomers saw Middle Island as a blank balance sheet. Maps of the island showed a fringe of coastal names and an empty interior, and the settlers set about filling it in. Mountains, lakes, plains, forests, fiords: all of them entered those first accounts as pounds sterling. Gold-miners found fortunes in the hills and rivers. Other settlers cleared and covered as much land as possible with sheep, 'the most remunerative investment for money,' exulted one report. After all, the real estate was almost free: 'The Government allows all persons to purchase land wherever they may please at a fixed price of two pounds an acre ... upon 55,000 pounds invested ... a clear profit of 36,578 pounds [can be] realised in three years' time, plus good annual dividends free from all deductions.'

The fact that the island was crisscrossed with Maori trails connecting their great industry, pounamu, with its markets, and dotted with kaika nohoanga, or settlements, was of no consequence. Settlers simply disregarded the tangata whenua.

They either took the land or negotiated its purchase, and there was not very much difference between the two. The so-called Kemp Purchase of 1848, for example, resulted in some 5.5 million hectares of Maori land being 'bought' for £2000, which, converted to modern currency, equals parking meter change. The Waitangi Tribunal found that the Crown had taken 14 million hectares of land from Ngai Tahu — more than half of the landmass of New Zealand. The iwi was left with only 14,470 hectares. The Crown, the tribunal said, had acted unconscionably and in repeated breach of the Treaty of Waitangi. But the Crown, at the time, consisted of the very settlers who were busy stealing Maori land, their hands, their arms, their entire bodies buried deep in the lolly jar.

So it was not surprising that the name 'Middle Island' suited settler ambitions very well. An anonymous land could be exploited. It needed no fancy name, no higher philosophy. Even the novelist Samuel Butler's objective in taking up the huge Mesopotamia Station in the upper Rangitata Valley was to double his capital and leave the country as soon as possible. He succeeded, and many of his fellow Europeans did too. Soon sheep barons bestrode mountains, valleys and plains, and wealthy southerners ruled the embryonic government.

Middle Island became the centre of their universe and their pot of gold. As Kenneth B. Cumberland and R.P. Hargreaves noted in 'Middle Island Ascendant' (*New Zealand Geographer*, 1955), 'The contrasts between the two major islands were sharpened, for now a greater proportion of the population was found in the Middle Island — almost two-thirds in 1867 when the search for gold was at its height … In the Middle Island the grazier and prospector penetrated both the dry, treeless 'continental interior' and the mountain highland ... In the late 1870s the golden fleece had become the cornerstone of the colony's economy.' And the Middle Island possessed the golden fleece.

Everything changed, of course. The gold ran out. The land, particularly the high country, was sucked dry, first by burn-off, later by over-exploitation. Middle Island's population dominance over the north peaked in 1881. Then people began drifting north. By 1901 Middle Island was no longer 'ascendant'.

Middle Island officially became South Island only in 1907. By then its fortunes had begun a slow decline. Yet when I was growing up in Christchurch in the 1960s the South Island still seemed Middle Island Ascendant. Farmers rode on the sheep's back. They drove American Fords and Chevs in an era when a 'new' car was one less than twenty years old. Christchurch was fat and happy.

I went to Canterbury University when it boasted the best-known academics in the land. It was the haven of choice for some of the nation's finest architects, artists and writers. If you wanted to be a doctor, surveyor, dietitian or dentist, you went further south, to Otago University. For a good time in a summer paradise, you went to Nelson, where you could not only parade on Tahunanui's beach, but pay for it by picking tobacco.

I never expected to move from the south. Why would I? The television studios were the most prolific in the country, it had thriving newspapers, the best live theatre and universities, great music. But by the end of the millennium the South Island's population was down to a quarter of New Zealand's and the ratio was falling.

A new golden fleece was proving elusive. Christchurch was once convinced that it could become the Silicon Valley of New Zealand. The West Coast still believes there is uranium in its mountains. At the top of the island, wonder crops, from blueberries to green tea, came and went.

Many a new candidate raised its head, ran the gauntlet, and collapsed exhausted. But the golden fleece still had to be somewhere ... didn't it?

Perhaps it lay in Aucklanders escaping a city where property prices had defied every law of gravity. Average home buyers there had only two choices: to take on mortgages whose repayment times were measured galactically, or to move somewhere south. The South Island resounds with stories of fleeing Aucklanders cashing in, or up, on their high property prices. In Nightcaps, an old coal town in Southland, I once met a woman who'd bought her house for $10 and was well pleased with her bargain. That time has passed, but I could still find a house in Nightcaps for only $170,000.

In Blackball, another old mining town on the West Coast, houses scarcely reached double figures before its renaissance. When I last looked, the cheapest house in that town was an original miner's cottage on sale for a mere $85,000. At those prices, the south might still be a bolthole.

In the shadow of the Rock and Pillar Range, as deep in the Otago hinterland as you can go, I met Nigel, who had the area's most unlikely occupation: controlling traffic. I was driving along a rough track leading to an ancient gold mine called Golden Point. The track crossed a road leading to the mighty Macraes gold mine, which outsizes Golden Point by a factor of approximately

10 million. Huge trucks crossed the track, carrying rocks from what the mine called a processing plant but I thought of as a dark satanic mill. They seemed to be driven mainly by women, unlikely successors to the grizzled chaps living monastic lives in their little stone huts at Golden Point. Every one of the trucks was capable of squashing my car to the thickness of a Zig Zag tissue.

Nigel's job was to keep me intact, and in the process of discussing my chances I learned that he'd sold his house in Papakura, south of Auckland, and bought one in Middlemarch, south of almost everywhere, for about a quarter of the price. Nigel's wife and children loved it. The move had made him prosperous and he was not so much happy as positively jolly.

Alternatively, perhaps, the new golden fleece could be found in cows, credited by one prime minister with economy-regenerating powers (he didn't have to swim in the rivers). Or in earthquakes, seen by some (usually people who didn't live with the terror or the sadness) as a golden goose for the billions of dollars in rebuilding costs.

It has to be said that the million or so South Islanders view changes with sangfroid. They love their land. If taken out of it, they long for the tussock, the high country, the great lakes and big skies, the crashing surf, their towns and cities, their lack of anonymity. Within themselves, they even speak differently. Southlanders roll their r's: 'earrrly to bed, earrrly to rise'. Central Otago accents are as crisp as their apricots. Christchurch affected an English inflection. The West Coast accent could shatter glass.

All of them have the differences of people who stay, who are content with their place. They like its style, pace, weather. They live in towns that have remained towns rather than outposts of cities spreading like deserts. These are places you come across suddenly, with town boundaries and community halls and swimming pools, where people take 50 km/h signs seriously and spend their lives and count themselves lucky.

To me they're familiar, and comforting, and I can't imagine New Zealand without them. So I decided on a quest, a search for the new golden fleece, the pot of gold, the unearthed riches that might change their fortunes in this great southern land. The bright future. Where might it be found now?

It immediately became clear that the Ngai Tahu, the people so assiduously robbed by the waves of new settlers, had already found it. Their injustices were addressed late in the twentieth century, when the government paid compensation of $170 million plus first dibs on any Crown property and utilities being disposed of, as well as every bit of pounamu or greenstone lying in the tribal area, which along with other items in the settlement were worth far more than the cash. The iwi took the money and grew an empire worth around $2 billion at last count. The dispossessed had become the possessed. They'd succeeded beyond any expectations but their own, and had done so without the usual clamour and flag-waving, much less the mansions on Waiheke Island or personal helicopter parks.

But others must have struck it rich, taken the lid off the pot of gold. Who were they, where did they live and most importantly, how did they do it? Could the south rise again, shake the dust from its garments, cock a snoot at the north and take back its crown?

The idea of a search, a quest for a golden fleece goes back a long, long way of course. In ancient Greece, a man called Jason and a bunch of his fellow heroes, the Argonauts, voyaged in his boat, the *Argo,* beyond the edge of the known world. Jason's mission was to find the golden fleece of a winged ram and remove it from the keeping of a sleepless dragon. The golden fleece symbolised nobility and power and Jason needed it to reclaim his fortunes. It was a deathly mission and it took him absolutely ages, dodging Sirens and so forth, but eventually he found the golden fleece, even if it didn't bring him much luck.

I lacked a boat called the *Argo* but I drove an aging Subaru. And the South Island has plenty of rams and quite a few sleepless dragons, if fewer Sirens. Emulating a man called Jason was fair enough too, given the name's popularity in the south.

I was ready to venture beyond the edge of the known world, or as many northerners know it, Cook Strait. Tally-ho.

CHAPTER ONE

City of Gold

Mataura was an odd place to begin the quest. The little Southland town had seen better days. Worse ones too. The good days were when the big industries — the coal mines beneath the town, the dairy factory, the freezing works, the paper mill — were booming. The bad days were when they closed down.

The dairy factory had started in 1887 and lasted almost a century until the books turned red and the accountants moved in. The freezing works had opened in 1893 and was still going, in diminished form. The paper mill was set up in the 1870s, using power generated by the Mataura Falls. Its series of owners read like a New Zealand business roll of honour: Bain, Coulls, Fletchers, Forest Products, Elders, Carter Holt Harvey. Asian competition wrote its epitaph. In 2000, after 124 years in business, the mill shut down and 155 people lost their jobs. Just when it seemed to have hit bottom, it was revealed that the old mill had been used by Bluff aluminium smelter contractors to store toxic waste.

When I last visited, a nearby fibreboard plant was still operating, but Mataura had an air of disappointment about it. Too many people had left, too little money was coming in. The former All Black Justin Marshall came from the town, and the famed racehorse Cardigan Bay. Both had left, of course. A few years previously, newspapers had reported that Mataura boasted the lowest-priced house in the land: it sold for $10,000. More recently a rather nice-looking villa of the style that would be rushed in Auckland sold for $9000. Even now, I could have bought the most expensive house on the market, a restored 1910 villa, for around $300,000.

Mataura was in decline, however gentle. It lay in ninth place (out of ten) in the government's official list of deprived towns. Yet I'd always liked the place, and today I was drinking coffee in a cheerful little café crowded with people who seemed happy enough with their lot and not at all deprived.

The town site had been part of the Murihiku Purchase negotiated with the Ngai Tahu in 1853 by Walter Mantell, a young government bureaucrat who seared his name in history by relieving Maori of their land. On behalf of the Otago Provincial Council, he bought the entire bottom of the South Island — all of the land below a line drawn between Milford Sound and the Nuggets. (Ngai Tahu complained that Fiordland was to have been excluded from the purchase, but that complaint, with most of their arguments, was brushed aside.) He paid just £2600 for this superb chunk of real estate and spent the rest of his life haunted by his broken promises to Ngai Tahu, as well he might have done: he'd told them they would have schools and hospitals outside every village, and substantial reserves. Instead they got almost nothing: no schools or hospitals, and reserves of just 1970 hectares.

Mataura has risen and fallen since then. Now it's a town on State Highway 1 in deepest Southland, offering no good reason for traffic to stop. Drivers can easily miss its most significant feature, its falls, as the arches on the town's old bridge hide them a little upstream. There the mighty Mataura River thunders over a sandstone ledge, falling some six metres so powerfully the water boils for half a kilometre below.

The falls are mesmerising. They're not high by New Zealand standards. The famed Huka Falls are double their height and, closer to Mataura, the Humboldt Falls in Fiordland dump water 275 metres from top to bottom. But Mataura's falls are more impressive for their urban setting. They are jammed between industrial buildings pressing so close on either side that they seem to be cliffs themselves, magnifying the river and echoing the power and roar of the falls. From a certain angle, the water seems to flow from their walls.

One of those buildings is the old paper mill, and people here worry that the toxic chemicals being stored inside, a by-product of the smelter, could be inundated by floodwaters (when the Mataura River rages, it's best to stay away), releasing dangerous ammonia gas to the general detriment of Mataura's remaining population. The smelter and the New Zealand taxpayer (of course) shared the cost of removing it in 2023.

The falls are what gave rise to the town of Mataura. In the early days of European settlement, the Mataura River was a natural barrier to every kind of traffic along the coast, perhaps less treacherous than its neighbour, the Clutha (then the Molyneux) but demanding equal respect. The problem was this: if you wanted to travel between, say, Invercargill and Dunedin, you had two choices. First, you could go by sea. That meant you had to sail out into Foveaux Strait, where the wild west winds fused as they crossed the Tasman and were funnelled through a passage so notorious that even now, in an age of sophisticated electronics and reliable machinery, it's New Zealand's most crowded marine graveyard. Then you had to round the bottom corner of New Zealand, where the fangs of Waipapa Point slavered. In 1881, they gobbled up 131 passengers and crew from the passenger steamer *Tararua*. If you survived all of this, you had to travel up a coast so accustomed to shipwrecks that the names on its points, capes and bays read like a maritime roll of honour. My own experience of sailing along that stretch of coast still awakens me on dark nights, for any language of ripping yarns — treacherous, wild, fanged, murderous — is enfeebled by the real thing.

The alternative was to travel overland, which involved you in a series of different adventures, almost as dangerous. The first of these was crossing the Mataura River. For a time travellers made do with a couple of shallow river crossings, but in 1859 the Otago Provincial Government built a wooden bridge at Mataura. It rested on a rock in the falls and was rickety. Travellers could walk across it, but the falls sprayed the walkway and it was always slippery, and vehicles and stock still had to cross by ferry.

The government men had the answer: they blew up the falls to ease the bridge crossing. Which, of course, ruined them. Thereafter, the river fell a little upstream, in a less poetic manner, but colonists did not have the time for poetry. The insult to the river didn't work in any event: the bridge was destroyed by a flood a couple of years later.

But the ferry remained, and a settlement grew around the crossing. There was a hotel, of course. It was built by the council and leased to the very first permanent inhabitants of Mataura, a man called John MacGibbon and his family. MacGibbon did well out of the council. He made money from his hotel, which had a captive clientele, and charged a toll to cross the river. He must have wept tears of disappointment when, in 1868, the council built a new suspension bridge downstream from the falls. A new hotel was built and named, of course, the Bridge Hotel. The original hotel was moved downstream and renamed Camerons Hotel; it was destroyed by fire in 1914.

A town grew around the new bridge, then a school and a railway line. Then a paper mill and a freezing works. In March 1897, the *Mataura Ensign* described a visit to the works, at

> a rate of progress which varied as the temperature of the different apartments fell away to the lower notches of the thermometer, or rose to a point which, while not pronouncedly frigid, brought back to memory that period of the year when red noses are more fashionable than comforting to look upon; until at last the sounds and scenes of … the busy outside world were once again contemplated by the visitors, and all appreciated, for a time at least, the genial rays reflected from Old Sol's glowing countenance.

The party then set off for the slaughtering department:

> Here were found … a bevy of bloodthirsty toilers, who despatched and 'dressed' (undressed is a better word) their

victims in a manner which for dexterity would put to the blush the most accomplished Armenian-killing Turk owning allegiance to the 'sick man of Europe' ... Every self-respecting fat sheep, prime lamb, and selected rabbit in the province would deem it a distinguishing honour to be introduced to the British consumer through the medium of the Mataura Freezing Works.

Ah, those were the days. Newspaper reporters could let their pens take flight.

Since then Mataura has seen its glory days come and go and its prospects tremble in the balance, but its proper place in history might lie just downriver, at a rather ordinary spot which, had Mataura been a little larger, might have been one of its suburbs. It's called Tuturau, and it was the place I'd come here to visit.

Tuturau's history far outweighs its size, which is just as well, for the place isn't very big at all. You might easily drive along the river and nip through it without noticing. It's a spot by and large known only to the residents of its scattered farmhouses, yet it enjoyed its place in the sun not just once or twice, but four times.

I drove through there scarcely knowing where I was. A school, a few houses, farms, Southland's lush green — it could have been anywhere in that velvety province, once covered by a latticework of small farming towns. It was a late spring day in November, drizzly. A roadside sign marking a historic reserve was the only indication to outsiders that this particular spot in the green might be important. At exactly the moment I reached it, the sky turned to iron. First heavy rain then snow battered the windshield.

It stopped a few hundred metres further on. I turned around, went back, and at the reserve it happened again: rain and snow, stopping immediately after I passed. I'm not superstitious, but I am, of course, a writer. Yet my wife Sally was with me. She curbs my excesses, but was as astonished as I was.

An obelisk on a nearby hill declared: 'The last fight between North and South Island Maoris [sic] in which the southerners were victorious took place in this locality in December 1836.' They'd fought the south and the south won.

It was not even a place: it was a 'locality'. The obelisk was the more remarkable for what it did not say, probably because the story was as much fable as history at the time it was erected, although both Pakeha and Maori historians have since confirmed it. A northern chief, Te Puoho, made an incredible journey from Golden Bay down the West Coast, crossing its wild rivers, penetrating its thick forests, risking cliffs and storming seas all but impassable even today. After crossing over the Haast Pass into Otago and Southland, he travelled down the Matarua River, knocked off what was called both a settlement and a pa (depending on which version you read) killed its inhabitants and took up residence, all with the intention of wiping out the South Island iwi, the Ngai Tahu — a scheme he described poetically as 'skinning the Ngai Tahu eel from tail to head'. The southerners were not to be trifled with, of course, and as soon as they were organised they killed Te Puoho before he could fire a shot.

The scene of this drama did not look like much. A sign in the reserve told part of the story. If it weren't for the obelisk, it would be just another hill in a province full of them. Yet this tiny place had seen ambition, courage, tragedy.

It was important for another reason, though, probably the reason the kaik, the village of Tuturau, was there in the first place. I crossed the road from the reserve and climbed a bank. Here the Mataura River shallowed, rippling across a shoal that offered a rare crossing place on the river. From the shore it did not look easy, and I would only have tried it as a last resort. But until the mid-nineteenth century, before the construction of the bridge at Mataura village upstream, it *was* a last resort, for this was the best, almost the only, place to cross the river — the reason for its second appearance in the history books. A rare and treasured facility on the mighty Mataura, Tuturau's ford was certainly why inhabitants of the embryonic Pakeha settlements in Otago and Southland knew the place.

The passage it offered across the river led to Tuturau's third, and biggest, claim to fame. By the 1850s, gold had already made fleeting appearances in European chronicles of the south. Traces had been found in the Molyneux (today Clutha) River in the early 1850s, and probably earlier. Maori knew it was there, but they could see no sensible use for it, as it was too soft for tools and no good for weapons.

In December 1856, Charles Ligar, who had been the Surveyor-General of New Zealand until he resigned that year, was searching for grazing land when he found gold in the bed of the Mataura while crossing the river at Tuturau. Perhaps he rushed out of the water shrieking 'Gold!'. But that seems unlikely: Ligar was a respectable gent. He merely reported that he believed there was 'a remunerative goldfield in the neighbourhood'.

From this distance, the fact that he reported it at all seems remarkable. Wouldn't you keep the news to yourself for as long as possible? Otherwise, you'd be sharing your find with every able person who could afford a gold pan, and a good few of those who were neither able nor solvent. But those early prospectors didn't keep good news quiet. They told everyone about it, and Ligar, who seems to have been an accidental prospector, did so too.

The reaction was predictable, at first. Vincent Pyke, variously gold-miner, civil servant, goldfields administrator, journalist, politician, businessman and historian (a truncated description but in short, Pyke was a twenty-four-carat all-rounder), reported: 'If Mr Charles Ligar had thrown dynamite in its most diabolical form ... it is questionable whether he would have created greater consternation.' Just like dynamite, the announcement went off with a bang — followed by a long silence. Dunedin decided to remain unmoved.

Little Tuturau had one last flash of fame. Its fourth appearance in the early history of the South Island owed itself to a man called Sam Perkins, a whaler from Fortrose, at the mouth of the Mataura River in Toetoes Bay. He was a venerable-looking gent, with the kind of white hair that people trusted, and in 1861 some 3000 miners did. He tricked them into following him from the rich diggings at Gabriel's Gully near Lawrence to Tuturau, for a fee. The miners forked over their cash to Sam. Most turned back, but he still had 500 men behind him when he reached the Mataura, supposedly the 'new Eldorado'.

In an era of wondrous discoveries when poor men could become rich overnight, less likely stories had proved to be true. Sam took them down to Tuturau. He showed them the spot then sought to depart with his loot, but not quickly enough. The miners might have been greedy, but they weren't suckers. They quickly discovered the truth and scragged Sam before he got very far at all. Evidently repentant, he suggested the miners shoot him — not such a bad idea when they were contemplating cutting off parts of his body.

The miners proved more civilised, however. They put him before a jury, which sentenced him to two dozen lashes, immediately administered. Only his hair was cut off. Sam died not long afterwards, drowned while fording the Titiroa Stream, but his story lived on: that part of the Mataura River is known as Sam's Grief and a horse trek, a cavalcade, still follows his track to this day.

Tuturau reverted to the quiet place it had been before, and remains today. After my visit I read a story in the local newspaper, *The Southland Times*, about two families from Tuturau, farmers who had been neighbours for 154 years. They'd arrived there in the mid-nineteenth century. One of those families got its capital from the goldfields.

*

Dunedin remained determinedly unexcited by the discovery of gold more or less on its premises. The city establishment was headed by William Cargill, a Scotsman who had become Otago's superintendent when the settlers won self-government in 1853. Cargill had two main goals: imposing religious adherence and maintaining order. The two had been forged into a growth somewhere inside his brain and, whatever their worth, they left little room for anything else. He scowled from his photographs, his brow lowering over a rather self-satisfied smile, the whole composition lurking below well-trimmed hair so rigidly brushed back that it looked like a gorse hedge in a gale. Cargill had been born in Edinburgh, 'Auld Reekie'. Some of his company wanted to call their new place of residence 'New Reekie'. Fortunately they were overruled.

Though publicly sanctimonious, Cargill was privately rather active. He fathered seventeen children and the ten who survived were expensive. New Zealand offered a solution and he took it. He arrived on 23 March 1848 with his family and 243 devout settlers and set about establishing the Free Church of Scotland at the head of Otago Harbour.

Immigrants had to be tough to survive in a place where a stiff winter southerly could freeze a forge. But Cargill ruled with a rod of iron. He used it to beat off complaints of intolerance and despotism and tyranny, and there was no shortage of those. Invercargill was named in his honour, possibly because it was far enough away from him to feel generous.

A monument to Cargill stands in Dunedin's Princes Street. Oddly, it is rather ornate, even light-hearted, the kind of thing you might see made in icing atop an expensive wedding cake. Spires and pinnacles jut out, the designer perhaps having had the spiky Cargill in mind. Political opponents alleged the gargoyles represented Cargill's children. When it was built in 1864, four years after Cargill died, it was supposed to be a lamp, a drinking fountain and a garden ornament. Neither the water nor the garden ever appeared. Although the structure stood above an underground toilet, passing drunks used the fountains as urinals and the light went out in the early 2000s. The monument was designed by an engineer, evidently roped in for his one and only shot at public sculpture. The newspapers hated it, of course; public sculpture has always been a popular target for editorials. A sign on the monument describes Cargill as the founder of Dunedin, although another plaque on a nearby rock acknowledges that the Waitaha, Kati Mamoe and Kai Tahu people had been using the same place for centuries.

Cargill's imprint is everywhere in Dunedin, not only in physical forms such as city architecture, but in the metaphysical too, for Dunedin can be a stern city. The ruins of Cargill's Castle still stand near St Clair beach. The castle was built by William's son Edward, a dead spit for his dad, a member of Parliament and mayor of Dunedin — for a year. The castle is an odd mix, rather like the Cargill family. It is described variously as Italianate and Gothic Revival, but it looked a little Mexican to me, as if Clint Eastwood might pop out and let fly with his six-gun.

Cargill and his southern burghers did not want gold to be found on their premises, and I wondered whether he was so disdainful of its discovery because he foresaw a loss of control. The new societies growing in the south were set on re-creating little Britains, ostensibly egalitarian but aping their British roots. Jack was as good as his master, until he became master himself.

This state of affairs was embodied by Edward Gibbon Wakefield, a middle-class, well-educated gent with a penchant for underage girls: parliament let him off for eloping with one but spat the dummy when he did it again, this time with a fifteen-year-old heiress. Ed was shunted off to Newgate Prison for a three-year stretch. It gave him time to ponder, not so much on his debt to society as what society could do for him. He decided his number-one objective should be to enrich himself, Edward

Gibbon Wakefield, and he had just the way of doing it. He formed the New Zealand Land Company, which was eventually involved in the establishment of Dunedin city, as well as Nelson and Christchurch.

The idea was to buy land as cheaply as possible from its Maori owners — this was before the process became popularly known as 'ripping them off' — and sell it to moneyed British owners. The hard work would be done by British labourers, servants and so on, who'd be offered a 'new life' and carted to the new colony cheaply. Thus a cross-section of British society would be moved halfway round the globe and preserved intact.

The company didn't last long and Wakefield's brother Arthur was killed in the 1843 Wairau Affray near Blenheim when he attempted to arrest the Ngati Toa chief Te Rauparaha and his associates for presuming to resist the company's fraudulent seizure of Maori land. But the notion of a transplanted British society found fertile soil in the new colony. Dunedin established a hierarchy before you could say *Dun Eideann* — Gaelic for Edinburgh, and the long version of Dunedin's name.

The gold discovery confronted the town with two social problems. The first was practical: if the working class ran off to the goldfields, who'd do the work? The middle class and the fledgling aristocracy would be left without labourers, without cooks and gardeners and people to fix things, and an awful lot of things needed fixing in a rapidly growing town. Not that Dunedin was anything to boast about, with its mud streets, poor buildings, high unemployment and few prospects.

The second was left unsaid. Southern towns with strong ties to the Home Country not only retained a hierarchy but also suffered from colonial cringe, which resulted in much bowing and scraping and constant attempts by citizens to assess who they should cringe before, and who should cringe before them. Such assessments were based on the suburbs people lived in, the schools they went to, the accents they spoke in, the clubs and societies they belonged to. New Zealand's egalitarian reputation came in handy for propaganda purposes, but in fact the brave new world down south had quickly established a social order and maintained it diligently.

A gold strike threatened that order. It made unworthy people rich. What was the purpose of striving and accumulating and setting yourself apart if some poorly educated down-and-out could become rich in the flash of a pan, literally? Gold gave working people an unhealthy desire for riches, an ambition that would eventually erode the proper social structure. Business people, farmers and, of course, 'the wider community', whose interests were always rediscovered in tricky situations, would all be inconvenienced.

The prospect of sudden riches would undermine the value of land that was then being grabbed by wealthy pastoralists, whose sheep and cattle would disappear into the gold-seekers' pots. A gold strike could wreck — not just wreck, chuck dynamite into — a proper social order, and only God knew what might happen then. Besides, gold was a frivolous substance. According to the editor of *The Otago Witness*, 'Flour is more necessary than gold, and may be more valuable.' That might not be the stupidest newspaper editorial ever written, given the competition, but it's certainly up there among the leaders.

William Cargill found the very idea of a gold rush distasteful. It was the devil's work. Gold was for the unworthy. Easy riches had no place in the Presbyterian way of things. So the Cargill-led establishment pooh-poohed Ligar's report. They sat on it, squished it. And when John Turnbull Thomson, Otago's surveyor, told the council a little later that 'the existence of gold is undoubted', they dumped his report into that magic disappearing box that bureaucrats always keep handy.

The Otago Witness either led the argument or reflected it. The newspaper derided early accounts of gold discoveries. It dismissed reports of a huge nugget on the grounds that the paper hadn't been able to find any witnesses, which would have been quite reasonable if they hadn't been so set on establishing their case: gold was just a silly story.

It seems amazing, to me at least, that Dunedin turned its back on the golden glow of its hinterland. But that's what the city did, at least until so many people were striking gold it was forced to admit the prospect of becoming enormously rich. Lloyd Carpenter, an academic at Lincoln University who has not only studied the subject but also has some experience of gold-mining himself, suggests another reason: the city had been founded by Presbyterians staunchly against gambling, and gold-mining was a gamble.

Yet the evidence piled up: gold here, gold there, until six months after Ligar's discovery, the *Witness* changed its view. Perhaps it was time to rattle the bones of those rumours, establish a body of evidence one way or the other. Why not offer a reward to anyone who could prove a substantial find? Even the Provincial Council, notorious for its short arms and long pockets, was at last poked into gear. All right, they said, £500 for a decent find, part of it to be paid when 100 ounces had been brought to Dunedin, the balance when production hit 500 ounces. To put that in perspective, 500 ounces would now be worth about $1 million.

*

Otago's first major goldfield would not be established near Tuturau, in fact, but further north. I found it by taking the inland route south to Central Otago, passing Lake Tekapo, crossing the Mackenzie Country and then climbing over the Lindis Pass.

You can get stuck on the Lindis. I've ploughed over it in mid-winter when abandoned cars squatted at odd angles at the roadside, or peered forlornly from ditches. Yet it's not among the south's famed alpine passes because this is dry country: it lacks the drama of Arthur's or the Haast. The Lindis's golden colours and gentle folds are essential rites of passage for budding landscape artists and still brighten living-room walls all over the country — they are as instantly recognisable as Mount Cook.

The highway climbs quite gently from Omarama, crosses the pass and drops abruptly into the Lindis Valley. At the bottom I could see, through the willows, an old road following the opposite side of the river. This was the wonderfully named Old Faithful Road, probably the road a man named Sam McIntyre was working on in 1861, when it was the main road through the valley.

Sam had prospected for gold in California and, as he and his road gang hacked away at the tough, stony ground with their picks and shovels, he was more and more certain he'd seen this kind of country before. Why, it looked just like the ground he'd mined for gold on the other side of the Pacific, didn't it?

So, in his spare time, he picked and panned and — bingo! — gold. Within days he and his mates had four pounds of the precious metal. A few weeks later, in April of that year, 400 diggers were working the field.

I visited the remains of the Lindis Hotel, which was thrown up during the initial excitement then rebuilt in stone ten years later. It became a boarding house, store, post office, school and private home and was finally abandoned in 1951. The Department of Conservation had restored the ruin, and I stood inside it working out its little rooms and thinking that it wasn't much bigger than the state house it had in a way become.

Relics of gold workings lay nearby, along with Wattie Thompson's old concrete hut. Wattie was the area's last goldminer. He worked Camp Creek after the Second World War, but his claim was wiped out by a flash flood in 1971.

No one, apparently, got rich in the new diggings, and soon something far more exciting, something really big, lured the miners away. A month after the Lindis reached its peak, Gabriel Read, an Australian, discovered gold at what became Gabriel's Gully in Central Otago. A truly enormous gold rush gathered momentum. Two months after that, the Lindis was deserted, abandoned but for a brief reprise during the Depression years, when the government turned unemployed workers into temporary diggers.

The departing miners must have been delighted. By God it was cold there. Gabriel's Gully wasn't much warmer at that time of the year, but it was far, far, richer.

In fact, Gabriel Read was not the first to find gold in an area that was to become New Zealand's fabled Tuapeka. That honour went to Edward Peters, aka 'Black Peter', a native of Bombay, now Mumbai. Peters was a handsome man, described at the time as 'Eurasian', meaning a mix of Asian and European — the term is now fortunately obsolete. The few pictures of him show wide-spaced eyes and a husky beard beneath a strong face. He looks both mild and good-natured, which was just as well, for he must have needed a sense of humour: he arrived in New Zealand as a cook on a sailing ship and was promptly thrown into jail for desertion.

Black Peter was certainly well travelled, for he'd been a gold-miner in California. On his release from jail he took up residence in Glenore, and worked as a shepherd, a hut-builder and bullock driver. In 1857 he took a team of bullocks across the Tuapeka River, which flows through Lawrence to join the Clutha at Tuapeka Mouth. He stopped for a drink of water at the point where the main road from Milton into Central Otago crosses the river now, and at that moment a thought crossed his mind, a notion that still reverberates the best part of two centuries later: what if there was gold in this here river?

He scooped some sludge in his pannikin. A speck of gold appeared. He panned in other nearby places, notably one called the Woolshed. He found gold there too. He took a sample to Dunedin, where officials declared it the best yet brought to the town. It indicated a workable goldfield and so the Woolshed diggings became the first large find in Otago but certainly not the last. Black Peter had started something huge.

In 1861 he claimed the reward, not for the last time. He'd discovered goldfields near the Tuapeka and Waitahuna rivers, and near Tokomairiro, and he believed the £500 bounty should go to him rather than Read. In that oddly courtly, courteous, curious world, Read would probably not have argued with him. The council gathered in its kilts. Black Peter's application was refused and a later one with it. (Read subsequently got double the amount of the original reward, £1000, demonstrating that even in those good old days when Jack was allegedly as good as his master, everyone deserved a fair go, even Australians ... except if you were 'half-caste'.)

More than twenty years later, in 1885, the provincial government granted Black Peter £50, on condition that the public contributed the same amount. Generous to a fault? I'd say so. The money was invested, and Black Peter got ten bob a week out of it, but he must have had a tight retirement, light years from the riches he'd discovered. He died in the Dunedin Benevolent Institution in 1893. Later historians dug him up as regularly as he once shovelled the riverbeds, but rather too late for poor Peters.

Edward Peters was never secretive. He was the opposite, in fact. If you wanted to talk gold, Black Peter was your man. He'd show the gold to you. He'd tell you exactly where he found it. A lot of people knew he'd found gold at the Woolshed, and newspapers often referred to the Tokomairiro goldfield as 'Black Peter's territory'. The Provincial Council even talked about it, probably not too loudly lest they had to pay Peters the reward due to him. Yet no one took very much notice. Why not?

Read had experience in both California and Victoria, Australia. He knew his way around. He came from a wealthy Australian family, was well educated and talked to the emergent middle class in Otago in their own language, and they responded with that odd mixture of pomp and naivety typical of a society making its way in a new world. Peters was from some godforsaken corner of the globe that had taken the British absolutely ages to get into working order. The locals couldn't even get his nickname right. Black Peter? His name wasn't Peter, nor was he black.

Thomas Gabriel Read was a much more accessible hero. He was the fourth of fourteen children. His dad, Captain George Frederick Read, was a successful entrepreneur in Hobart, Tasmania, who owned several big farms, had other business interests and was even head of a bank. Gabriel was of good British stock. He'd worked on the Californian fields and returned home to the diggings in Victoria, but he was a bad fit: he hated the lawlessness of the miners. Otago, he believed, was more civilised and besides, he knew there had to be gold in those bare hills.

But here was another conundrum: he both felt for the poor and never sought to get rich himself. You could argue that he was free from the desperation that drove other gold-diggers. Perhaps. He'd also fallen on his head when he was hunting as a young man. This was said to have changed him, for the better or the worse depending on your view of his later life.

Everything about him — his behaviour, his letters, his recorded conversations — indicated someone concerned about his fellow man. He was kindly and thoughtful. Notably, for a place where greed was not so much an unfortunate condition as a job qualification, he lacked avarice.

He'd decided to come to New Zealand on a whim: he was passing a Port Chalmers–bound ship in Hobart and hopped aboard. He read about the Tuturau discoveries when he got to the area, but his inquiries discouraged him. He was about to go home when he was offered a job on a farm. He stayed, and that in turn led him to the Tuapeka. Read took Edward Peters seriously. He followed the man's footsteps.

At that time, farming in Otago was moving inland. First, the coastal strip had been developed. As more moneyed immigrants arrived, they began moving inland to bigger blocks. Further inland again, in the vast open spaces, on the slopes and hills and mountainsides of Otago, settlers began to lease the land for truly huge runs. The runholders could have the freehold of the block of land their homestead stood on. The great land grab had begun.

But now the newly landed gentry faced a sudden invasion of gold-miners. Their problem was that their leases did not exclude mining, so there wasn't much they could do about it.

On the edge of his biggest discovery, Gabriel Read set out for the Tuapeka, with a tent, blankets, spade, butcher's knife, food and, of course, his tin dish for panning gold. There, he met George Munro, a shepherd employed by two of the biggest leaseholders among the budding land barons of the region, James Smith and James Allen. His bosses' reservations about diggers either hadn't reached him yet, or he'd taken no notice of them. He took Read in, fed and housed him for the night and after breakfast the next morning showed him to the top of an adjoining gully.

There, near Lawrence, Read tried his luck, as he later recounted in a passage ending with his loveliest quote:

> I followed the creek down till I got on the flat and saw no favourable opportunity of trying a prospect for some time. The drift was deep and cumbered with boulders and little or no loose gold lower down. Getting opposite the Blue Spur the prospects began to brighten, just when I had deemed it

meet to make a fit for my tent, as darkness was fast coming on the scene. At a place where a kind of road crossed on a shallow bar, I shoveled away about two and a half feet of gravel, arriving at a beautiful soft slate, and saw the gold shining like the stars in Orion on a dark frosty night.

That last sentence summed up Gabriel Read. He likened his find to a constellation named after Orion, a giant huntsman in Greek mythology. Read, too, seemed to be hunting a higher purpose.

He was delighted by his find, though not by the riches he'd fallen into, but rather their possibilities. In a letter he wrote, 'I became the sole possessor of a secret which provided a panacea for the evils which were impending over the Province.' He was, in fact, a true altruist, a pious man who believed Providence had guided his footsteps to the place which forever after carried his name: Gabriel's Gully.

Nor did he keep his find secret, although he could have enriched himself beyond any dreams of the time simply by working for a few weeks on his own. I was amazed at Read's willingness to share his discovery (I would have kept it to myself, for as long as possible). He wrote a letter to the Otago Superintendent, Major Sir John Richardson, containing his second most famous quote: 'I found at many places prospects that would hold out a certainty that men, with the proper tools, could be munificently remunerated — and in one place, for ten hours work with pan and butcher's knife, I was enabled to collect about seven ounces of gold.'

Seven ounces in ten hours! I tried to work that out and got lost in the tangle of gold weights, troy ounces, grams and so on. The closest I could come to the answer was that it was an awful lot of money for ten hours work, even by today's standards. It would have been a fortune then.

Seven ounces in ten hours. It was rhythmic. You could march to it, and immediately hundreds, thousands did.

'Seven Ounces in Ten Hours' instantly became another legend.

Read's letter admitted that, while working in secret would have been to his benefit, he felt it his duty to report his findings. The historian A.H. Reed offered one explanation: 'Read's first thought was for others, not for his own enrichment.' In the history of gold-seeking, said Reed, never had such disinterested generosity been shown.

Gabriel Read's letter to Richardson showed what he suspected might happen if he bragged about his find: 'The plain would have been deserted by all the adult inhabitants the next day and the farmers would have suffered seriously from a neglect of agricultural operations.' At the same time he told Richardson that if he believed the news to be 'of any benefit to the public interest', then the superintendent was at liberty to shout it from the rooftops, or at least forward his letter to the *Otago Witness*, which Richardson promptly did. It was published on 6 June 1861, with the *Witness* declaring: 'Should this turn out to be a remunerative goldfield, Mr Read, in justice, will be entitled to a reward.' Which, unlike the less socially acceptable Black Peter, he got.

The rush Read expected never eventuated, however. That was another weird thing about all of this. Those early prospectors did not keep their gold strikes secret, no matter how much it might have enriched them, but no one seemed much interested anyway.

Another letter from Read to the superintendent confirming the extent of his discoveries, and his conviction that he had indeed discovered very rich goldfields, was, in A.H. Reed's words, 'couched in such terms as surely would have roused to fever heat any other community but the now distrustful Dunedin people'.

By then, the autocratic Cargill was dead, but his legacy lived on. No one came to Read's party, or at least, not for a little while. It was business as usual for the phlegmatic Dunedinites, and Gabriel's Gully was as silent for a time as it is now, except when a busload of tourists arrive to marvel over the scene.

Then a provincial councillor brandished five pounds of gold he'd obtained from Read's claim and the cork was out of the bottle. Dunedin went from a city of sceptics to one of believers. As much as that Presbyterian city could go off its head, it did. Cargill's grave was said to have trembled, probably not so much with indignation as the sheer weight of booted men tramping past it.

Fever broke out. Every man who could walk or ride left the city. And of course, the dire predictions came true: the cost of goods and services doubled, Dunedin was stripped of its labour force, public works and private enterprise ground to a halt.

The *Witness* reported on 13 July 1861: 'The residue of the depleted township — amounting to a few hundred persons — watched the first gold escort ushered into town with five hundred ounces of gold.' Oh, how conflicted the editor must have been. On one hand, his worst imaginings had come true for a change. On the other, the city, its businesspeople and the *Witness* itself would soon be gorging at the trough.

The article continued:

The arrival of the first Gold Escort produced as much excitement as the limited number of persons remaining in Dunedin rendered possible. The Escort brought in above 500 ounces, and an additional 100 ounces was brought in by private persons accompanying the escort. The reception that his Honor [the Superintendent, no less] met with on the Diggings was satisfactory, and the diggers are of the most peaceful and orderly character. As yet no difficulties have occurred, but the necessity of the appointment of a Commissioner to settle claims is apparent to all, especially the diggers. The produce of the field, which has arrived in town to this date is about 900 ounces and as it is the produce of only about a dozen parties, the paying nature of the Gold Field may be said to be an ascertained fact. It is stated that fully as much gold remains on the field as that brought by the escort. The number of persons on the field cannot be correctly ascertained, but on Thursday there were believed to be about 700; and, as many were met on the road, about 1000 persons may now be there.

Those men understood the business all right. You took your shovel, you dug a little, you swilled the dirt in a pan-full of water and, hey presto, with luck you were rich. That certainly beat mending a fence, or carting wood, or swinging a pick on a primitive road.

It was not called a gold rush for nothing. Thousands arrived and the Tuapeka wilderness was soon supporting 11,500 diggers. By 1870 Dunedin was unchallenged as New Zealand's largest and richest city. Scots leaders who still bemoaned the loss of the settlement's 'old identity' were ridiculed by the people who'd moaned the loudest.

Dunedin became a cosmopolitan city overnight, in every sense. An exotic mix of races now made up its population. The Europeans included French immigrants, Germans, Belgians, Danes and many more. Chinese miners flocked in. The entire southern hemisphere was represented.

The Dunedin establishment called the immigrants the new iniquity, and had to share their city with people who were not Presbyterians. Catholics built a church, Jews a synagogue, Anglicans a church that soon began to fall down and was then slowly developed into a cathedral that was finished only in the new millennium.

Fortunes were made and, as the legend always has it, lost. But, in the end, it was the miners who built the city with the gold they dug up: in 1866, the combined production of all the goldfields reached 735,000 ounces, worth some $1.5 billion at today's prices. In a single year. That's a record still standing today. It was soon obvious that the good burghers of Dunedin had been, to say the least, blinkered.

The wealth attracted the nation's finest architects to design the nation's finest buildings, and grand houses spread across the cityscape (though slums also developed in the inner city). Railways were built, harbours constructed, the port grew. It was the world's leading instant city: take a muddy patch of hills and add gold.

After ten years, the economy slowed, but Julius Vogel's 1870 immigration and development scheme, which borrowed heavily to finance assisted immigration and public works (including more than 1600 kilometres of railways in nine years), brought in thousands more to Dunedin and Otago before recession set in during the 1880s. By then, Dunedin had grown into the biggest, most magnificent city in the land.

*

Everyone in the old photographs of Dunedin notables seems to look as stern as William Cargill. Being forced to stand absolutely still for very long periods was bound to produce gloom in the standees, I suppose. They put a rather dour stamp on the city, which has lasted to this day.

Yet the city's forefathers were a mixed lot. They might have been God-fearing, like the Reverend Thomas Burns (nephew of Robbie, the poet); or allegedly artistic, such as the poet Thomas Bracken, author of the dreary 'God Defend New Zealand'; or visionary, like Julius Vogel, the eighth premier of New Zealand, a founder and first editor of the *Otago Daily Times*. Or slightly bent, like John Hyde Harris, mayor of Dunedin, lawyer, judge even, who married Cargill's daughter, became an unsuccessful land speculator and a wretched landlord, was eventually bankrupted and served a year in the pokey, yet seems to have remained one of the Dunedin establishment throughout.

Johnny Jones was an even more unlikely case. He was born in Australia, and that was just the start of it. He grew up with sealing and whaling, married and eventually had eleven children, became a part-owner of three whaling ships, purchased a whaling station in Preservation Inlet at the bottom of the South Island, then acquired almost every whaling station in the south, including one at Waikouaiti. There he established the first farm in Otago, expanded his fleet and 'bought' huge blocks of land from the Ngai Tahu chief Tuhawaiki in 1838, including one stretching all the way from Waikouaiti to Wanaka. Then, with a bunch of shady businessmen, he bought everything in the south not yet sold. For that he paid just £200.

At the time New Zealand was part of New South Wales, but this was too much. The New South Wales governor George Gipps declared a foul and took a carving knife to Jones's holdings.

In spite of that, Jones continued to build his empire, which he ruled with a stern hand, an iron fist and a terrible temper. Photographs of him show a square face and shrewd eyes with a touch of humour, which might have fooled some of his adversaries. All the while his men were driving seals to near-extinction, although the whales, somewhat smarter, started giving that section of the coast a wide berth. The result was the same: soon, massacring marine mammals was not paying as well as it had done. Johnny was feeling the pinch. His empire tottered on the brink.

He concentrated on farming and business, and poked his stubby fingers into many more pies. He became a ship-owner and newspaper proprietor (his syndicate owned the *Otago Witness*). In 1854 he bought one of the best houses in Dunedin, twenty-five room Fernhill, and moved into it. It was so majestic that Jones lent it to the city to accommodate the Duke of Edinburgh during his visit in 1869. That added the royal seal to his rise through society, which he then exited, dying the same year. Six of his eleven children and his wife, Sarah, had beaten him to the grave. His eldest son used his legacy to set up what became the

Union Steam Ship Company. As a last stamp of respectability, the Dunedin Club bought Fernhill, moved into it in 1874 and remains there to this day. Jones's station up the coast, its red-painted farm buildings complete with schoolhouse and three accompanying long drops pristine despite their advancing years, is now a popular visitor attraction.

As a city father Johnny Jones was, in a word, raffish. I liked him. It's a pity Dunedin did not take on more of his character.

*

I moved to Dunedin as a young newspaper reporter and part-time student. I'd previously worked in Waipukurau on the *Central Hawke's Bay Press*, which advertised itself as 'the country's smallest daily'. It had expanded under an ambitious new editor from the metropolitans, increasing the number of reporting staff to one. Me. I had a compelling reason for going there: no one else would take me on.

After two years, however, the lines between cattle sales and county councils had begun to blur and Waipukurau's eccentric and sometimes catastrophic social life had taken its toll. I'd looked around for another job and found one at the *Dunedin Evening Star*, again because … well, let's just say they were in no position to be particular.

I soon fell in love with Dunedin, which surprised me, because my introduction to the city was not encouraging. I found a room in a boarding house where my first night's sleep was permeated by the stench of urine. In the morning I discovered it came from the mattress. 'He was a boozer,' was the landlady's excuse as I departed, suitcase in hand. Possibly she thought that as a journalist I'd understand.

Next, I hooked up with a group of students needing a flatmate. Two women, two men. Fine with me, but not with the University of Otago's Council, evidently direct descendants of the city fathers who'd suppressed the news of gold strikes. The council had brought in a ban on mixed flatting. They were in loco parentis, they explained. In loco William Cargill, I thought, reflecting on the hammer-headed city founder. Unfortunately our landlord was a lawyer who, he explained solemnly while ogling one of my well-endowed flatmates, felt honour-bound to accept the council's strictures.

The poet James K. Baxter expressed his views on this situation in 'A Small Ode on Mixed Flatting':

> A thousand founding fathers lie
> Well roofed against the howling sky
> In mixed accommodation — Hush!
> It is the living make us blush
> Because the young have wicked hearts
> And blood to swell their private parts.

To which we exclaimed, '*Gaudeamus igitur*!'

The problem sorted itself out. Two of us left the university. I was thrown out for lack of academic progress. The word 'lack' surprised me, for I'd made no progress at all. Then we all quit the flat anyway. I found another one, more peaceful, beside the Leith Stream, which despite being pretentiously named after Edinburgh's Water of Leith, was hardly more than a drain.

I was getting to know Dunedin, and it was a delight. The gold rushes so stolidly resisted had created a beautiful city and notably given the settlement the confidence to build its magnificent Gothic First Church. Some fine buildings had not survived the late 1960s, a bad time for good architecture, but Dunedin Railway Station remained, and the University of Otago, and the banks whose buildings reflected the solidity and trust that banks once enjoyed. A medieval-looking prison coexisted with an equally gloomy 'lunatic asylum', as it was known then, not far up the road. Breweries and factories and plants survived from the industrial revolution fuelled by gold money. Otago Boys' High School and dozens of splendid old homes, including Larnach Castle on the peninsula and Cargill's Castle, looking down on its luck even then but still occupied, told of a raffish past. Even my newspaper occupied a historic building (appropriately, some said, just over the road from the jail). It's now home to its former arch-rival, the *Otago Daily Times*, the *Evening Star* having gently bowed out after 110 years.

I worked for the *Otago Daily Times* later. We'd knock off at midnight or in the small hours and go to one of the obliging city pubs, all, of course, occupying historical and improbably delicate old buildings.

To go from the *ODT* to the police station, you walked down a narrow lane beside the cells. Barred windows let into the dank inside, so walking down that thin dark thoroughfare was always depressing, and even a little scary. One of the reporters who worked for the *ODT* liked smoking a little weed, regarded by the establishment then as the leading edge of drug culture. The reporter got careless and was nailed one night as he sucked a joint in a doorway. The law being an ass, he was packed off to jail and sacked into the bargain. Legend has it that another reporter was told to take his letter of dismissal down to the cells, and he simply poked it through one of the barred windows in the lane on his way to the pub.

The gold rush transformed the jail too. A simple wooden building had done the job until the miners made their merry way into the legal system. They were professionally adept at tunnelling, and a more substantial stone building was called for. When the British invaded Parihaka and took the pacifist Te Whiti and his followers prisoner — no great feat as they offered no resistance — about 140 of them were sent south, and some of that number were jammed into Dunedin's first jail to wither and rot with tuberculosis. Later the thirst for justice demanded more spacious quarters and a new administration building and cell block went up near the turn of the twentieth century (it later became the police station). The magnificent High Victorian Dunedin Law Courts stood next door, the whole becoming an efficient machine: you stood in the dock, received your sentence and then were whisked off to your cell, with great savings in shoe leather.

Oh, the magistrates were stern gents, terrifying to a young reporter, and so upright! Yet justice could be tempered with mercy if you belonged to the same club. One city businessman, wealthy, prominent in those city organisations which were then, and probably still are, effectively private clubs, was arrested for bashing his wife. What to do? The authorities thought they'd resolved the dilemma by setting up a hearing after usual closing hours, obviously with the magistrate's agreement. Presumably the idea was to chastise the man and send him off into the darkness without the affair becoming public. But a passing reporter was curious about the lights: what could be going on this late in the day? So the plot was revealed, and the suppression of the man's name — the magistrate's last, desperate good turn — did no good at all, since it was all over town by morning.

I was always surprised that thousands of talented young people passed through the university and hardly any of them stayed. This affair gave me an answer: the old boys' networks suffocated the place.

Justice in those medieval-looking buildings always seemed a little strange. In the mid-1990s I sat for three weeks in the High Victorian Gothic–style Supreme Court covering the Bain trial for the *NZ Listener*. David Bain was charged with murdering his entire family — his parents and three siblings — one savage night, in their house in Andersons Bay, Dunedin. The whole thing was curious: the talented, spiritual, cultured family; their cluttered ruin of a house; their relationships; their personalities; the father exiled to a caravan; the mother consulting crystals on whether to buy apples or apricots; the strange way the family worked. (The house, incidentally, was burned down in a ritual almost as curious as the murders themselves, the fire brigade watching, the public standing in the firelight as if it were Guy Fawkes Night.)

The Bains's lives were re-enacted amid the elaborate architecture of the courtroom, composed of docks and benches and passageways and hidden entrances in curly whorled wood, as the tiny robed judge popped in and out of the woodwork like Punch, and the defendant sat with his eyes fixed on one particular spot on his old bench. My companion for the whole trial, James

McNeish, seemed to me such a strange old bugger that I wasn't surprised when his subsequent book, *The Mask of Society: The Bain Murders*, came to the same conclusion about the family as I did: they were weird.

The jury found Bain guilty, and both McNeish and I agreed they were right, but a series of appeal court hearings eventually ended with Bain's convictions being set aside. The verdict was debated and compensation for Bain reviewed by a retired Australian judge, who concluded that, on the balance of probabilities, Bain was 'not innocent'.

Well, what was the government to make of that? A resolution as strange as the case itself, as it turned out. The government declared that no compensation would be offered, but a payment of almost $1 million would be made if Bain agreed to halt any further litigation against the government. So this dreadful thing was left suspended in space. It seemed to me to be a uniquely Dunedin event: serpentine, set amid its theatrical architecture, as if some eccentric component had leaked from its history and inked the present.

Across the road from the law courts stood Dunedin Railway Station, designed by George Troup, known to his colleagues as 'Gingerbread George', whose severe Victorian countenance certainly would not have cracked a smile at the quip. Troup earned his soubriquet for the station. Oh, what a fantasy it was. Designed in a style known officially as Flemish Renaissance — a term usually reserved for art — it had towers, dormer windows, stained glass, wrought-iron balustrades, cherubs, majolica tiles, a superb porcelain-tiled floor in Roman key patterns, and a colonnade that was quite useless in Dunedin weather for it admitted the rain and ushered in the wind smartly. The only people who walked there were serious students of architecture.

Penurious Dunedinites, direct descendants of those who had abjured the miners, thought it all extravagant, too fancy and, especially, too costly. The building earned George Troup a reputation for frippery among architects, who in my own experience are a bitchy lot who cannot be relied upon for a good opinion of any design but their own. Fortunately George (he did not become Sir George till 1937) paid them no heed and went on to design other railway stations, many of them still standing, which gave the New Zealand railway system a unique character. (All they lack these days are trains.)

His masterpiece, Dunedin Railway Station, is a building to be loved, stroked and wallowed in like a spa. When I last visited, it was packed with tourists, many of them from two cruise ships in the harbour. A million or two selfies were being taken around the intricate ticket booths while, on the next floor, in an exhibition of Otago art, a woman was busy taking a picture of a picture of, yes, Dunedin Railway Station.

*

I last visited Dunedin in spring 2019, when the giant mountain buttercups and the yellow kowhai bloomed, pink valerian sprang from every crevice and the sweet smell of broom filled the air, and I fell in love all over again.

I wanted to know what had happened to this once-opulent city, to its hopes and dreams. I stayed at Wains Hotel, in what was once the centre of the city's business district, the Exchange.

Job Wain opened his first hotel in Dunedin in the 1860s, at the height of the gold rush, and built this one in 1878. It seemed the right place. Its columns, capitals, the carved figures of Bacchus and Neptune, mermaids and balustrades summed up an opulent new society. Now the hotel was being renovated, and scaffolders politely kept their backs to our room. Oh, Dunedin, I thought, always proper.

All around the hotel are fine buildings built on gold money, many of them banks of course. Yet it wasn't so much the grand buildings that impressed me most, but the smaller ones, the shapely two- and three-storey buildings filling the spaces between the bigger structures — the detail, the fine print.

By the end of the gold boom, in the 1880s, the downtown area had been jammed with hotels, banks, insurance companies, breweries, theatres. The names of their styles roll around your mouth: Gothic, Renaissance, Italianate, Elizabethan, Jacobean, Georgian. The city has more fine historic buildings than you can shake protection orders at, and they reduce their modern neighbours to indifference.

Their owners established local commerce and industry on such a scale that they became central to the young nation's economy and suppliers to much of the country. Engineering, woollen mills, clothing manufacturing, importing and warehousing operations all abounded. Jobs were abundant and rich people steadily got a great deal richer.

All of this was summed up for me by a customers' desk from the old Bank of New Zealand, dating from the 1880s and now preserved in the Otago Settlers' Museum. It was a magnificent thing, crafted by a gifted carver from dark Australian red cedar.

In its day, six customers could sit at it, each in absolute privacy, and conduct their business in splendour. It took a while to walk around it.

It seemed to represent the glory of Dunedin's golden age, the city's grandeur and wealth, and it had survived the bank itself: built in 1883, the building had closed in 1998, and now stood empty, along with the fine insurance building next door.

I thought the answer to my question lay in that desk, somewhere. What had happened to this city? Not very much, thank God. Like the desk, it had endured.

*

As the gold rush ended and the focus of the economy shifted to sheep farming, Dunedin, despite its charms, dwindled. The entrepreneurs, the business people attracted by gold who had set up manufacturing and engineering industries, mills, breweries and factories and created jobs and made themselves and the city rich, by and large moved on. Fortunately for Dunedin, they couldn't take their buildings with them. Shifting north was a little like death in that respect.

Yet, right through to the late twentieth century, the city remained both self-satisfied and covetous, quite sure of its proper place in history and equally certain that its golden years were not behind it. As a youthful reporter I covered the city council for the *Otago Daily Times*. It was full of dull old men in grey suits with names going back to the gold-rush era, from families who'd shaken free of the prevailing antipathy towards the miners and taken the money. (There was only one woman on the council, Ethel Emma McMillan, a Labour MP, a nice old soul who nevertheless could induce a coma at the press table after five minutes on her feet.)

The councillors belonged to an era when Dunedin was always first: first daily newspaper, first university, first art school, first medical school, the best, most ornamental and most expensive buildings in the land (including First Church, which still stood grandly over the city and harbour), first campaign for better working conditions, resulting in the first sign of the New Zealand Labour Party, first frozen meat shipment exported, arguably the first internationally recognised artist, Frances Hodgkins.

The city council was quite certain that Dunedin would rise again. Charged with the task of giving effect to that ambition was a body called the Otago Council, similarly composed of men in grey. Their job was to put Dunedin back in its rightful place, or, put another way, to find the golden fleece.

They sought it here, they sought it there. They thought of beet and exotic trees, of shoes and ships and sealing wax, of cabbages and kings. They chased baubles as children chased bubbles, usually finding they went pop and disappeared. All those hopes and dreams. If ever there was a quest for the golden fleece, the Otago Council held the copyright.

Irrigation. Montane wax. Limestone, building stones. Sands for ceramics and foundries. Scheelite (the last of the lonely scheelite miners toiling in tunnels above Glenorchy at the end of Lake Wakatipu were soon to disappear), gold again (of course), hydro-electric power (the council seemed blind to the growing opposition to dams and their consequences). Why, look at all that undeveloped grassland, and even more tussock land, they said: it should be covered with sheep and cows. Sugar beet (a perennial favourite). Forestry. Tourism.

They knew there was another golden fleece out there, somewhere, if only they could find it.

Their chief executive was a man called Jolyon Manning, whose eyes shone with vision. He held the world record for the number of times a person could use the word 'Otago' in a single day, and he'd developed his own pronunciation, rather like *Itaaaaaaaaago*. When he said it, his eyes widened, his face shone. I was not surprised to learn, later, that he was a lay preacher. He was absolutely, relentlessly optimistic about Otago's future, and never missed a chance for a commercial. Naturally, we mocked him. He knew it, but didn't seem to mind.

Years later, he was a fellow passenger on the last train to Clyde, which left from glorious Dunedin Railway Station. It was a nostalgic trip, packed with people who became more tearful as the journey went on and the bar became busier. The line originally ran through the goldfields all the way to Cromwell until the Clyde Dam flooded the Cromwell Gorge and drowned the railway with it. Now here we were, marvelling at why a government, even one as benighted as the one now ushering in a new economic order, could be shutting down what was obviously one of the great wonders of the world, especially when viewed through the bottom of a glass.

Oh, the imagination of that line! The spectacular curves, the ornate tunnels, the viaducts (the most notable of them the wrought-iron Wingatui), all of them so intricate we celebrated an organisation that could create it. The Notches, a puzzle of bridges and cuttings. The sweeping S-bends of Tiger Hill. The enterprise, the adventure of it! Now, in the grip of the vandalism following the neo-liberal reforms of the 1990s, the last gasps of the twentieth century were turning into sighs.

They closed the line from Middlemarch to Clyde after that trip. I expected Jolyon to be a little melancholy, at least. But he wasn't. He foresaw the line's new life as a tourist attraction, now the famous Otago Central Rail Trail, and perhaps even the success of the surviving line between Dunedin and Middlemarch. Now privately operated, it probably carries more passengers than it ever did.

Jolyon Manning eventually struck it rich. In the early 1960s he bought a dry, schist-strewn piece of land on Bridge Hill above Alexandra in Central Otago. Over the next fifty years he and his wife, Enny, planted trees where people had said trees could never grow, exotic trees Jolyon believed could become plantations and make Otago rich again. Otago never quite warmed to the idea, but Jolyon was eternally optimistic. He toiled over his arid block in the freezing winters and the hot dry summers, and the land, named Jolendale Park, grew rich and green. It was his dream in miniature, and it worked. The trees flourished. Residents and visitors marvelled over it. It won permanent protection from the QE2 Trust. It was always open to the public, but the Mannings later gifted the whole thing to the community.

The experimental trees never grew into the large plantations Jolyon had dreamed of, which, along with the tall buildings and the bright new industries and the other, later harbourside fantasies of the city, proved illusory. Yet, almost alone among the suits, Jolyon had found gold.

*

I had my own take on Dunedin. The city's weather could be truly horrible, but you expected cold winters this far south. There were always a few days each year when cars skidded off the northern motorway into snow drifts, highways were blocked, the city was cut off, people skied down Baldwin Street (said to be the world's steepest street), kids tobogganed to school, and so on.

It happened every year and probably I'd have been disappointed to get through a winter without those things. Friends in other cities would ring after the television news showed a farmer carrying frozen sheep across a paddock, or a truck jack-knifed off the road, or passengers from abandoned buses huddling in the snow, and inquire after my health and wellbeing. I'm fine, I'd say heroically, and crawl back under half a tonne of blankets with a hottie. It was a way of life.

Really, it was the summers that were bad. You'd get up on a summer morning, look out of the window at a bright blue sky and shout, 'This is the day, let's go', and you'd pack some lunch with your togs, hop into the car and set off. But before you could say 'sandwich' it would cloud over, go from blue and promising to cold and grey — that particular cold and that special grey that, when they got together, made you huddle into a little ball and insist that it was only a cloud blotting out the sun, it would pass. But it never did. On summer weekends, I'd get up so early trying to cram a summer's day into a single morning that sometimes it hardly seemed worth going to bed.

And the sea! I never knew why Robert Falcon Scott's expeditions called in to Port Chalmers then left again. He could have got the full Antarctic experience right there, in Otago Harbour.

Even in midsummer the water was icy. I had some of the shortest swims of my life on local beaches, charging in laughing, emerging screaming. But the water was wonderfully clear. So clear, a local surfer once told me, that you could see the great white sharks coming for you from kilometres away. Sharks killed three people off Dunedin beaches in the 1960s and a man attacked by a great white in 1971 at St Clair beach needed ninety stitches in his leg. As well, newspapers reported, his surfboard was broken. Wisely, he never surfed there again. In all, Dunedin counted five great white shark attacks off its coast.

The city council placed shark nets off St Clair and they stayed there until 2011, after arguments about whether they were effective and, of course, how much they cost. Sharks were still seen occasionally but no one had been attacked for half a century and a new generation of surfers followed a policy of laissez-faire. Those 1960s and 70s attacks were often later attributed to a lone, 'rogue shark'. Like *Jaws*. *Boonga boonga bong bong!*

*

Deep in the crevices of the southern city lies the conviction that sharks are still circling. In 2013 the citizenry bent a beady eye upon a new waterfront hotel whose plans showed it rising above the ancient wharves like the monolith from the dawn of man in the opening sequence of Stanley Kubrick's *2001: A Space Odyssey*. Consent was declined on the basis that it was a blight on the city's heritage. A seventeen-storey version nearer the city centre was rejected in 2017 because it didn't look right and was a blight on ..., etc, etc. A later, a more curvaceous version, of a hotel resembling cockleshells, emerged in 2018 (and still shines from the heavens), along with plans to turn the city into a Centre of Digital Excellence.

Back on Earth, the city's most successful modern venture got away to a shaky start. Dunedin's new stadium, the Forsyth Barr Stadium, rose trembling from the ground just in time for the 2011 Rugby World Cup but oh — shades of the gold rush — what moaning went on about it. The cost! The uselessness of it! The sheer impudence! The city fractured. The golden fleece indeed. People took to the streets.

Surveys showed people didn't want to pay for it, especially when like many a grand project in New Zealand it ran millions over budget. Both the city council and the Otago Regional Council were taken to court for spending public money on the stadium. Both won.

Yet, eventually, everyone agreed that possibly, or even probably, the stadium had been A Good Thing. In 2018 it was calculated that major events at the stadium — the concerts, the games — had boosted the local economy by $77 million, and that was just in that year. Oh, how everybody loved it now. How they shouted out with glee!

There was a surge of optimism in the city. When the population hit 130,000 for the first time in 2018, people jumped for joy. 'Dunedin is riding a wave,' declared the *Otago Daily Times*. The university accounted for some of its characteristics: a higher female population, a younger median age, a high proportion of people under twenty-five. City fathers, and probably mothers too, were ecstatic.

Then the *Otago Daily Times*, ever-vigilant, asked the question: was Dunedin the hottest town in the south? You might describe that claim as ambitious, or even breathtaking, given that the city shared space in the country's geography with Queenstown, whose progress through the statistics would put a meteor in shadow. The evidence produced by the *ODT* was record house prices and a tourist boom. Old Dunedin hands put most of that down to hot air, which, God knew, Dunedin needed more than most. Want a family home, but priced out of the markets in the north? Go south, join the queues. Yet median house prices at the time had jumped by 15 percent to a new high of $430,000, which wouldn't have bought very much in Auckland but might have got you a reasonable three-bedroom in Christchurch.

It was the lifestyle, said the indefatigable. That and the Ed Sheeran effect — all those concerts. All that sport. All that moaning over the price of the new stadium? Who said that? And construction was about to take off. A big hospital rebuild. A huge harbourside redevelopment, a piece of urban art in the form of a new bridge, new university buildings.

One survey even threw up Dunedin as the best city in New Zealand to live in, calculated roughly on that safe, warm feeling of community and neighbourliness, cultural richness (although my own, informal survey showed it the least Maori of all our major cities) and civic pride. Its closest competitors were Wellington, Rodney district and Porirua, with Auckland not even in squeaking distance. You could make of that whatever you liked.

CHAPTER TWO

All that Glitters

I went looking for Edward Peters, aka Black Peter, the man who started it all by finding the first serious goldfield in Otago. Once there were several ways of getting into those old goldfields from Dunedin, most of them difficult, all of them arcane. Some survive, but the main route now, and certainly the most popular one, is to first drive south from Dunedin to the little town of Milton, where once great gangs of gold-miners gathered on their way into the interior. Except for the relatively new prison on the highway into the town (the Otago Corrections Facility, aka the Milton Hilton), the main landmark here is the Gothic church designed by the Victorian architect R.A. Lawson, who also designed the Seacliff Lunatic Asylum north of Dunedin. The asylum was then New Zealand's biggest building, which said something about the country's sanity in those days.

I've always thought Milton an admirably eccentric little town entirely suited to its place in history. State Highway 1 runs in a straight line through it from northeast to southwest, except for a kink in the town's main street known, of course, as 'The Kink'. The popular explanation is that one surveyor was working on the southbound road and another on the northbound, and they didn't quite meet in the middle.

Turning right after Milton towards Lawrence, you came, just before a deep cleft called the Manuka Gorge, to the fabled goldfields at Glenore. Here, in 1857, Black Peter scooped up his pannikin-full of sludge at Hopkins Crossing near the Evans Flat Mill and found the speck of gold that eventually started the biggest gold rush of all.

None of this was apparent. To any casual passerby, Glenore no longer exists. There's hardly a sign of it, much less a signpost.

I followed a road that hinted at a cemetery. It soon became a track and disappeared into a slushy place where gravestones poked out of pine-forest scraps. Quite a large area, not very many headstones. I pushed open a steel gate, trudged through thick wet grass to a couple of big headstones, and was trapped by blackberry so firmly that I began composing my own epitaph: 'He came, he saw, he got caught up in the place.'

Eventually I freed myself, saw more headstones a hundred metres away and read inscriptions to people who no longer existed and who had lived in a town that had vanished, completely. None of them belonged to Edward Peters, but one marked the final resting place of Archibald Anderson, a farmer with links to Peters — Peters presented some gold to a man named Dawson, who'd helped drive sheep to Anderson's farm. (The gold was made into a ring for Dawson's wife and survives in the Otago Settlers' Museum.)

Not far down the road was a little white cottage with a stand selling rhubarb. I got a bunch, looked for someone to pay. That person proved to be Archibald Anderson's great-great-granddaughter, Nicky Anderson. I told her I was tracking Edward Peters. She told me where I could find his memorial. Where did he live? I asked. 'Why,' she said, 'right here. This was his house.'

The cottage was tiny, just a kitchen, small living room and bedroom, but comfortable and probably quite substantial for its day. Nicky's life seemed little different from Peters'. She lived simply, largely on what she could produce. She seemed to me to be a far better memorial to the old miner than the quite recent monument to the all-but-forgotten hero, a large rock in a place called Mount Stuart Reserve down the road. It was a quiet spot shaded by old trees, but the rock seemed as obscure as Peters himself. A plaque celebrated his place in history: 'The Discoverer of the first workable goldfield in Otago at Glenore in 1858–59.'

Lawrence lies further along the road. It's a nice small town, with several nice old buildings, none of them as grand as you might expect of the former capital of the richest goldfield in the land. My favourite story about Lawrence is the tale of two lions that, in 1978, escaped from a circus in the town. Sultan and Sonia (these were New Zealand lions, after all) were young, and frightened, and apparently not even desperate to get away — they eventually took up residence in the porch of a house. But Sonia had knocked down a small boy and badly gashed his face, so they were eventually shot by the town constable. Still, waste not, want not. They were stuffed and placed in Otago Museum.

Lawrence's big attraction is, of course, Gabriel's Gully. It is marked, tracked, signposted, choreographed and tramped over by battalions of tourists. That is just as it should be, of course, for Read's discovery put the gold in the golden fleece. Yet I could not help comparing the daily worship at Gabriel's altar with the rock commemorating the poor man who started it all, Edward Peters.

Between them, they'd been responsible for wealth beyond the telling. They'd discovered vast amounts of gold, opened the way to fortunes, enriched a city and towns throughout the south. In the new millennium they would have surveyed their territories through the great glass cliffs of Queenstown mansions and traversed their holdings by helicopter. Yet they both died in poverty, Edward Peters in the Dunedin Benevolent Institution, aka the poorhouse, in 1893, Gabriel Read a year later in the New Norfolk Hospital for the Insane, in Hobart. He suffered from bipolar disorder. His widow, Amelia, inherited his estate. It amounted to £96.

Around the same time, a shadowy duo was sneaking about, far upriver near present-day Cromwell. Horatio Hartley and Christopher Reilly were mysterious then, and still are. Both men came from America, Hartley a Californian and Reilly an Irishman originally from Dublin. They met on the California goldfields and arrived in New Zealand in 1862, when the cries of exultation from the Tuapeka, as the goldfield around Lawrence came to be known, could almost be heard in Dunedin. They seem to have brought cool heads to this febrile society.

They wondered: if so much gold was being found in the Tuapeka, might it have come from further upriver? Perhaps they were not the first to reason this way, but upriver they went, digging here, panning there, all very quietly, progressing to a place not far from where Cromwell now stands at the junction of the Clutha and Kawarau rivers.

The rapacious life on the Californian goldfields, where every kind of swindle, theft and violence was common, had taught them a little. They had none of Edward Peters' benevolence nor Gabriel Read's generosity. They worked in secret. They found some decent colour and then they kept on going until they struck a lode just across the river from modern Cromwell.

Downstream, miners and townspeople alike were surveying their falling returns glumly and predicting an end to it all. Hartley and Reilly weren't in the business of giving employment to out-of-work miners. They were, instead, out to make as much money as they could in as short a time as possible, for they knew that sooner or later they'd be sprung. While the miners downriver were wringing their hands, the pair were accumulating about six ounces a day, which, in modern terms, was a whole lot of gold.

But miners were by profession a nosey lot, and a pair of Americans working away in silence and staying more or less in the same spot were bound to be noticed eventually. And so they were, by an Australian, a digger from Victoria who brought his Australian instincts to the job. They did their best to con him into thinking they were not doing at all well. But he was an Ocker after all, and he could smell bullshit in the sharp winter breeze.

Hartley and Reilly knew their game was either up, or would be up very soon. Off they went to the Gold Receiver in Dunedin and startled that official by dumping sacks full of gold on his desk.

'An old woman could scratch more gold out with her fingers than all the miners in the Province could get elsewhere!', the pair told a newspaper reporter, clearly throwing all caution to the winds. The *Otago Daily Times* carried this story:

> The utmost excitement prevailed in Dunedin yesterday on the subject of the new gold field. Knots of men were gathered at the corners of the streets discussing the subject, and the various stores and outfitting shops in the town were crowded with purchasers, procuring outfits for the new rush.
>
> Horses and pack saddles have risen in price about 50 percent, in fact the latter are fetching three or four times the price asked a few days ago.
>
> We question if the excitement which prevails in Dunedin was equalled even by that which was occasioned by Gabriel Read's discoveries.

The city was in ferment. The ship *Lombard*, bound for Auckland, was deserted by many of her passengers at Port Chalmers. The crew quit en masse.

Hartley and Reilly meanwhile promised to tell the world where they got the gold from, but only if they were paid a reward of £2000. A lot of grumbling and mumbling followed, of course, but the answer was succinct enough: yes.

It was a sound investment. Back they went, in the company of Major Jackson Keddell, who, as a warden, acted as a kind of goldfields' policeman. His job was to verify the story. He found a group of angry miners on the spot, who, according to Vincent Pyke (then the chief commissioner of the goldfields and de facto their leading historian and storyteller) 'expressed very plainly their disbelief', threatening to throw Hartley into the river and/or give him fifty lashes. One account had Keddell drawing his sword to restore order.

But Hartley waded into the river, stuck his shovel into the bed, panned the shingle and there it was — gold!

So a new goldfield was proclaimed, and given a name that still resonates more than a century and a half later: the Dunstan.

Despite the history they created, Hartley and Reilly simply faded from view. Reilly wanted to make a more enduring mark on his adopted country. He started survey work for a seaport, Port Molyneux, at the mouth of the Clutha River, on the site of an old whaling station. But he soon left the port, taking himself off to Tasmania, then Adelaide, before disappearing from the face of the earth. The port thrived until the great flood of 1878, when the Clutha River carved out a new channel, blocked the harbour with a huge sandbar and formed a new river mouth to the north. Port Molyneux ceased to exist virtually overnight, its pubs, shops and all the industry of a port vanishing like Reilly. Today the port is just a sign on the road that carries traffic through to Kaka Point and the famous Nugget Point lighthouse. Of the once-busy Port Molyneux only an old schoolhouse remains, opened in 1865, closed in 1999 and much later, when I last checked, turned into a wedding venue.

Hartley was said to have taken himself off to the Coromandel diggings then returned to Otago, impressing one and all with a lone trek through the wilderness between Queenstown and the West Coast, 'a feat of foot which few men could do'. He popped up again in Australia and New Guinea, then he went home to the United States with quite a fortune, most of which he bequeathed to his hometown school district in Tacoma, Washington, leaving only a little to his widow and even that on condition that she not remarry. She declared him insane. He died in San Francisco in 1905.

Oh, but their legacy, and Black Peter's, and Gabriel Read's, and Thomas Arthur's for that matter. In 1862, Thomas, a shepherd, was working the Shotover River (then called the Overshot) with another shepherd, Harry Redfern. He was equipped with a milking dish and a knife; in other words, his gear was about average for the day. Between them the pair reaped around 1000 ounces of gold, worth about $2 million today. In two months. Even the richest cocky in the even richer New Zealand legend would get off his quad bike over that. It certainly beat shearing, another reason why the pastoralists weren't overjoyed.

Yet few traces of their endeavour remain in Central Otago, and even fewer at Hartley and Reilly's famous site on Brewery Creek. In fact, it's unlikely that even the miners themselves would recognise it today. A memorial marks the approximate spot, and heavy traffic dashes past on a new highway. The place where they struck gold has disappeared under the waters of the flooded Cromwell Gorge.

Long after the Clutha's gold ran out, the New Zealand government had a bright idea. New concrete dams could still wring wealth from the old gold rivers. This was the jewel in the crown of the 1975–84 government ruled by a man called Rob Muldoon. He and his lieutenants exhorted the nation to think big about all sorts of things, including trains, smelters and a succession of high dams on the Clutha River. The plan caused a great deal of fuss, to which the PM twitched a cheek and told his opponents to jump in the lake, a large one of which he was planning. In the end the scheme boiled down to the Clyde Dam, built between 1982 and 1993, downriver from the spot where Hartley and Reilly scored their fortune.

The dam sits on the river like a scowl. It drowned orchards and homes and old gold workings and Hartley and Reilly's famous site and much of old Cromwell beneath newly created Lake Dunstan. For a while people worried that the shaley hillsides in the flooded gorge might slip into the lake and cause an unstoppable wave that would pour over the top of the dam then charge through Clyde and Alexandra and right down to the Roxburgh Dam, doing God-knows-what damage.

But that hasn't come to pass and a new prosperity has taken over. New Cromwell and old Clyde rediscovered the golden fleece in hydroelectricity and flourished in their new lakeside locations. Clyde huddles under its monstrous concrete neighbour but it has a picturesque town centre full of nice old buildings and seems unworried. It's a rather sleepy little town fading into new subdivisions with perfect gardens exuding confidence, their owners, presumably, too young to remember either Muldoon or the Great Wave. A plaque set in a footpath commemorates an earlier resident: not Hartley or Reilly or anyone else from that era, but Fleur Sullivan, a well-known Otago restaurateur whose first restaurant, in an old stone store, lies nearby.

Cromwell, where miners once huddled in tents, still has its stone shelters but now they have four bedrooms and double garages and commonly cost a million dollars and more. Some, at least, are still striking it rich.

Hundreds of dredges, some of them massive, followed the miners along the Clutha in the 1890s and early 1900s and even staged a comeback in the 1930s and 40s, when their tailings — great piles of stones sluiced out of riverbeds, ransacked for gold and spat out again — once again reformed the landscape. You can stand at Earnscleugh near Alexandra and marvel over a changed land: whole ranges of foothills created by the tailings. Today they'd set off another full-scale environmental war, but after a century or so they've become part of the view.

The new highway now carries traffic past Cromwell and on to the Kawarau Gorge, past the remains of little rock dwellings where miners once huddled. It passes Roaring Meg, where a gold-miners' hotel, the Kirtleburn, stood until it burned down in 1880. Its owner saved only a bag of flour and a case of spirits. (The name Roaring Meg may have come from a rather noisy woman once carried across the river by gold-miners, and the merest glance at that foaming water will tell you why she roared.)

The highway runs on to Arrowtown, named for the Arrow River nearby. Here, a man called Thomas Low stopped to take a drink one day in 1862 and grabbed a tussock to steady himself. But the tussock came out of the ground and in the raw earth beneath it he saw a big nugget. Tewa, aka Maori Jack, a tall and kindly man from Hauraki, had found gold in the Arrow in 1861 and talked about it openly, and Low, along with many others (for it didn't take much to spark a rush) had followed his tracks. Europeans always made the history books before Maori, and credit for finding the goldfield went to William Fox, a big man, both tough and vicious. In 1862 he and a few other diggers worked the field secretly, amassing as much gold as they could before word got out.

Even more than the country they worked in, scorching in summer, frost-bitten in winter, the marks of the miners' passage amazed me. These men had only what they could carry, primitive tools and a few basic items, yet they created buildings, water-races, waterwheels, houses, hotels. One hundred and sixty years on, some of it could still be seen. The White Horse Hotel in Becks near Alexandra has endured almost unchanged (albeit with a lot of restoration) since John Nixon Becks built it at a river crossing in 1864.

In the space of a few decades the miners created a way of life, achieving a permanence sometimes not matched in a modern New Zealand of flimsy building materials, where buildings collapse because they can't perform one of their basic functions: keeping water out.

With my twin sons I once walked the Croesus Track from the old West Coast mining town of Blackball over the Paparoa Range to Barrytown on the coast. We walked along an old tramway, took a side track and there, deep in the bush, was the first stamping machine I'd ever seen. A stamping machine swallowed great chunks of rock and battered them to pieces for the gold that might be inside. It had to be huge, strong, and very, very heavy. I marvelled at the effort it must have taken to haul it into the mountains and through the bush. Yet stamping machines could be found all over the goldfields, abandoned, isolated and as enduring as the standing stones of Britain.

The Moonlight Track branched off the Croesus, following a route pioneered by George Fairweather Moonlight. When I first read Moonlight's story, I had to keep reminding myself that he'd been real and not a character from a Jack London novel. Moonlight was a Scottish gold-miner who, among the many, actually made a lot of money. He became a legend even among miners used to loneliness, deprivation and hardship for his solo forays into dangerous country, and he left his name on creeks and other places throughout Central Otago and the West Coast — at one time the Buller area was known as Moonlight Country. The Pessini gold nugget, claimed to be New Zealand's biggest ever (the West Coast town of Ross avowed the same title for its own nugget, the Honourable Roddy; the two seemed to be the same weight) was found in Moonlight Creek.

Moonlight spoke with an American accent, dressed in American clothes and gave streams along a new route he found from Nelson to the Grey River American names such as Shenandoah and Rappahannock. The route and the names endure as State Highway 65. Moonlight built the Commercial Hotel in Murchison, a version of which still stands, and became the town's unofficial sheriff.

A series of misfortunes culminated in his return to prospecting. In 1884 he didn't return from one of his forays into the bush. His daughter started a search. Months later his remains were found near Glenhope, in a place called Cow Creek, northeast of Murchison. He'd died of exposure. I could not even imagine the bleakness of his death. How cold must it have been to kill someone of such endurance? In a place so lonely I could not find it, even on the map.

*

My own earliest experience of gold occurred at the European Hotel in Charleston. I was travelling with my father, who knew the proprietor, who must have been the famed Mick Sheldon. He showed me a jar half-full of gold nuggets, which apart from being unreasonably heavy made no impression on me at all. What a stupidly dull business it seemed. Nor was I impressed by the hotel. It was ... old. Cold, too, and almost empty. We ate in the bare kitchen, just the three of us.

My father loved staying in odd places like this, and now I do too. He told me there had been eighty hotels in Charleston in the good old gold days. Eighty! But numbers varied. Some said there were only thirty-seven. A more authoritative study put the number at ninety-nine. The European was quite big, which was perhaps why it was the sole survivor. It was two-storeyed and made of wood, whereas some of its competitors were reportedly little more than canvas. Even when I was there, the European looked fragile, but it lasted until after Charleston celebrated its centennial in 1966. Then, old and shaky even among the old and shaky, it was pulled down.

*

Gold diggers put an enduring stamp on the country. Miners in the rush following Hartley and Reilly's discoveries took the same routes into the Dunstan that modern traffic follows: through Lawrence and Gabriel's Gully to the south, or along the Pigroot, running from Palmerston to the Maniototo, now State Highway 85. The Dunstan Road, then called the Mountain Road, was more difficult. It crossed four mountain ranges: the Lammermoors, the Rock and Pillar Range, Rough Ridge and the Raggedy Range. But it had one outstanding advantage: it was shorter, and that made it more popular.

Even now it's a tricky route, so primitive it has the highest category listing from Heritage New Zealand, requires a four-wheel-drive vehicle and is closed over winter and sometimes well into spring. I drove over it twice, in spring, without meeting another vehicle, although the rock formations had been so sculptured by gales, rain and snow that it was often hard to tell: some objects appeared to be cars, wagons, pioneers, horses, dinosaurs, gargoyles, Neanderthals, but all of them turned out to be rocks.

About halfway, the road dropped into a green valley full of cows, and for a little while I was back among farmhouses and barns, as well as an old stone hotel, the Styx, with stables and a gaol dating back to gold-rush days. But soon I was among the stone sculptures again, with the car groaning as if it were scaling a mountain (it was) and climbing in and out of trenches at the same time (it was doing that too).

I made it to Rough Ridge, whose name showed restraint on the part of the geographers, for it was rough in the truly heroic sense. It ran off the top of the Dunstan Road, without a signpost or anything at all indicating this might be a way to somewhere else, and the gate was uninviting.

I failed to reach the Serpentine on my first attempt. My car was slipping, sliding and bouncing so much I expected the roof to be covered with head-sized bumps and look like a bag of marbles. Feeling lonely and discouraged, I decided to save it for another day, which didn't arrive until a couple of years later. Same route, same spectres, same bounces. It was a heavier truck, though, and it reached the Serpentine.

It must have been the coldest, most desolate, most vicious,

most uninhabitable gold town in this whole uninviting landscape. Some of it survives, buried in the high-altitude tussock; if you wanted your house to withstand the gales, you built low. There is even a church, still standing, still roofed, at the highest altitude of any church in the land.

When I'd fetched back my heart from my mouth, I inspected the church: small, perfect, its roof held down with rocks and cables and steel stakes, all but empty, its history scorched onto the hymn board. The town's miners paid £100 to build the church, got drunk for its opening, which annoyed the preacher, and thereafter stayed away in such numbers that the empty church was eventually sold as a private home. That was surprising. I'd have thought the church a refuge from the desolation and grind of the mining town, which was either stupendously hot or freezing cold and always, always, leaning into a gale.

The Millers Flat correspondent of the *Otago Daily Times* once struggled up to the town and reported, 'Never did I witness a more forbidding habitation.' As for the miners, 'They were an unwashed and uncombed lot; the debris of ages seemed to have accumulated on their hands, face and clothes.' Not surprising, given the conditions they worked in. In August 1863, the same newspaper reported that forty — forty! — miners who'd pitched their tents under a cliff had been killed when an avalanche buried them, 'an accident of a fearful and most melancholy nature'.

When the gold-panners left, the heavy machinery arrived, and stayed. The huge stamper battery and waterwheel moved from mining settlement to settlement until they came to rest here, where they still stand proudly in the cold amid the relics and ruins, generations after the last miners departed, occasionally being photographed by a posse of tourists brave enough to make the journey in their air-conditioned four-wheel drives.

In the surrounding tussock lie the remains of the town, its cottages, stores, butcher's shop, post office. 'Which was which I could not say,' wrote the Millers Flat correspondent. 'Drink was served in any of these establishments.'

A more or less whole town survives in the Nevis Valley too. It is called Nevis, of course. You get there via Bannockburn, a former gold-miners' town itself. In the hot, bare, once-gold-bearing rock of Bannockburn, vineyards and orchards have taken root, and a miner's hut would fit easily into any one of the three bathrooms of the average Bannockburn house.

Carricktown, a little further on (again, for the adventurous) is still full of mining bric-a-brac, despite its short life. It was never a rich field, but hundreds of miners lived in its stone huts, built dams and water races and the stamping machine whose remains survive. The road through the Nevis Valley is closed over winter, usually from June to September, a blessing without a disguise: if crossing icy rivers twenty-seven times is not enough, frosts that can last up to three weeks at a time should convince any sane traveller to settle for a hot toddy in front of the six o'clock news instead. The road at Duffers Saddle is claimed by some to be the highest public road in the land. It drops into the Nevis Valley following an old Maori trail.

The Nevis might not have been the least hospitable valley in the country, but it was well up there. You needed then, as you did now, a deep respect for wealth to live there, and in its heyday in the 1860s, 600 people had that ambition. A workforce of 500 Chinese miners then worked over the tailings for another forty-odd years until the end of the nineteenth century. You could still find miners in the Nevis until the 1950s, and a few hopeful souls stayed until the new millennium. Their houses, pubs, schools and cemetery have been preserved like mammoths in the Arctic ice. A gold dredge still lies in the river, occasionally clanking. The last time I was there a sign announced the surviving settlement's permanent population: three.

Skippers Canyon, north of Queenstown, hasn't changed very much at all since the first gold-miners climbed peaks, scaled cliffs, crossed rivers and dropped into its gullies. They were lured by the Shotover, 'the richest river in the world,' which sliced through this land like a rip saw.

As with the Serpentine and the Nevis, people come to Skippers Canyon to experience the conditions those early miners faced, without heated seats and Bluetooth. Its main concession to the twenty-first century is a road, but it's not much of a road at all really — a thin, winding thing so tricky to navigate it is rated among the world's two dozen most dangerous routes. It's probably the most signposted route in the country, a forest of poles proclaiming perils to the left and right and imminent death should you be foolish enough to press on. The miners didn't even have a road, for it was only built when the rush was over, and they faced innumerable dangers. When they weren't falling over cliffs or drowning, they were being decimated by scurvy, as in 1863, when they could not obtain any fruit or vegetables.

The most remarkable story here, though, starred two Maori, Zachariah, or Hakaraia Haeroa, and Raniera Erihana, aka Dan Ellison, and was originally recorded by the historian Vincent Pyke. Moving along the Shotover, they came across some

European miners working a remote gorge. Opposite the miners was a beach of 'unusually promising appearance'. But sheer cliffs behind it rose 150 metres and the freezing torrent ran in front of it. Inaccessible? Everyone thought so, until the two Maori plunged in and swam across.

Their dog followed them but was swept downriver and onto rocks, where it huddled pathetically as only a dog knows how to do. Dan took off after it, reached the animal and, by golly, what was this in the rocks? Gold, that's what, and lots of it. They collected 300 ounces that day, now worth nearly half a million dollars, which must still be a record for an afternoon's work.

There followed a sad tale, probably apocryphal, of Dan bring ripped off by an assay clerk and losing the lot, but, even if it was true, he'd made his mark. That spot on the river is now called Maori Point. And today the name Ellison, borne by leaders and landowners around the Otago Peninsula, resounds through the south.

Another old gold trail runs from the Wairau River valley near Blenheim northwards across a range and down Cullen Creek to Linkwater, between Queen Charlotte and Pelorus Sounds. Prospectors found gold in Cullen Creek in 1888, then in the ranges above it, and before very long 1000 men were working the diggings. A whole town, Cullensville, sprang up, with three hotels, two restaurants, billiard saloons, bootmakers, banks, shops, bakeries, a school and even a port at The Grove at the head of Queen Charlotte Sound. There's nothing left of Cullensville now except a few signs. But all along that trail you can find shafts and tunnels and the stumps of trees the miners felled to make the pylons of a cableway, said to be the longest in the country, that carried rock from the workings to a battery that crushed it to powder. On the Wairau River side of the range are the remains of another village which once housed 200 miners and seemed to match perfectly the appalling, steep, dangerous conditions they worked in. I walked around it, which did not take long, and thought, 200 men? Here? In a space scarcely big enough for an Auckland townhouse?

Gold-mining was always a clunking, monotonous, laborious business interrupted occasionally by the glitter of success. The old mining villages are picturesque, but, oh, those stone houses must have been cold and uncomfortable, accommodating single-minded men living for the most part very boring lives. I was astonished by the enterprise, the courage and stoicism of it all. Certainly it was a way out of poverty, and greed played its part — the desire for gold lies somewhere deep in the human psyche.

But those villages have crumbled, the tunnels and flumes have gone and such fortunes as remain are creations of the tourist industry. The remaining roads and rocks of the mining villages are shrines to something, but I'm not sure what. Was it really a golden era? Or just a collection of stories blown up and cobbled together by a nation whose rather dull European history was short of legends? A short-lived adventure that boosted the new colony's fortunes but left only one lasting monument, Dunedin city?

*

Yet gold-miners survived, or a few of them did, their business now one of hard hats and heavy metal.

The Birchfields are famous on the West Coast. You can scarcely move along its long, skinny length without encountering their name, as branches of the family are prominent in farming, mining and local government. There was once even a town called Birchfield, but it has gone now. I drove along the highway north of Westport to the intersection where it once stood and found no trace of it beyond a couple of houses, not even another West Coast ghost town.

Evan Birchfield is one of the biggest gold-miners surviving in New Zealand, certainly the biggest private miner, even if claims like that make him hunch. Around 120 people work for his company, and he is one of the main employers on the Coast.

I found him near Ross, on State Highway 6, the main road south to the glaciers and the Haast Pass. I turned off the road past a coal yard, took a drive up a cutting and arrived at a kind of parking yard for huge machinery, a vista of hydraulic arms and caterpillar tracks and diggers. I drove towards a gateway marked by two giant cogs, pressed a button on a raw steel plate, waited while a rusty steel lattice-work gate slid out of my way, drove past a huge green shed where one of Evan's two army tanks pointed its gun at me, and found him in a room that could go from courtyard to glass-roofed hot-house at the flick of a switch and seemed to accommodate the West Coast's mercurial climate perfectly.

Evan sat on a vast sofa in front of a huge open fire (still allowed on the Coast, of course) and lit a cigarette of normal proportions, asking politely if I'd mind. Considering the range of hazards he surrounded himself with, I thought the risk of lung cancer the least of my worries.

He pointed in one direction, to the Tasman Sea, looking quite peaceful this quiet morning: 'Jane's view' (his wife's). Then he pointed in the other direction, to the yellow forest of diggers and dump trucks: 'My view'.

Evan is quintessential West Coast, if you regard a central feature of Coast character as rather eccentric honesty and a total lack of skite. And he likes to laugh.

Knowing first that he made his money from digging deep into the ground and second that he'd take no offence, I can call him filthy rich. But his house was no Herne Bay mansion, and where was the helicopter? The Aston Martin for him, the Tesla for her? 'Jane said we should go up to the Gold Coast,' he said, 'so we went on holiday to our place up the Grey Valley.'

Yes, he even took his holidays right there on the West Coast, on his Grey Valley farm. He was happy there, with a dump truck and a couple of diggers so he could mine a bit of gold in his spare time. He had a Portacom for a bach and from there he could admire his nice green paddocks. He liked the earthworks side of farming but not the stock. He sat back contemplatively. 'I'd sooner the smell of diesel than cow shit.' Engineering made him happy, not golf, nor fishing.

He was the kind of man you'd meet in a bar, especially if you were in the bar of the Empire Hotel, Ross. He laughed easily, and often, and he sat in his eyrie with the ease of someone who knew his place and loved it, a successor to those raggedy-arse men with their shovels and shanties who once scratched a living and sometimes a fortune from the ground below.

The town of Ross was built on the gold mined here. What was claimed to be the biggest gold nugget ever found in New Zealand (challenged only by the Pessini nugget from Moonlight Creek) was dug out of Ross ground. It weighed 3.1 kilograms and was called the Honourable Roddy. It was presented to King George V for his coronation in 1911 then, apparently, lost by the Palace. ('Another nugget? Confounded colonials!')

You do not have to spend much time in the Ross hotel bar before someone tells you there is more gold lying below the town than was ever dug up around it. That story, in various forms, can be heard all around the Coast, whose inhabitants believe quite literally that their houses, roads, schools and, especially, their national parks, all sit on untold fortunes. The story goes that if you dug a hole through the floor of the bar in the Ross hotel, you'd strike it rich.

Evan has spent a lot of time in the bar of the Ross hotel ('Drinking is my only hobby') and he told this story: 'When a bus tour came by, the publican used to pull up the floorboards and climb down with his shovel and he'd get a pan and drop some gold he had in his hand into it and pan it and show it to the tourists. One day my two sons pulled up outside while this was going on and the publican hopped out of the hole and cried, "I'm in trouble now, the gold-miners have arrived and this is illegal." One of my sons said, "What's going on here?", and one of the women from the bus got really bolshie and shouted out, "You can't touch us, we're tourists ..."'

Ah, the West Coast stories, you just can't beat them. But Evan Birchfield reckoned part of that one, at least, was true: 'There's more gold left in Ross than was ever taken out.' The place has been worked over. Most of the property the Birchfields own around Ross contains old workings. Evan thought those old miners pretty messy, and not that thorough. Some of his best gold has come out of their abandoned tunnels.

The sign that announces 'Ross, Gold Town' is good for the tourists who pile into the town, but for some of its 300-odd residents, at least, a little conflicting. Evan employs a lot of the locals, but on the other side of the king's shilling some residents were objecting to a new gold mine he was planning so close to some Ross houses that residents would be able to spit on it. Some of them were doing just that as his application went through the regional council's arcane processes.

Evan bent a leery eye on locals worried about contaminated water and other side effects: 'They want all gold-mining shut down and pushed out.' A little late, possibly. Ross is surrounded by gold mines bigger than the town, which forms an island of houses and bush amid the workings and heaps, a giant pit and the hills of rock thrown aside when heavy machinery bored into the gold-bearing alluvial gravels the town was built on.

Evan reckoned there was, probably, $2 billion of gold underneath the town. To get at it, it seemed he'd have to move houses, shops, pub, everything.

'Hence the tank,' he said.

Yes, he was joking, although once he thought about building a whole new town of Ross, giving its 300-odd people new houses on new streets with every kind of modern service, and making them part of a holding company so they'd get a share of the profits from mining the streets and back gardens of the old Ross. His sums went like this: the new town would cost, say, $30 million. There was $2 billion worth of gold under the town. It might cost three-quarters of that sum to extract. That was still half a billion dollars left over.

But Ross, like most West Coast towns, consisted of people with their own ideas on life, whether living it or escaping from it. 'You'd need the whole town aboard,' he said. 'Just one person could stop it, and I don't think you'd ever get that ... Back in the nineties when we were mining in Ross we got the blame for everything that went wrong. I always say I'm glad we weren't mining in Ross when Jesus Christ was on the cross because we would have got the blame for that too.'

He lit another cigarette, showed me photographs of gold. It looked like a lot to me, one nugget the size of a twenty-cent coin. An old miner would have been very happy to see that in his pan. To Evan, it 'wasn't too bad'. It came from a test he'd done up the Grey Valley. 'There's more gold here on the Coast than we've ever taken out,' he said, again.

Evan told me about two beach leads he'd been investigating. A lead is gold-bearing gravel along a route, often an ancient creek, which miners always hoped would lead to its source. You found one, you followed it up. Evan believed he'd tracked one right up to the golden bonanza, the modern equivalent of the Eureka moment. For a second, he seemed delighted. Then his face changed, closed. 'I'm not allowed to divulge ...' For a moment he looked just like one of those old miners must have looked, torn between the glory of his discovery and the need to keep quiet, probably, in this case, due more to another impending council hearing than another miner eavesdropping from the next tent.

He was silent for a while, in this lovely house with its twin views, his livelihood on one side, the sea on the other, the car, the ute, the tanks, the respect. Then he pressed a button, and the courtyard became a room, the big fire blazing, cosy, the wild West Coast kept nicely at bay.

The quantity of gold Evan was digging dwarfed all that went before — the Tuapeka, the Dunstan, the Shotover, the giant nugget under the tussock, the Honourable Roddy. It was different, too, finer than grains of sugar. Sometimes he still found big nuggets but: 'I always reckon big gold is no gold at all because once you start getting the big stuff you're coming to the end of the lead.' Alluvial gold came from eroded hard rock, washed and sorted by rivers and glaciers which concentrated the gold and often made richer deposits than its sources.

They'd found a huge nugget weighing ninety-nine ounces in the Ross mine — almost as big as the Honourable Roddy — and they'd washed out other nuggets the size of hen's eggs. 'But the problem when you get big gold,' Evan said, 'is that you don't get a lot of it.' Oh, the crashing of dreams when the old stories of fabulous finds met the toughened steel of Evan's crushers.

Still, he'd fostered a few dreams in his time. Once he was suction-dredging for gold on his Grey Valley farm and he found a creek with a line of nuggets. (A line? He was so casual about it.) He suggested his two sons, young then, get into the creek and check its bottom. 'They got that excited when they saw the nuggets they were almost talking underwater. Every so often a hand would come up with a nugget.'

He pressed the button and the room became a courtyard again. He lit another cigarette and contemplated the ranks of scrapers and drillers. He was an unreformed man, and proud of it. 'Because we're successful we tend to get picked on,' he said. 'Jane and me, we've both worked since we were fifteen. We sometimes worked sixteen hours a day, sometimes in the dead of night.' He talked of one team who went on the booze and didn't turn up for work, so he worked both day and night shifts for forty-eight hours. 'I was that pleased when they came back.'

The trouble was, I thought, that he was in a controversial business. He wanted to dig up the ground and wash it for gold or coal, both carrying grave environmental consequences. Yes, yes, he agreed, he didn't expect to win any popularity contests.

Did he believe in human-induced climate change? The West Coast ran more climate-change deniers per hectare than, probably, anywhere else in New Zealand. Evan did not so much as pause. 'No. But I'm a director of the family's coal mining and I'm not allowed to comment.' When you are talking coal on the West Coast, you are still talking Birchfields. As I said earlier, they are everywhere.

If you were searching for the golden fleece, I asked, and he, Evan, was allowed to get at all the gold on the West Coast, would New Zealand have a debt problem?

'No, no, it would not. There's even gold under this house here.' I looked at his yard with new respect.

*

I went to see Tony Kokshoorn, Mayor of Greymouth, and found His Worship in his office. I walked up the stairs, opened a glass door and went straight in and there he was, behind his desk, probably the only public official I'd ever talked to who didn't count gatekeepers, secretaries, public relations hacks and assorted guard dogs among the trappings of office.

He was proud of that. His hair sat like iron and he carried his tight smile so low that it seemed to be fitted into his chin. This was one of the few times I'd seen a face I'd genuinely call chiselled, if a little unfinished in a way that made it look as if he'd done it himself, this being the West Coast. His accent seemed sculptured too. It became a national institution during the Pike River coal mine disaster, when, in November 2010, twenty-nine men were killed.

This was his last day in office. I'd postponed meeting him from morning to afternoon, but he didn't seem to mind. 'You're my last official function in office,' he said. I fancied I could hear a popping noise, as in tops coming off bottles of Monteith's.

That day, that very afternoon, at sixty-four years of age, he was retiring. His office had a stripped-down look. There was nothing personal left on the shelves, nor his desk: no photographs, nor framed certificates.

Everyone called him Koko, he said. It was pronounced *cockoh*, not like the hot drink. Koko looked stripped down and fit himself. He prided himself on it, and on love of country, which, in his case, meant the Coast.

'I'm going to live and die in this place,' he said. 'There's a lot to be done still. I'm a great believer in going at a thousand miles an hour and my enthusiasm is just starting to wane after fifteen years as mayor and twenty-one on council. I've got miles of energy. I've got ants in my pants. I got kicked out of school. Well, I didn't get kicked out, I got the best reference I could get and the reason they gave it to me was to make sure this kid wasn't coming back the next year.'

All of this by way of hello. He'd sat down and dropped into an autobiographical routine as if he were performing for an audience of one, starting from the very beginning. It was as if I'd turned on the radio. All I had to do was sit back and tap my feet. Whereas, what I really wanted to know was why the Coast was in such a mess, where did all the money go, how had the golden fleece evaporated in the damp air. When we got around to the subject, he was absolutely certain. The Coast's decline had started in the final quarter of the twentieth century, he said.

The extractive days of mining coal and cutting down native forests were now coming to an end. The Pike River mining disaster hadn't just been a grave for twenty-nine men, it was a tombstone over both the coal-mining industry and the neoliberal economic policies introduced by the Labour government. Well, Koko didn't say all of that, I did.

Koko said that the Coast had been in recession all of his working life. He said only 10 percent of the Coast was open for business now. Without jobs, the Coast was exporting its children. The population was in sharp decline: it had dropped by a quarter. House prices had collapsed. Small towns such as Ruru near Lake Brunner, where Tony was born, had disappeared. The Coast had become, as one newspaper headline proclaimed, the ghost-town capital of New Zealand. Yes, tourism was flourishing and tourists had their place, only a lot of Coasters wished that place wasn't the Coast.

Koko wanted the extractive industries back again. Coal might be the devil in climate-change hell, but you didn't have to burn the stuff, you could use it for carbon fibre and other products that wouldn't ruin the planet.

As he spoke, plans were being revealed to reopen the famed Blackwater mine, once the second richest in New Zealand. It had got started when a group of four prospectors were taking a spell early last century and one of them idly dug his heel into the ground. In that remarkable way of southern gold strikes he thereby discovered the Birthday Reef, named for King Edward VII's birthday the same day. Vast amounts of gold were extracted from the reef, which still lies beneath the ghost town of Waiuta near Reefton. The mine closed in 1951.

It then changed hands more often than a used Toyota. Even OceanaGold, which as well as the Macraes mine worked the Globe Progress mine near Reefton until it 'transitioned' (closed) in 2016, had a crack at it, coming to the same conclusion as everyone else: the project was just too difficult.

Waiuta went back to doing what it had done very well, brushing up its relics for tourists. Then an Australian company announced plans to investigate reopening the mine with the help of some government funding, proving again that what glitters might not be gold, but is always entertaining.

Koko also wanted to get back into the Coast's forests. By God, he wanted those forests, and he wanted the hydroelectricity that could be generated by the rivers that flowed through them. He wanted the rare earth minerals lying in conservation land, minerals crucial to the future, for batteries, for electric cars. 'We have to get access to our resources,' he declared. 'Our biggest problem is that we've only ever had access to 16 percent of our land. The other 84 percent is tied up in the conservation estate.'

For him the golden fleece lay buried in land controlled by the Department of Conservation: gold, lithium, maybe uranium, all the rare minerals.

But, could anyone cut down rimu trees half a millennium, even a whole millennium old, with a clear conscience?

Koko had the answer to that, and it was astonishing.

'We know we were the bad boys,' he said, 'but can we cut down the last rimu and say it's going to be another 500 years before we get another one? Of course we can't.'

Instead, here was his plan. You didn't have to cut down the trees. You lifted, say, half a hectare of forest and soil from the ground, put it over there, dug the gold and minerals out of the ground, then put the forest back in the hole.

'You don't even notice it,' he declared. 'When you've jumped through all the hoops to mine gold or anything else, you can rest assured the environment is protected.'

What could I say to that? Nothing, of course. I hadn't expected to like him: too much the old West Coast. But I did like him. He was straightforward and honest about his beliefs, even though he knew he was talking to a nonbeliever. Besides, I'd always been a sucker for charm.

'If New Zealand wants us to be its environmental conscience,' he said, 'they've got to give us something to survive on. The trouble is, Wellington and Auckland will argue every day about how congested they are, how crowded, how expensive, but they won't give up one job and outsource it to the West Coast.'

Even the Inland Revenue Department could be relocated to Greymouth, in his view, and there could be no greater tribute to West Coast hospitality: who else would invite the tax men into their home?

The telephone rang. Koko was proud that everyone could ring him direct.

'Oh yes,' he said to the caller. 'Well, that's no good. I'll see what I can do.' He hung up, called his works manager. There was a women out on such and such street, he said, who was worried that ducklings were dropping through the grate into the storm-water drain. Could the manager take a look, see what he could do?

He hung up. 'Actually,' he said, 'you're now my second-to-last official duty. Saving the ducklings is my last.' And His Worship rose from the table, shook my hand, and went off to his farewell function.

*

We know now why the dragons guarding the golden fleece were sleepless. Armies of Jasons, squadrons of Argonauts want to dig for treasure, drill for it, suck it from the bowels of the earth and the depths of the sea by whatever means they can: gold, coal, oil, rare and precious minerals, substances that to most are the detritus of centuries but to an ever-hungry market are exceedingly valuable. Adventurers threaten the environment, the earth, the sea, the climate we live in, the air we breathe. There just aren't enough dragons.

*

One day in 2019 when he was Mayor of Dunedin, the city built on mining, Dave Cull stood before a town hall full of miners and told them, 'To be clear, if you're promoting fossil-fuel exploration, extraction and exploitation — and especially its expansion —

then understand you are at odds with this community and my council that represents it.'

The town hall stands at the centre of the city, in the heart of the grand old buildings from the gold-mining era. Between it and the sea is a suburb called South Dunedin. It is not so grand. In fact, it makes up a good proportion of the city's 3000-odd houses, a record number in New Zealand, which are threatened with flooding as a result of fossil fuel-related climate change. The town hall itself risks inundation.

As Mayor Cull spoke, outside the hall chanting protesters linked arms and tried to stop delegates to the minerals forum from entering. One even superglued her hands to the door. It was the kind of protest mayors usually tsk-tsked over while imploring delegates and guests not to allow their views of this wonderful city to be soured by the importuning few. But in this case Mayor Cull told the miners the protesters were 'expressing the overwhelming view of this community and my council … We don't have any right to trade in our children's and grandchildren's futures just to make a quick dollar now.'

I talked to him about that speech later. Yes, he'd been importuned, but he was unrepentant.

Miners, however, are one of the most persistent species on earth, and they always return, often assuming new forms, like geological werewolves changing shape to suit the times.

Some of the protesters carried placards objecting to proposed mining at a place in the Otago hills called Foulden Maar. A maar is a wide, low volcanic crater, and this one lies near Middlemarch, a little town with a gas station, B&B, store, cafés and several churches huddling beneath the Rock and Pillar

Range. Middlemarch can be very hot in summer and very, very cold in winter. Its population varies between 150 and 300, so jobs here are important and the mining company, Australia-based, Malaysian-owned, was promising jobs. It already owned land at Foulden Maar but wanted a neighbouring farm too, and for that it needed government consent.

I went looking for Foulden Maar and immediately got lost in a desert of soft brown hills, taking a maze of little roads over Sheepwash Creek, along the Moonlight Road to Butter and Egg Road (whoops, wrong way) and back to Bald Hill. Eventually I found the right road and there it was, a small yellow patch at the bottom of a green basin in the Foulden Hills. Despite a landscape of grotesque shapes, of capering demons and squat, hollowed rock houses, you would not pick it as the remains of a volcano, but things change in 20 million years and that was roughly how long ago this one was formed. The crater became a lake, which lasted for perhaps 100,000 years, and in that time became home to a form of aquatic life called diatoms, tiny creatures that, on dying, sank to the lake bed and, with various kinds of leaves, plants and marine life, had formed layers of sediment so deep that drilling hadn't yet reached the bottom of it.

Two kinds of people wanted that sediment. The first group, scientists in various disciplines, were interested in the amazing range of leaves, many of them still autumn-coloured and quite intact, from trees and plants, even orchids, now long extinct. The plants formed a ghostly signature that made this site one of the most significant in the southern hemisphere. Geologists argued that the deposits were an underground treasure trove for researchers, unique on the planet. They thought Foulden Maar ranked with Pompeii, the Roman city buried by the eruption of Mount Vesuvius in 79 AD.

The scientists were doubly affronted by the intended use of the trove by the second group, who were, of course, modern miners. They planned to grind up the preserved treasures of many millions of years for pig food.

Over the centuries those diatoms had formed a powdery, off-white mineral that miners call diatomite or, when it is mined, diatomaceous earth. It is mostly silica and it has been used in such things as pottery for thousands of years; today it is used to make all sorts of products, from insecticides to toothpaste, from dynamite to kitty litter, from soil for bonsai trees to fertiliser to dental fillings, from swimming pool filters to insecticides to insect repellent. It is quite valuable, but the rare black diatomite found at Middlemarch was worth considerably more than usual, because it was particularly rich in natural organic matter.

So the mining company was prepared to spend quite a lot of money. Black earth was black gold, and hard for this part of the country to turn its back on. The miners promised riches far outweighing gold: oh, the money they'd bring in, the jobs they'd create.

Well, the old gold-miners might be remembered in song and verse. People might wander around their old towns and diggings nostalgically. But I didn't think they'd be as dewy-eyed over the real thing, thousands of men and women doing their best to dig up or tunnel into every hill, cliff, crevice, gully, riverbed and paddock in sight. It had taken a century and a half to quieten that damage into the picturesque, and in the twenty-first-century people just wouldn't wait that long.

Academics objected. Politicians argued. Eventually the company settled the matter itself. It collapsed into receivership and its plan went with it. The whole history of mining suggested the miners would come back again, so Dunedin City Council led a charge to have it protected from miners and bought the site in 2023.

From the air, this part of the country looks like a human brain, smooth rounded lobes riven with sulci. Its bleakness makes it the most remote part of the nation, more accessible than Fiordland but less familiar. Most people have no reason for going there: its only real sign of life is the old Central Otago railway to the west, now the famed bike trail. The area is without landmarks other than its strangeness. You can drive through it without knowing where you are.

It is very beautiful though. The most similar landscape is the volcanic plateau in the middle of the North Island, though at least the Army lives there, which makes it seem positively bustling compared to these hills.

I'd first visited the Middlemarch region as a writer for the *New Zealand Listener*, when I stayed at the old stone Stanley's Hotel at what was Macraes Flat then and is now simply Macraes. I was interested in a planned new gold mine. The pub was cold and the toilet and shower down the hall, but the building dated from 1882, so what did I expect? In the evenings the public bar was crowded with locals, which was puzzling, for in the daylight it was hard to spot a house outside the tiny village around the pub.

The talk was all about the grand new gold mine soon to open. Some were against it, most were for it, and it was a rowdy night. The new mine was hard to imagine then, in this abandoned, lovely stony wilderness. Environmental reports had been dismissive of concerns, or most of them at least: in sum, even a mine as big as this one would be lost here.

More than two decades later, here I was again. I didn't remember the two big stags' heads dominating the long, narrow public bar, nor the boar's head, but then it had been a long night on that first trip. Perhaps a dozen people were in the bar this time, and they all seemed in favour of the mine, partly because they made their living from it, partly because they rated their employer, OceanaGold, highly. Every worker I talked to was content with his or her lot. The money was good, the jobs were secure and, in this part of the country, that was to be neither sneezed nor sneered at. The company seemed to me to engender the same emotion in its followers as evangelistic churches: yes, they made money, but they had a higher calling.

Outside, a bus full of Australians pulled into the car park at Frasers Pit, the vast amphitheatre at the centre of the great mine, so big it seemed to hollow this country. It was a huge hole in the ground, and it had the same overpowering effect as the Grand Canyon, the difference being that Frasers Pit was, well, a hole in the ground.

It dived down in a series of benches to a portal leading to tunnels. At its bottom machines scurried about the entrance to a tunnel, looking, from this distance, like mice around holes in a skirting board. Half a kilometre above sea level we tourists gazed at charts of the tunnels resembling cardiographs, tunnels that zigzag down to 289 metres below sea level.

The mine's processing plant runs twenty-four hours a day. It crushes, grinds, treats with chemicals and cooks 6 million tonnes of ore a year, reducing millions of years of natural weathering in about thirty minutes. The gold it recovers, in grains too small to be seen by the human eye, with something like the consistency of talcum powder, finally emerge from a smelting furnace as bars of gold bullion that are then flown to the Perth Mint and further refined into gold of 99.9 percent purity.

If the topography resembled a human brain, it had been lobotomised here. The roads through Macraes led into landscapes of cliffs, terraces, valleys, lakes, escarpments, plains — every shape imaginable in this world or, for that matter, any other. The land had been cut, dug, sculpted, hammered, pounded as its faint traces of gold were wrung from it. You could drive for half an hour or more along the roads penetrating these workings without seeing the end of them.

In its information for visitors, OceanaGold declared that 'natural systems thrive in a changing landscape'. A 'changing landscape'? Waves of gold-miners, the originals in the nineteenth century then those jobless, desperate men forced to take their picks and shovels into the hills by the Depression, left a few grooves and ponds and tunnels, but they made no real impression on the land. The new miners, astonishingly, were making the same claim. The waste rock, they said, was being 'shaped to reflect the natural angles of block mountains that are a feature of the surrounding landscape'. The most polite way of expressing my own opinion of that claim was, 'Oh yeah?' I questioned the company and received no answer.

Yet the company was doing a great deal to keep opinion on its side. It had set up a community development trust and given it the old hotel to run, along with funding to restore other old buildings; it had paid for a medical centre, given money to local schools and an education trust, to community organisations and sports clubs.

Not far from Stanley's Hotel, deep in a gully in Deepdell Creek, was an old mine called Golden Point. It had the only complete, working stamper battery surviving in New Zealand. It had pounded ore until the 1950s. Around it stood the mine manager's house and three mud-brick workers' cottages, all of them mean. The best I could say of them was that they'd probably kept some men alive, although considering the miners' lives, their inhabitants might not always have thought that a good thing. The desperate dwellings of the Depression miners must have been even meaner. Living in this dark, cold place would have been more miserable than I could imagine. It was not just half a century but light years removed from the well-paid, comfortable lives of their successors.

But when I asked myself if mining could be the golden fleece again, I thought of Macraes, and Pike River, and Foulden Maar, and the other mining controversies that have wracked this country, and thought, 'God, I hope not.'

CHAPTER THREE

The Fleece

The McLeans of Coll were unlikely sheep nobility. In the 1840s, the widow Mary and her five children were literally starving to death on that tiny island in the Inner Hebrides. Coll lies off the west coast of Scotland, a little west of Mull, far enough north to be cold and close enough to the Atlantic to be wild. It's about twenty kilometres long and five wide, a chip of land whose inhabitants in those days had one common objective: staying alive.

For some 500 years, Coll was owned by a branch of the Clan Maclean. In the late sixteenth century another branch of the Macleans invaded the island, and an internecine battle was fought at Breacachadh Castle. The locals won the day and settled the family spat by chopping off their cousins' heads and throwing them into a stream, still called the 'stream of the heads'. The original castle, whose name was pronounced rather like a sneeze, presides over its dominion of sand and rock to this day.

By the mid-nineteenth century, life on Coll was unrelenting drudgery, consisting almost entirely of gathering or growing enough food to sustain life and keeping out enough of the weather to avoid death. The McLean family shared the island with perhaps 1000 other people. Alexander McLean was a man of his time, his various occupations — farmer, fisherman, cooper — all part of living in a subsistence economy. He did not live in it as long as he'd hoped, however, for one bitter winter his small boat was wrecked and McLean so badly hurt that he later died. His widow Mary McLean, née Maclean (for her father was Laird of Coll) and the five surviving children took over the family business, which was, yes, staying alive.

Coll was not the best place to achieve that. Even in the twenty-first century it supports only some 150 people, and they can leave any time they like. Two centuries ago, Coll was all the islanders had, the place they lived and died in, for their land was everything, their living and their soul. A patch of ground was a gift, and the McLeans lived on fish and the potatoes they grew.

In the 1840s two disasters struck the Hebrides. First, the market for kelp, a seaweed, collapsed. Then potato blight struck the islanders' main crop. The era became known as the 'dark forties' as people began to starve. The McLeans were reduced to living on seaweeds such as dulse and carrageen, and the choice became clear to Mary: leave or die. Almost everyone on Coll faced the same dilemma. Most of them left, even Alexander Maclean, heir to the island. He took himself off to South Africa. Others chose Canada. Mary McLean decided on Australia.

Mary was fifty-three years old. She was desperate, and she must have been brave. The family, her three sons, John (or Jock, who was twenty-two), his brothers Allan (four years younger) and Robertson, and two daughters, Mary and Alexandrina, packed their belongings onto their backs and walked over the dunes to Arinagour at the head of Loch Eatharna, still the island's main settlement. They took a boat to Tobermory on the Isle of Mull and joined hundreds of islanders desperate to go to, well, wherever ships would take them.

Coll never recovered. Its twenty-first century tourist literature rather desperately says that Coll 'definitely has lots of wild, raw nature that thrives due to the solitude ... What it does have is quite special and often quite intangible.' The novelist Alexander McCall Smith thought so. He bought the Cairns of Coll, a little to the north of the island, vowing to protect them forever. (As an aside, McCall Smith's grandfather, George Marshall McCall Smith, ran the Hokianga hospital for thirty-four years, a tempestuous and often controversial regime which ended in 1948.)

The McLeans found a ship to Australia. They were an enterprising family, and their narrow escape from starving to death was an excellent incentive to do well. The talents they'd needed to survive on Coll — essentially determination, hard work and enterprise — were ideally suited to a new colony. The boys worked first as shepherds and, eventually, the family made their way to the new goldfields, Bendigo and Ballarat. They had a small farm and opened a store for miners, both buying gold and carrying it. The story goes that a Chinese miner, Fan So, swam a river to warn John McLean that a band of robbers planned to murder him and steal his gold, establishing a lifelong allegiance that would last until Fan's death. Within a decade the McLeans had made enough money to buy two sheep stations in Victoria.

Then came news from New Zealand, incredible news: great swathes of land were being given away for virtually nothing to anyone with the enterprise and the desire to take them up. Could that possibly be true?

Well yes, it was. An accommodating government (at least to the mainly British settlers), with a fine disregard for character and splendour, had declared the land beyond the coastal plains — the rich, vast, tussock-covered expanses rising to the mountains — to be 'waste land'. In the main, these were presumed to be vacant lands. The Maori owners or occupiers of the land, the Ngai Tahu, were either seen off with mere handfuls of cash or simply ignored.

For very little money, a prospective farmer could have tens of thousands of hectares. All a run-holder had to do was find a good spread of vacant land, roughly mark its boundaries (to the nearest few hundred hectares) and charge off to Nelson, Christchurch or Dunedin to make it theirs. (In those early days Nelson included Marlborough, and Otago included Southland). They had to promise to stock the land within nine months, although this was soon relaxed to a year. The government would then lease it to them in perpetuity for a peppercorn rental.

Sharp and adventurous colonists knew a good deal when they saw it. The 1850s saw a land rush in areas of the South Island quite as dashing as its equivalent in gold. Runholders or squatters soon claimed plains, valleys, foothills, even the more accessible mountains. Within a very few years they'd occupied every space where a ewe might cobble together a feed. Most of Canterbury, for example, was gobbled up by just 200 large estates in a very short time. Otago followed, then Nelson.

This was an astonishing period in New Zealand history. A brave new (European) nation was making its way, giving every one of its (European) citizens a fair go, but providing some of them with a brisk head start and thereby establishing a colonial aristocracy. For the rewards were huge. Wool was a way to riches as fabulous as any gold-miner might dream of. Gold-seeking was more democratic: anyone with a shovel and a pan could do it. But the big difference, of course, was that when you'd dug up the gold there was no more of it, whereas there was always another sheep.

A canny squatter could expect to recover his investment in a mere four years of farming. Profits could reach 30 percent a year. The South Island economy moved rapidly from gold to sheep. The era of the golden fleece had well and truly begun.

The McLeans weren't just canny. Having dealt with privation, starvation, deprivation, aggravation and ruination on Coll, not to mention a drought crippling farmers in their new home in Australia, they were what modern entrepreneurs called motivated. And here was land for the taking!

The family sold up and shipped to New Zealand along with sheep, cattle, horses, Fan So and some capital, and set about laying claim to, well, pretty much everything they could get their hands on. Their first farm was on the Waimakariri River near Christchurch, at a place still called McLeans Island. Other huge farms followed, causing some resentment. A would-be member of Parliament complained about a huge McLean property called Laghmor (named after their tiny village on Coll, although verily it was far more than just half a world away from home), which ran from Ashburton south to Hinds. He argued that this vast estate employed only a manager and four shepherds. Wrong, said a newspaper article. The station employed sixty or seventy shepherds and other hands who were all doing much better than they would if the estate, and others, were broken up by designing politicians.

Then John McLean heard about a huge swathe of land deep in the back country, beyond the Lindis Pass. Some said a shearer told him about it, some claimed it was the Ngai Tahu chief Te Huruhuru.

The first European across the Lindis Pass was the Otago surveyor John Turnbull Thomson in 1857. He named it after Lindisfarne Island, near his home in Northumberland, England. John McLean followed Thomson's track. If he'd been accompanied by Te Huruhuru, he would have known the pass as Okahu.

Either way, McLean climbed a peak near Lake Hawea which is still known today as Grandview Mountain.

Oh my!

For a man who'd grown up on a tiny, rocky island, even one who'd passed through the great reaches of Australia, this was something new. Below him lay Lake Hawea and, further to the west, Lake Wanaka and, beyond them both, the great ranges of the south. More important to him were the tussock-covered slopes that lay to hand: fantastic sheep country. Many thousands of hectares and only one diminutive Pakeha, John McLean. And his mother, brothers and sisters.

He made his sketch, hastened back to the coast, lodged his claim.

In those days it must have taken quite a bit to give the Waste Land Board pause. It was used to doling out large bits of the South Island. The McLeans' claim, however, made them contemplate their teacakes quite solemnly. All that country for one family? Never mind. The number 8 wire tradition was well on its way. If in doubt, improvise. What if we divided the claim into four, they mused: one for each McLean brother, and one for sister Alexandrina? The board wasn't there to get in the way. It existed to facilitate, to encourage farming and settlement in the far reaches of its dominion.

In the end Morven Hills Station, an amalgam of stations, became the biggest run in New Zealand. It covered somewhere between 162,000 and 202,000 hectares, anything up to 2000 square kilometres, more than five times the size of Great Barrier Island, almost as big as Stewart Island. The entire island of Coll covers only 100 square kilometres.

Morven Hills was 75 kilometres long from north to south. Its boundaries ran alongside Lake Hawea down the Clutha River beside what is now Lake Dunstan, then back up the Dunstan Range to the Lindis Pass. Combined with the family's other runs it wasn't so much a farm, more an empire.

The McLeans still had to stock the land to meet the Waste Land Board's demands. An inspector was sent to check. A famous story, which might even be true, had the inspector being taken out onto the run to admire a flock of sheep grazing on the pastures. That night John McLean poured whisky with a liberal hand. Meanwhile the station's shepherds were moving the flock to another block so that the next day, when the inspector was checking in that direction, sheep again stretched as far as his eye could see. Another night, another bottle, another pasture, and the same flock was moved under cover of darkness. Everyone was happy. (Madge Snow, whose family had farmed Morven Hills from 1914, remarked to me, 'That story has been told by generation after generation. I'm quite sure it's true but it gets embroidered every time around. He couldn't have started with so many thousand sheep when he'd just bought the property.')

The tale may have grown as a satire reflecting the farmers' view of bureaucrats generally, for in the McLeans' case the requirement was ridiculous. Nevertheless, their flock rapidly increased, eventually reaching more than 140,000 sheep.

*

I was searching for remnants of the sheep aristocracy, the land barons who once bestrode the nation and gave rise to the legend of the golden fleece. Morven Hills seemed a very good place to start.

I wondered, first, how an apparently penniless family got so rich so quickly, for the McLeans' legend grew as rapidly as their flock. The story of the fortune they made on the Australian goldfields was easy to tell, hard to prove. Robert Pinney, one of the high-country historians, asked the same question. In his book *Early Northern Otago Runs* he cast doubt on the tale on the grounds that it was impossible to make such a fortune without capital to work with.

Was the family legend embroidery? Well, the best part of two centuries on, it had no serious competing story. But there had to be some reward for being the Laird of Coll's daughter, and where had Mary found the money to ship her entire family to Australia? That must have been expensive, even then.

In the end, what did it matter? The hardworking McLeans had the spirit, the enterprise and the courage required to succeed in a hard land, and Morven Hills in the Lindis was the capital of their empire.

It was a bright spring day when I drove around the huge bluff at the foot of the pass. The Lindis Valley was at its best and brightest, the trees a delicate green, the soft hills golden.

The Lindis might have been remote, but it was an artery into the interior. Beyond it, the road divided just south of the tiny town of Tarras. It was the district capital in the days of the great stations; now it's just a few shops in stone buildings, a school, a scatter of houses and the war memorial hall and community centre, its grandest building. From Tarras, one route led to Cromwell, the other to Wanaka. The Lindis Pass was critical to those routes, to both locals and through traffic, and had been for centuries. Even now it was wild enough to imagine the Ngai Tahu plodding this ancient trail from the coast to the lakes, probably the same route taken by John McLean.

Morven Hills station itself grew into a small village. The homestead was built of stone of course, for its rocky landscape was one of the marvels of the region. Stone walls, corrugated-iron roof, a simple cottage, later expanded with adobe bricks.

Madge Snow, who farmed the property for many years with her husband Max, believed Sir George Grey, twice New Zealand's governor, slept in the old homestead. If he did, he would have been cold. The house was small, and its walls were thick, but in winter it froze.

Madge noted that 'the stonemason must have forgotten that he'd crossed the equator, as he set the house facing southeast.' The veranda faced the river 'but it's on the cold side of the house, so never sees the sun'. That alignment was not uncommon in those days. Christchurch's planners were also equatorially challenged, the city's street grid perfectly designed for the refrigerant easterly to pipe through in one direction and the vicious sou'westerly to prowl in the other.

The huts for shearers and shepherds were also built of stone, that staple of Coll. As was the big cookhouse. A temporary woolshed was used until a proper stone one was built. You could not look at that woolshed today without realising that the time of the golden fleece was not just an era, it was a philosophy, even a religion, and this was not so much a woolshed as a cathedral. Certainly some southern cathedrals — the rather narrow Anglican cathedral in Christchurch, for instance, or the modest building in Nelson — lacked the proportions and grandeur of the Morven Hills woolshed.

This was the Temple of the Golden Fleece, in heartland fleece country, a huge stone affair, one of the biggest woolsheds in the country, a shrine accommodating thirty-four shearing stands. (A shearing stand is the place where a shearer does his work: one stand for each shearer. An average farm now might have, say, four stands.) Only the Teviot Station woolshed, built by John Cargill (son of Otago's despotic first superintendent) was bigger, and that was burned down in 1924, either by thieves, envious neighbours or a stray cigarette, you took your pick. Its stone ruins now stand in a paddock, looking like the New Zealand version of a medieval castle keep.

I'd seen the Morven Hills woolshed often enough, on my way over the Lindis Pass; it stands on a terrace a few hundred metres from the highway, partly hidden, beautifully mysterious. It always seemed to slow the car by the sheer force of its presence. It dwarfed the other buildings.

John's humble homestead, still occupied, was overshadowed by the stables. A hut that was first a school then a blacksmith's shop then a store, still stood, and the long cookhouse lay behind.

This village of stone buildings went back to the grand era of high-country sheep stations. A different age. Now, the gates were locked because, Madge said, one weekend someone had stolen all the saddles and bridles and other gear in the old stables. 'It's sad,' she said. 'In my times, we left everything open.'

Richard Snow, Madge's son, farmed the property now and kindly allowed me to nose around as long as I liked, and I did, going up the curving drive past the new farm homestead (new, that was, in Morven Hills terms), to cower below the massive woolshed. Officially, it was nineteenth-century Australian Georgian, which sounded grandiose for a woolshed. I stood before it, awed by its superb proportions, its power, antiquity and workmanship, by the arcane practices it accommodated. Shearers had always been a race apart, a people with their own traditions, laws, customs.

Inside, the thirty-four stands had been reduced to six, for modern shearers using power-driven hand-pieces are much faster and more efficient than the old blade shearers. This was a working woolshed, not an artefact. Everything here had a purpose.

I had worked in woolsheds from time to time and I'd always loved the smell of wool and sweat and sheep shit; the still, poised feeling of an empty shed; the rituals that were almost religious; the hierarchies established over the ages, with an interloper like me right at the bottom. Here, I was awed by the generations of lanolin varnishing the floors, the wooden gates and pens worn smooth by hundreds of thousands of sheep, everything stripped for action and ready for the next show, the silence of a place that, for a few weeks a year, was the beating heart of the run.

In April 1874, 140,000 sheep were shorn here. That was the heyday of the golden fleece. The present farm manager, Joe, reckoned a blade shearer might average a hundred sheep a day, meaning the gang would shear 3400 sheep. They would have been on the station for forty-one days, well over a month. Armies of shearers, shed hands, rousies, cooks — hundreds of people had to be housed and fed.

Today I could see the evidence: a store account for ten tons of flour, ten boxes of tea. A wool cartage agreement, in fine handwriting, dated 6 October 1875, for transporting the Morven Hills clip, some 900 bales, to Oamaru. That must have been a magnificent procession, a dusty caravan leaving no one in any doubt about what was riding on the sheep's back. The shed — what a diminutive term for such an edifice! — accommodated and celebrated the highlight of the sheep farmers' year, when all the work and planning and tedium and worry was squeezed into bales and sold.

Morven Hills woolshed was a piece of history in full working order and far more imposing (and graceful) than the old homestead nearby. Perhaps the McLeans regarded it in the same way, for they added an odd touch of grandeur. The building had two doors into it. One was for the men, the other for the boss, and if a shearer went through the wrong one, according to Madge Snow, he was fired. The two doors were still there, one of them squeezed into a corner and blocked off. It had the feel of a servants' entrance and, looking at it, I tried to imagine that the boss had been eating seaweed not so long before.

Madge believed the woolshed had been built between 1861 and 1863, just as the Lindis gold rush over the road was losing steam. That was bad for the miners, but good for John McLean. Up to then, the miners had been a nuisance. Now they were increasingly unemployed and McLean had just the job for them.

'Jock McLean said, "Come on, all you people, let's build something," and that's when they built the woolshed,' Madge said. 'I'll stand by that because when you look at the shed it's not a building that could be put up by three or four men: they needed a team. He fed them, they had the cookshop and the sheep in the hills. He might have paid them a small wage, but he got them all working and the woolshed was built. Jock McLean was very enterprising, but no one gives him any credit for it.'

The McLeans were motivated not only by their struggle to survive on Coll: they were genetically equipped for the job. Francis Fuller, a military gent who lived in Canterbury for a time and published a detailed account of colonial enterprise and investment in his book *Five Years Residence in New Zealand* (1859), noted that 'the colonist who has come from Scotland is generally observed to have succeeded better than those from other parts of the United Kingdom, as the mode of education and the principles of economy inculcated in North Britain induce more self-reliance, and they apply themselves more readily to the circumstances of a thinly peopled country, than do those practised only in the more densely peopled districts of the British Isles.'

Go the Scots!

I asked Madge Snow why the McLeans had built such a small house when the woolshed beside it was majestic. Their efforts went into the working parts of the farm, she replied. The place they lived in was less important. Perhaps because both John and Allan McLean (Robertson returned to Scotland and died in 1871) were bachelors.

Later Madge told me, 'After McLean left [early in the 1870s] it was just a series of managers, and a manager isn't going to take care of your property or plant it up and make it beautiful. That's why it's so bare. Max and I did it up, but I'm not into old buildings. We lived in it after we were married, from 1954 to 1958, four years. Although the walls are very thick, it was cold. When you're first married, it's home, and it's exciting, and I liked it. We had a Shacklock range — Dirty Dora we called it because it smoked so much. It was home. Then the time came when the farm was getting bigger and we needed a married couple and we had to have a house for them, and we thought, why don't we have the new house.'

When I met Madge, she was living in a house she and her husband Max had built on Beacon Point, the peninsula jutting into the lake beside Wanaka town. She was eighty-five. The house had been built on a large section of almost two hectares they'd bought in 1983, now full of trees and flowers, every planting recorded, every one part of a grand design in Madge's head so it was that most lovely of gardens, apparently without pattern but actually so artfully designed that when you walked into it, the garden took over your senses. The composition surrounded a large, very comfortable house, the kind of home built by people used to space, and you immediately felt peaceful in it.

Well removed from the Lindis extremes, it was surrounded by colours — red, silver, yellow, even green (for Madge disliked native trees) — and heathers arranged like cushions. She looked through rhododendrons to the lake and mountains and talked about Morven Hills. 'I loved the life. I just loved the life. Having people come in was part of your life. I had a little idiosyncrasy: I always had a kettle boiling on the range because I had been used to it on Dirty Dora, where the kettle was always bubbling away. When we built the new house, my mother said, "You are wasting power." It was just something I did, a hangover from the old days. You welcomed people, you were pleased to see them, and I loved to cook. I still cook and I love it and I think all girls should learn to cook.'

She laid out homemade apple and cinnamon muffins and shortbread and I decided there was certainly something to be said for a philosophy like that. Madge, so full of life, died in 2021, aged eighty-nine.

*

I wanted to see one last artefact at Morven Hills, one that showed just how brutal life could be at the ragged end of the golden fleece.

John Polson from Sutherland in Scotland was working as a shepherd on the station in the bitter winter of 1869. He and his wife, Christina, lived in a stone hut, thought to have been built by John McLean around 1865. They had one son, Roderick, who was fifteen months old when Christina gave birth again. Roderick had been born without any medical care, for the Polsons' hut was fifty kilometres of hard country from the nearest doctor. They'd expected to get through this birth on their own, too, except that, instead of one baby, there were two. They were born prematurely, quite common with twins. Snow lay deep on the ground. First one baby boy died, then the second. I thought of my own twin sons, and their difficult, premature birth, and felt the anguish.

No one could reach them. John could not so much as dig their graves in the icy ground. The twins were named George and William. They lay frozen until the ground thawed enough for John to break into it. He marked the grave with a slab of schist bearing only the date, 1869. One hundred and forty years later, the Polsons' descendants placed a new stone on the grave, properly inscribed. This story had told me more about early life on that hard land than any other I had read.

I went looking for the hut. Even now it was not easy to find. A narrow shingle road led off the highway and up a valley with the snow-specked wall of a mountain at its end. I passed several farms, stopped to ask a farmer if I was going the right way (although in truth there was no other way to go), opened (and closed) several deer gates blocking the road, and finally spotted a tiny hut huddling well back, on the cold and shady side of its ridge.

The gate was locked, but I'd spoken to the farm manager, so I climbed over a deer fence. The hut sat near a stream and huge, old, fractured willows. It was small and strong, about five metres long and four deep, its walls, I guessed, about half a metre thick. It had been there, now, a century and a half, and it was low: anyone but a child would have had to duck through its only door. The lintel scarcely came to my neck. There was one small-paned window at the front, and another in a side wall, and these two openings admitted the only light.

The hut had just one room, with a wooden ceiling, and tin roof. Small as it was, the little fireplace inside must have struggled to warm it, and firewood would have been scarce in this barren place. Even now, on a late spring day, the gauge in my car had recorded an outside temperature of five degrees. The cold seemed to seep out of the cottage as if I was standing next to a fridge with the door open.

It was as lonely as it felt. I could hear a tractor working down the valley, out of sight, but otherwise it was completely silent, and I was startled when a couple of starlings fled squawking from a nest somewhere in the stonework.

I walked around outside for a while, looking at the valley and the hills, imagining the abandonment and the despair, and the two tiny bodies under the ground nearby, and left with the wind wailing in the fences.

*

Perhaps the McLeans, despite their gravelly beginnings, had begun to show symptoms of a common phenomenon among the newly landed gentry, one summed up by Oliver Duff, a former editor of the *New Zealand Listener*. Duff was writing about Canterbury, whose immigrant lists on the locally revered First Four Ships were literally set in stone in the city square. Its squatters were the best and most foolish men New Zealand ever imported, he said, for 'they had no sooner performed miracles of enterprise and endurance than they forgot that they were the creators of a brave new world and sent back to England for their top hats'.

The McLeans steadily acquired even more land. They were very good at it. They took up Waitaki Plains and Redcastle in North Otago, and the land that became Waikakahi Station near the coast and a little north of the Waitaki River. John based himself at Morven Hills, but Allan took up residence at Waikakahi, taking Fan So with him.

Then he reached for his top hat. The Morven Hills homestead was at best functional, but Waikakahi was grand. It ran to twenty-one rooms, which was big, even if not as imposing as many of the mansions built by the nouveau sheep barons.

Allan's style there was an emphatic rejection of poor, bleak Coll. He wore plum-coloured suits and rode in a white 'wagonette', an open carriage which for some reason he called the Yankee Express. He named his homestead 'The Valley'. But his masterpiece was the mansion he built in Christchurch and called 'Holly Lea'.

'I don't know much about Allan McLean,' Madge Snow told me. 'He's a shady character to me. He had an illegitimate daughter. He left her money in his will. He left Morven Hills and they must have split, he and Jock McLean.'

But, duplicating an English manor house in the middle of Christchurch city? Did he have delusions of grandeur?

'That was Allan,' she said. 'I don't know anything about that side of the family. I think he was having it on with his housekeeper. He never married, but he had this daughter.'

His daughter was Mary Henderson, who was later supported by the McLean Institute, founded by Allan, until she died in 1962. McLean made provision for her in his will, but it was niggardly compared with members of his family born on the right side of the blanket. He left money to nieces, nephews, friends and members of his staff, particularly his long-serving housekeeper Emily Phillips, who got a life interest in Holly Lea and an annuity of £3000 until her death in 1919. Three thousand pounds in 1919, according to the Reserve Bank's calculator, was the equivalent of $300,000 today. Handsome indeed, although reassuring, for Allan had at least broken the family mould: apart from their mother and sisters, the McLean men seem to have had no women in their lives. I found it interesting that the only known partner, of sorts, had been kept secret. Mrs Phillips, incidentally, sold her rights to the McLean Institute for £2000 ($200,000 now) in 1913 and moved to Waimate, which was not far from Waikakahi.

Unlike Allan, John was interested in public affairs, and became a prominent citizen and a member of the Otago Provincial Council and the Legislative Council. He also became a major shareholder in the Bank of New Zealand and, with his brother-in-law, George, and Mr Justice Gillies, exposed a scandal that shook the young nation. The bank, one of the country's most trusted institutions, had lost all of its reserves and a third of its paid-up capital through a villainous mix of lending to the old boys' network on over-valued assets, a Sydney manager who was a notorious gambler embezzling a great deal of money, an Adelaide branch that 'squandered' funds in a 'reckless and disastrous way', 'suspicious' advances in the North Island, and 'rash' advances in the South Island without adequate security. Oh, the mess, the scandal, and all under the noses of directors such as, yes, John McLean. No one went to jail, apparently. It was a good time to be a prominent New Zealander.

Though the family's New Zealand history was dominated by the two brothers, their sister Alexandrina also made her own way. She married a young up-and-comer, George Buckley, and they had a son pompously called St John McLean Buckley, who, after a short-lived Oxford education, returned to New Zealand and busied himself on his Uncle John's several farms. St John Buckley followed the family's developing tradition and built his own brick castle, Redcastle, still carefully preserved in the grounds of St Kevin's College in Oamaru. Another monument to the golden fleece, the mansion was built of red brick with burnt-orange roofing tiles imported from France and its interior was sumptuous by the standards of the day. In his old age, and still a bachelor, Uncle John moved from Morven Hills to Redcastle to live with Buckley and his wife, Frances.

When John died in 1902 he left his property and money to Buckley. Alexandrina died a fortnight after John did. Brother and sister were buried in a family grave in Addington Cemetery, Christchurch, still marked by an obelisk the height of a country church.

Fan So, the family retainer, died in 1885 and was buried in Oamaru. The headstone declared him to have been a native of China who was for thirty-three years 'a faithful servant'.

*

By the 1870s Allan and John McLean had become the owners of New Zealand's largest flock. But the days of the great runs were ending, partly because of poor farming practices — the runholders' technique of torching tussock to encourage regrowth that the stock could eat was ruining the land and encouraging a plague of rabbits — and partly because the nation was seeking a fairer model. In response, the reforming Liberal government of 1890 began breaking up many of the vast runs into much smaller farms.

The government had made an election promise that it would put more farmers on their own properties, partly in response to an expanding market for New Zealand's meat and dairy products, and partly because it was an equitable thing to do. Its eye fell upon the huge estates of the land barons and the McLeans became targets.

They may not have fitted easily into the popular view of entitled landowners, for they were in every sense the New Zealand dream: impoverished men escaping desperate circumstances who had worked hard to create a new life in this country and had been successful, probably beyond their own wildest dreams.

Too successful perhaps. Later philosophers would have asked why two men, both of them bachelors, should have become so rich from a public asset that could provide a living for ten families. Or a hundred.

Modern observers might also have accused the government of self-interest by keeping a canny eye on their voter base, and of setting a time bomb for future generations by taking millions of acres of Maori land for the same ends. But its reforms also encompassed old-age pensions, minimum wages and maximum working hours, arbitration procedures for managing industrial disputes, and voting rights for women, thereby establishing a precedent for endless claims later that New Zealand was 'leading the world'.

Breaking up the big estates for smaller farms and giving the new settlers financial support was part of that process; a popular part of it too, because a wider public had come to resent the way the bespoke land barons now bestrode great swathes of countryside and treated them as fiefdoms.

Echoes of the Liberal government's reforms would be heard a century later when a new revolution swept through the high country. Successive governments reviewed the traditional pastoral leases that had created the farming fiefdoms. New deals gave farmers freehold title to the more easily farmed and profitable parts of their properties in exchange for giving up the higher, wilder areas, which then went into the public conservation estate.

The policy was popular at first sight as a win-win offer: farmers emerged with valuable freehold, the public got some of their land back. It wasn't that easy, of course, and inevitably some, usually the farmers, won considerably more than others, usually the public. By 2006, farmers, initially resentful, were the scheme's most avid defenders, while the public, jubilant at first, were calling it a turnip.

*

In 1914 Madge Snow's father Hector Gibson bought Morven Hills with his friend and partner George Henderson. The two already owned the neighbouring Breast Hills. Hector was only twenty-six. He'd been head shepherd at Morven Hills and now he owned that too, although it was a much smaller version of the great estate. The two stations had been whittled down to 20,639 hectares, still held under pastoral lease: that is, the government owned the land, the farmers rented it. Hector and George farmed the two properties until after the First World War, when they divided their holdings and Hector took Morven Hills. He later added the Malvern Downs station, down the road near Tarras.

Madge Snow grew up there. She believed Hector had bought the property to be closer to his future wife, Eileen Jolly, who worked at the Tarras post office ('Isn't that what men do?'). He died in 1938, only forty-eight years old, and at the age of thirty-five Eileen became the owner of two farms and, Madge wrote later, 'two small children, very little money and a huge mortgage'.

She also inherited a great deal of work. By Madge's accounting, she worked seven days a week, every day of the year, from 1938 until 1953, cooking for and looking after the men on the farm, always three of them and often more.

Madge said, 'My mother worked so hard. I was lucky: my father was very fair. I was born with a silver spoon in my mouth.' Perhaps it was a cooking ladle? I asked. After all, Madge too had cooked and cleaned and cared for her family and the dozens of people who worked on the farm through the seasons, through power cuts and snowstorms.

'That was my life,' she said. 'Only Max, he had a funny heart and his health gave out. He had a bad head injury too. He went downhill after that. [He died in 2008, aged eighty-three.] Otherwise I'd still be at Morven Hills, because I loved the life. I just loved it.'

*

Waikakahi, 'The Valley', was Allan's pride and joy, and when his partnership with brother John broke up, he kept it. He'd made it into one of Canterbury's best stations, carrying almost 70,000 sheep. He lived in his twenty-one-room homestead with his housekeeper, Mrs Phillips, and was known for his lavish parties. He might have been a little homesick, for he dubbed a town, on the main trunk line running through his property, 'Morven'. It was still there when I visited, a little huddle of dilapidated buildings at its centre.

Waikakahi was bought by the government in 1899 and was its second biggest purchase in Canterbury; it was divided into 122 farms and 11 grazing runs and the town of Morven. (The government's biggest purchase was William Robinson's Cheviot Hills estate at the present town of Cheviot.) Allan was not happy with the government's deal. The story went that he negotiated all night, got up in the morning, left his home and never returned.

I'd planned to be at the old homestead at three in the afternoon after driving through the tangle of little roads on the north side of the mighty Waitaki River. Rats might work out ways through mazes, but I was no good at it. I stopped a passing car, got directions that included that fatal phrase 'You can't miss it.' I missed it, had another try, got the blank look.

I'd been calling it 'Waikakahi', then realised the local people probably used Allan McLean's name for it. I stopped a man in a council truck, asked the way to 'The Valley', and was immediately successful. He got out a map, showed me roads that seemed to form a series of triangles. 'Go to the top there, hang a right here.'

And then there it was, a big gateway proclaiming 'The Valley', set in trees so thick they formed a tunnel entrance. It disgorged me into a massive Victorian garden from a storybook mansion, English trees more than a century old spreading away on either side, glades, dells, glens, bowers all glimpsed through the thick trunks and bright spring flowers of another age. The driveway circled around acres of lawn with Allan McLean's great house at the very top: a big, two-storey weatherboard house, with one large and two smaller gables on the second storey and a broad veranda shading the bay windows of the ground floor.

I looked at it for a long time, wondering why it wasn't more ... satisfying. Then I realised the gables seemed asymmetrical. The two smaller ones appeared to be different sizes, but that might have been an illusion caused by the middle one being jammed against the largest, giving the house a rather pinched look. It was quite simple, and had none of the pomp and ceremony of McLean's Mansion in Christchurch. Still, it was undeniably imposing.

I climbed the wide concrete steps to the veranda, spacious as an arcade, seized a great iron knocker. *Bang, bang, bang.*

Nothing from inside, although I fancied I heard an echo. I turned down the side veranda, just as imposing, and ran into a man with a big beard and matching ute. 'I'd given you up,' he said, and instantly I felt at home. He wore boots and a shirt supporting the Australian rugby league side the Rabbitohs. He had Rabbitohs stuff everywhere, even though he supported another team. I'd long since given up trying to understand rugby league addicts.

He was Richard, son of the long-time owners of The Valley, Mr and Mrs Bailey, and he ran the 270-odd-hectare sheep farm that was the residue of McLean's great estate of 20,000 hectares. The house had been kept just as it had been in McLean's time, Richard said, except for the chimneypots, two great lumps of masonry housing the flues of many chimneys, like the pipes in a ship's funnel. They'd been taken down because in this shaky country only God knew what damage they might do to the house in an earthquake. Each of them weighed 1.9 tonnes. Now they lay beside the woolshed, part of which was the original household stables where Allan might well have kept the Yankee Express.

Richard's grandfather had bought the place before the Second World War but sold it. The family bought it back after the war. By then, the homestead had been empty for some time. They'd owned it ever since.

Richard had grown up with the garden. He knew the trees, the stubborn pine over there, slowly dying after a blizzard years before, a giant redwood more than a century old and fifty-five metres tall. The great thing about the place, its rarity, he said, was that it had never been messed about. No one had taken down walls, added rooms. The Baileys had left it alone, lived in it as it always was. It was pretty much the same as it was on the day Allan McLean had climbed into his carriage and left it forever.

The house was amazingly simple by modern standards, without swank or gadgets. Yet it was still the house of a man whose every need and whim had been seen to by platoons of maids and cooks, manservants and navvies. The huge front rooms were as he'd left them, repapered and carefully touched up by the Baileys. Here was the billiard room, and the dining room with butler's pantry behind it, and a door leading to the kitchens. And a huge living room, probably the place where a despairing McLean sat with government agents all night, haggling over the disposal of his property.

A staircase led up to McLean's bedroom. Richard said, 'I've lived in houses smaller than this room.' It opened to a bathroom, throwing into question the claim that McLean's Mansion in Christchurch featured New Zealand's first en suite. For this man, an en suite was routine.

Where was the housekeeper's room? Richard gestured towards the big bedroom. She'd had her own room, but all the rumours about Allan's and her relationship were contained in that gesture. There was no room for doubt when you were standing on the thick floorboards of The Valley's upper storey.

The servants' rooms lay at the back of the house, the small bedrooms with their own staircase down to the kitchen, scullery, bathrooms, and so on, effectively a second house with all the amenities for a troupe of domestics seen only when needed. The crofter's son from Coll, from the family who'd allegedly escaped penury with little more than the rags on their backs, had gone up in the world and was intent upon putting the old world well behind him.

The house was not ornate, though. Its style was colonial simplicity, with little intricate woodwork or extravagant decoration. It was big, not vast. After all, it was built for just one man. Looking at it another way, of course, you might ask, all of this for just one man?

*

I went to Christchurch to see the house Allan had built there, although it was not a house in the usual sense. It was his castle, far bigger and more magnificent than The Valley. According to legend, when he first visited his architects, England Brothers, he was handed a stock plan for a four-roomed cottage. 'Not four rooms. Forty!' he snorted. Even that was a serious underestimate, for McLean's grand home was fabulous by the standards of the day and is monumental even now.

It's a huge, three-storeyed pile. A fifty-three-roomed Jacobean fantasy of 2137 square metres, or enough room to swing whole clowders of cats. It has nineteen bedrooms and six bathrooms — not so many bathrooms by the standards of a modern entrepreneur's pile, perhaps, but nine toilets seems sufficient.

It has servants' rooms that today would constitute a small apartment block. Domes and towers. Its cast-iron pinnacles are a French fantasy. Its upper storey sprouts a brickscape of chimneys and so many windows that housemaid's elbow must have been endemic.

Inside are cornices and coffered ceilings and chandeliers. A huge staircase rises heavenwards from the ground floor, featuring enough wide, sweeping stair-rails to excite the heart of any small person with bannister-sliding on their mind. Originally, walls were covered with fabrics such as satin brocade and velvet. There were white and black marble fireplaces, chandeliers, porcelain bathtubs. There wasn't just the whiff of golden fleece here. The place reeked of it. It was carved, gilded, ornamented, brocaded, marbled, velveted, mirrored, Persian-carpeted, monogrammed. A rich man's wildest dream, the biggest wooden house in New Zealand built on two hectares of gardens.

He called it 'Holly Lea.' More pragmatic locals dubbed it 'McLean's Mansion'. Here he lived in luxury, surrounded by riches, and must have felt himself far more than half a world away from Laghmor, his village on Coll, which consisted of perhaps five 'black houses,' little, low stone cottages with thatch or turf roofs and virtually no windows.

But he didn't live in his mansion for long, only thirteen years. He died in 1907 aged eighty-five, and was buried in Addington Cemetery alongside his mother Mary, his brother and his two sisters. A newspaper obituary said he'd never taken part in public affairs, was of 'retiring disposition', had been confined to his house since he'd caught a cold twelve months previously, and had gone to bed one night and been found dead by his footman.

Under his will, Holly Lea, McLean's Mansion, became the home of the McLean Institute, 'a home for women of refinement and education in reduced or straitened circumstances', supported by a very handsome endowment. I wondered whether his debt to Emily Phillips had anything to do with that.

Imagine the interviews for prospective residents. Even in Christchurch, never wanting for pretension, they must have been fascinating. The reduced or straitened circumstances would have been easy enough to establish, even the education and good character, but refinement? A century later, you could still smell the sweat on that one.

Whatever it took to get in, the effort was worth it. The indigent women moved into their grand new quarters. They had to hand over their assets to the institute and, with a few exceptions, stay broke: windfalls such as legacies had to be surrendered too.

As the ladies passed through the front door, they were flanked by hat stands bearing bears carved from mahogany. Elaborate mirrors reflected their every move. A huge grandfather clock signalled teatime. They could arrange themselves prettily on burgundy settees or wing chairs set upon Persian carpets and surrounded by paintings of exotic landscapes few if any of them would ever have seen, and rather ironic given the beauty of the country the McLeans had lived in. The southern landscape was regarded as inferior to England's, and Europe's, and its merits wouldn't be properly recognised for the best part of a century.

The women dined at a vast oak table and ate off fine china with monogrammed cutlery. The rough lad from Coll had travelled far from his roots and probably more than a few of the ladies had too.

The mansion was sold to the government in 1955 along with the furniture and fittings, most of which disappeared into that grey scrapyard of official business. Given his feeling about government, Allan McLean must have twirled in his grave.

The grand house became a hostel for trainee dental nurses until 1977, then accommodated the Salvation Army and the St Vincent de Paul Society. There was much chatter in the early 1980s about turning it into a house museum, but it came to nothing and the mansion was sold into private hands in 1987. There it remained, a city landmark, a curiosity for visitors, until the Christchurch earthquakes, when it went from curiosity to calamity in a moment.

The first earthquake in December 2010 shook the building, the second in February 2011 wrecked it. The brick behind its wooden panelling behaved as brick does during earthquakes: it collapsed, along with the building's enormous chimneys. The superb interior was destroyed too. Yet the rest of the old house was so well built that it remained intact — well, more or less. McLean's Mansion still looked whole. I drove past it, thinking it a tribute to the resilience of wood.

The building was locked and barred. The Christchurch family who owned it wanted to demolish it. But a mysterious organisation of 'urban explorers' crept in and published photographs in the hope it might be restored rather than pulled down. The photographs revealed terrible damage, but in the event, the explorers got their wish. The mansion was a listed heritage building, and Heritage New Zealand did not want it destroyed. They and the explorers were backed by Christchurch's people, who erupted into the kind of clamour only residents of the Garden City seem capable of. The owners went to the Environment Court, and lost. The mansion was to stay upright.

The building sat there as the controversies continued to swirl around it. Should it be restored? Should it become another drain on the public purse, by now thoroughly pummelled? Christchurch loved an argument and for a time McLean's Mansion, in a city full of ruined buildings, seemed likely to fade away through … well, neglect.

At the eleventh hour it was sold to another trust, the McLean's Mansion Charitable Trust, which set about restoring it. They expected to turn it into a private art gallery along the lines of the Pah Homestead in Auckland, a large, elaborate pile built on an ancient Maori pa site, originally modelled on Queen Victoria's Osborne House and later turned into an art gallery housing the James Wallace Arts Trust collection, some of which would be lent to the Christchurch trust.

One still blue day in winter, the kind of day you cannot imagine spending in a ruin, I went to see what was left of Allan McLean's dream of nobility and his tribute to this astonishing period in New Zealand's colonial history. The mansion was still closed to the public, and I was escorted through the ruins (wearing a hard hat after a safety briefing) by Richard Herdman, an engineer from York with both intelligence and humour in his blue-green eyes and endless patience lodged somewhere deep within.

Richard was exactly the sort of man you wanted around a project like this. He was an island of calm confidence in a sea of wreckage. He was undaunted, apparently, by the burden that now lay on his shoulders. His record of restoration read like a roll of honour in this city. It included some of the city's most loved buildings, such as the Victoria Clock Tower and Mona Vale, two treasures that lie deep in the city's psyche.

He led the way over a mountain of bricks. Tens of thousands of them lay in what had been the front garden of McLeans Mansion, a huge tonnage that might literally have driven the mansion into the ground had it not been so strongly built. I'd never seen so many bricks crammed into one small area.

Initially the mansion seemed more intact than I had thought it would be, but I soon changed my mind. The rampaging quakes had been assisted by vandals and thieves who'd stolen lead off the roof, letting in years of water. A disaster. Broken plaster, ruined roses. We walked up curved steps into an entrance hall and I wondered at the courage of people who'd take on a job like this. Yet even shrouded by dust and disaster it was still elegant.

The Yorkshireman's take was that the mansion had been built by a man from a place where they built houses to last. One where New Zealand's ten-year guarantees would be, at best, a joke.

The main staircase swept up to the first floor, undiminished by the huge graffiti mural on the landing. The kauri timbers had stood up well. Among the debris I could see skirting boards almost half a metre high and intricately moulded, thick kauri doors that each took two men to lift. In that age when giant trees were freely available for felling, weatherboards and even the house's wooden frame were kauri. The toilets were grand affairs, their bowls intricately sculpted porcelain that must have been hell to clean, even for McLean's army of servants.

The first-floor room Richard believed to have been Allan's must have been vast by the standards of the day and was big even now — his dressing-room would have made a good-sized bedroom. The bedroom featured an innovation: an en suite bathroom that must have been a Christchurch first, at least. Narrower staircases led from either side of the landing into the house's two distinctive towers. Both accommodated good-sized rooms. The speculation was that McLean used to climb them for a hawk's-eye view of his domain, and quite possibly he included the city as part of it.

The mansion had already been deteriorating, in a courtly sort of fashion, before the earthquakes. In a sense the earthquakes saved it by forcing a decision on the city in a way a slow crumbling would not.

The weight of the huge concrete and brick fireplaces had driven them into the ground below. The floors in between, held up by their piles, had stayed more or less in place. The result was a house-scape of valleys and dips, the mansion sagging most in its northeastern corner, which seemed to give the building a list. Plaster had been shaken from the walls, leaving the sarking beneath bare, like an old actor waiting to be dressed. Some of the original features had been laid bare too: later hearths under the fireplaces had covered the beautiful tiles of the originals, which were now exposed for the first time in, probably, the best part of a century.

Richard stayed calm. He'd start by levelling the building on its foundations then move upwards. It was going to be a long job.

I wished him luck and, just out of curiosity, went to Waimate, where the housekeeper, Mrs Phillips, spent the rest of her life, near Waikakahi, near Morven Hills, near Oamaru, deep in the country of the golden fleece.

She was a wealthy woman, living on her pension of £3000 a year, a handsome sum then, and clearly possessing some capital besides, for she built a mansion of her own. Te Kiteroa still stands, overlooking Waimate. It's a toss-up which was grander: Mrs Phillips' house or Allan McLean's The Valley. Her house was more symmetrical, in some ways swankier. It boasted turrets, five reception rooms, five bedrooms with en suites and two more, servants' quarters and lots and lots of panelling. It also had two separate cottages, one for her gardener and the other for her chauffeur. She built it in 1913 and lived there in great style until she died in 1921.

The housekeeper had followed her employers. They'd gone from crofters to sheep barons; she'd gone from keeping house to owning her own mansion. And all of them, masters and servants, on the sheep's back.

The town she looked down on, Waimate, has inherited a style of its own from those glory days. It stands not far off the main highway, State Highway 1, but traffic needs to take a lengthy detour to visit the town, and only a tiny proportion of it does.

Waimate seemed grand when I was young and camped there with the Scouts, pitching our tents in Kelceys Bush in the hills behind the town and going out in the dusk to watch wallabies feeding on the paddocks in little steps and hops. Much later I had afternoon tea with a retired minister of religion who told me the town's big problem was losing its kids. They had to leave home to find work, and the town was greying. Statistics show a town much older than the average, with many fewer young people. The town council in 2019 refused to sign a climate change emergency declaration and also decided it was best not represented by a pest and removed the wallaby from its logo.

Like many small towns, though, it dreams of a golden future, this one by way of a big new dairy factory just down the road at Glenavy. A population surge was prophesised. The hotel was to be redeveloped, a new medical centre built and, oh dear, several old buildings demolished. Waimate is full of listed buildings, which include the local grain silos, as well as Quinn's Arcade. It was always my favourite, built of bricks from Quinn's own brickyard between 1905 and 1907, a fine-arched stained-glass window dominating its frontage, through which you passed into an ornate plastered interior that housed one of New Zealand's first shopping arcades, perhaps even *the* first, as well as the Arcadia picture theatre (where 'talkies' were first shown in 1930) and a billiard saloon. A fire in 1955 began its decline. Since then many had had a go at restoring it, but it slowly descended into flats and now sat locked and silent, a symbol of past splendour patiently awaiting the next round of hopes and dreams.

The town is cared for though. Wide streets, nice public gardens, kempt houses, broad avenues of old trees, and a statue. Not the usual statue of brave soldiers or past men with various stories of derring-do. The subject is a pioneer, however: Dr

Margaret Cruickshank, the second woman in New Zealand to qualify as a doctor and the first to practise. Except for a year in Britain, she lived in Waimate for the rest of her life, which ended in the flu epidemic of 1918. Her statue is one of only ten celebrating individual New Zealand women in this country: even Queen Victoria stood alone in Wellington until 2013, when she was joined by Katherine Mansfield.

*

Monuments to the era of the golden fleece survive all over the South Island. Midway along the Waitaki Valley in a location called Otekaieke lies a place known as Campbell Park. Once a station spreading over valleys and hills, it was originally established by William Dansey, who left his name on the famous pass. A bridle track still runs from the park to the pass.

Dansey had only been there a few years when along came William Campbell. Eton-educated, scion of a wealthy Scots family, he bought the place in 1865, importing Scottish workers and materials and building a huge house, a castle everyone called it, with thirty-five rooms and matching stables in Scottish baronial style, severe enough to make me shiver as I looked at it from the outside, much less from within. Its history was just as creepy.

The family holding company became New Zealand's seventh biggest landholder, but William Campbell was soon caught up in family scandals. Life, he decided, was best viewed through the bottom of a glass, and he rapidly became a rich drunk. His great run was broken up in 1908 and the cheer that went up around the country was only matched by the sigh of relief. It was not a venerated relic of its era.

Campbell Park grew into, well, a town really, with a suburb of cottages, gardens, vineyard, 200-seat restaurant, gym, tennis courts, even a jail and an airstrip. Early in the twentieth century it began a new career as the government-owned Campbell Park School for Boys. That didn't go well either; the school closed in the 1980s and the government was left to settle dozens of abuse cases in a scandal that has continued well into the twenty-first century.

Various owners followed and the castle and its surrounding landscape became a set for films including of course — did any part of the country miss out on it? — *The Lord of the Rings*. The castle's architectural style seeped into nearby churches and buildings, so that although the park lies a few kilometres off the main road, you can sense it as you drive through the valley.

Much of the South Island's early European history of vast sheep stations being literally given to the wealthy and adventurous was summed up by William Robinson. Robinson owned a huge station in South Australia and came to New Zealand with bags full of cash and a spear wound inflicted on him during the massacre of some thirty or forty Aboriginals. Photographs show classic English looks: wavy hair brushed back from an austere face and a long nose above a smile that was almost a sneer, the whole composition looking (I suppose he supposed) rather aristocratic.

Robinson bought a huge sheep run, Cheviot Hills, which ran over the hills and far away. It occupied the land between the Hurunui and Waiau rivers from the coast to well inland, which, if you look at a map, was a fair slab of South Island — indeed, the second-biggest block in a land where self-styled squires could pick up vast areas for a pittance.

He was known as Ready-Money Robinson because, according to legend, he carried the money to pay for his land in a wheelbarrow. Another version of the story insists that after his cheque had been declined by land officials, he cashed it at a bank, demanded small change, and notes, put everything in a sack, returned to the land office and dumped it on the counter.

One way or the other, he built a vast mansion just outside Cheviot. It was a huge affair, built around a central courtyard, surrounded by a park ranging over the hills. Its corridors and courtyards, bedrooms and halls spread over 1418 square metres, its hallways alone accounting for 376 of them.

His sheep were so profitable he even built a port, Port Robinson, for shipping his wool. The project was as adventurous as its owner. The coast there was not accommodating, being dangerously straight, with only a tiny snout of land in whose fragile shelter Robinson built his port. It included a chute, at the top of which boats were loaded with bales. They then shot down the chute into — *splash!* — the water, and were then rowed out to the waiting sailing ships, precariously anchored in this exposed spot against ocean swell and the hard onshore winds.

Amazingly, Robinson managed to ship many thousands of bales through this alleged port and only one ship was wrecked, the *Maude Graham*, a schooner that broke its anchor cable; the ship's anchor now sits outside the Cheviot Museum. The port slowly crumbled and finally disappeared into the sea only quite recently, unlamented and, except for the efforts of a local resident, unrecorded.

Robinson owned a town house in Christchurch, where he spent more of his time. He employed a 'coloured' butler, Simon Cedeno. One Monday morning in 1871, Cedeno stabbed one of the two maids, Kate, with a silver-handled bread knife (the handle got more of a mention in newspaper reports than the blade did). Though bleeding heavily, she escaped, so Cedeno turned on the other maid, Maggie, and stabbed her to death. They'd been teasing him, he told the court, which did not think much of that as a defence and sentenced him to death. Cedeno was duly hung at the infamous Lyttelton Gaol. It's hard to say now who history remembers best, Robinson or his butler.

The golden fleece served Robinson well, however. He died in 1889, the most prominent of runholders and one of the richest men in the land. The house he built at Gore Bay for his wife, Eliza, still stands today, a model of colonial simplicity. His manager's house on the outskirts of Cheviot is intact too, a mansion itself by modern standards. But although his mansion near Cheviot outlived him by forty-seven years, it burned to the chimneys in 1936, the bannisters and curlicues, gables and corridors, panelling and heavy doors all reduced to ash. Only the foundations were left. I traced them in the Cheviot Hills Domain, parkland that now covers Robinson's rich gardens. Like foundations everywhere, they didn't seem as big as I'd imagined, and gave little hint of the great house they'd once supported. The front steps lay beneath the local cricket pavilion.

Robinson possessed the golden fleece all right. But when he died his station set another, rather different pattern. This was, and is still, dry country, but after Robinson's death in 1889 the station was divided into fifty-four freehold farms and the town of Cheviot. Robinson's 77,000 sheep also went under the hammer.

A model of Robinson's great house was on display in the Cheviot Museum. I stood before it, imagined the house itself and found it unimaginable. It soared out of the New Zealand context. It was on a scale of its own, a pinnacle of pastoralism, a headstone to the era.

Of the port, only the name remained.

*

One of the most famous squatters of the era was Samuel Butler, then the wayward twenty-four-year-old son of an English vicar. He'd been harshly treated by his parents, who seemed to have regarded themselves as God's headmasters and were handy with a whip. Their crippling piety was leavened only by a good Anglican regard for money.

Butler loathed his father and his rages. Naturally, he was keen on leaving home and there was no better way of distancing yourself than putting half a world between you and your folks. His parents agreed, rather readily. His father put up the money for a journey to New Zealand, specifically to Canterbury, the England of the antipodes, where Butler senior prayed that his son might be influenced by the new land's dedication to the Church of England. More handily, the Reverend Butler also promised to advance his son the capital he needed to set himself up as a runholder.

Butler arrived at Lyttelton in 1860. By then scarcely any big areas of land remained unclaimed. The new legion of squatters was inspired by many things, notably a yearning for wealth, but Butler junior was probably spurred on by his desire to leave a healthy distance between himself and an angry man with a stick. There was no evidence of any previous thirst for adventure, or talent for it, nor any kind of qualification for sheep farming barring that farmers' staple, an urgent need to make money.

Yet Butler bought himself a horse and began poking into the inaccessible parts of Canterbury, those places seen as too difficult or too remote to farm. Even now their roaring rivers, deep valleys and high cliffs, their gullies and mountainsides and their frequent accompaniment of gales, storms, ice and horrible winds are largely avoided, even by citizenry equipped with four-wheel-drives, puffer jackets, huts, gas stoves and de-hy food.

Butler had a horse, tea and a bit of damper. He journeyed deep into the mountains. He was, probably, the first European to see Arthur's Pass, then just a grassy saddle which he was sure might lead to the West Coast (as it now does), but which otherwise held out no prospects for him.

He climbed to the top of another pass in the Southern Alps, later named the Whitcombe Pass after a fatal attempt by a surveyor of the same name to find a route to the Coast. Butler merely observed that it was no good for sheep and went back down the hill again. But the pass and its approaches became one of the settings for his famous novel *Erewhon*, whose hero journeyed up to the saddle and found a 'Stonehenge of rude and barbaric figures'.

Butler never really had much taste for Canterbury. He sketched 'ye horryble glaciers' and 'ye vexatious gullies' and he hated the prickly matagouri and the spiky spaniard. Still, he kept at it until he found some empty land far away in the upper Rangitata Valley. It was cold up there, so close to the mountains, so chilly he later declared that words froze as they left speakers' mouths and had to be melted in a frying pan so others could hear what they were talking about.

Perhaps it was too cold for sheep he thought, but the most important thing was, it was there. He built a rough hut, like an A-frame, beside what is now Forest Creek. The stream was misnamed, for by any standard except those of the mountains it varies between a river and a torrent. I went to the site of his hut and all but froze just looking at it. It wasn't even winter, the season when Butler built it.

Butler's place was forty kilometres of rough country away from his nearest neighbour and a week's journey by ox-cart from Christchurch, providing the huge rivers crossing the plains could be forded. Still, Butler drew up his map and claimed everything in the immediate vicinity, naming his run Mesopotamia, 'the land between the rivers'. The property expanded as he bought other runs until it spread over 24,000 hectares.

Butler got his station up and running quickly but then spent most of his time in Christchurch, for he was more artist, writer and musician by nature than he was a farmer. In the budding city, he was known as a man of culture and perception and a bon viveur. He became rich, doubling his capital in only four years, then sold up and went home to England, both too accomplished and too muscular to be beaten up by the pater.

Modern successors tend to look down on his farming talents. To me he was remarkable: an Englishman from a sheltered background who displayed courage, enterprise and talent, New

Zealand's own David Livingstone. In one way he was an apostle of the golden fleece. He illustrated the point that wool was the short-cut to wealth, and that a man might not even have to work very hard to become rich.

In another way he was an exception. Many of the new runholders became addicted to grandeur, even hauteur. They built big houses in the English tradition, not the low, relaxed houses of a sunny country, but the tall, tight, crimped places they might have thought of as stately homes. The aspiring egalitarian tradition of their new home country could, in that country's vernacular, go and get stuffed. Some affected English manners, kept squads of servants and held tea parties that might have been copied from Jane Austen. A few stones and the remains of an adjacent dairy are all that mark the passing of both Samuel Butler's country residence, little more than a stone cottage (which crumbled away to nothing in the 1920s), and his tenure.

His neighbours were more permanent. John Acland and Charles Tripp were young English lawyers who set off in 1854 to make their fortune in the colonies and succeeded, probably beyond their wildest dreams. They knew very little about sheep farming, so little they both worked as farm cadets at first to learn the trade. It was a fleeting education, for by 1855 they were looking for a station of their own. They had only £2000 each in capital and, like Butler on Mesopotamia a little later, they'd found that all the easier-to-work land had already been grabbed.

They simply took a stab at boundaries in the wild, unknown country of the upper Rangitata, applied for the land and, of course, got it. Their various stations soon covered some 100,000 hectares. They were high-country pioneers, and like Butler they quickly prospered. Unlike Butler, they stayed. Four generations later, Mount Peel station is still being run by Aclands, although it's a great deal smaller than the original spread.

Heritage New Zealand believes John Acland brought the homestead's plans from England. It is a huge brick Gothic affair, gabled and steeply roofed, with verandas everywhere, imported architecture but attractive. It sits amid lawns, trees and fine gardens in the English tradition, with a little stone church, the Church of the Holy Innocents, beside it.

The partnership split up in 1862. Tripp took himself off to the south, retaining a couple of their stations there. They may not have started in rags, but they'd gone to riches in what must still be a record time in this country. Tripp occupied a homestead, large and handsome, on Orari Gorge Station. The story goes that when he visited England in 1862 he could not convince his sick father of the wealth yielded by the golden fleece or that he was now rich and successful. So he sold Orari Gorge, transferred the money to England to prove his worth to his dad, and bought it back again when he returned to New Zealand. Tripp family descendants still farm Orari Gorge, and other runholders' homes from the period dot the countryside.

William Rees, known as the founder of Queenstown, left his mark all over the place. Frankton, the town on Lake Wakatipu's elbow that is becoming the working person's Queenstown, was named after his wife, Frances. Cecil Peak and Walter Peak were named after his sons. His woolshed became a hotel, still standing on Queenstown's foreshore and now called Eichardt's. Central Otago has a Rees River, and Rees's statue stands on Queenstown's Rees Street. Yet the unsentimental tourist hub lets nothing get in the way of progress. The homestead on Rees's former high-country farm at nearby Kawarau Falls vanished without trace and was replaced by a Hilton hotel.

*

The number of sheep in New Zealand used to be a joke. Sixty-six million sheep, three million people. Twenty two sheep for every Kiwi. It got worse: the flock reached just over 70 million, peak sheep. After that the numbers changed but the ratio remained more or less the same and was much appreciated around the world, especially by the British, who seldom missed a chance to throw the sum at visiting New Zealanders.

But sheep numbers dropped as the twentieth century faded away. When last I counted they were down to fewer than 27 million, the lowest number for three-quarters of a century. New Zealand farms fewer sheep, although they are more productive — more lambs, more meat, more wool. Even the ewes have cottoned on to the new deal: work harder, work smarter, or you're down the road to the knacker's yard just like any other redundant worker.

No one talked about the golden fleece any more. The world preferred synthetic fibres. The price of wool dropped. Meanwhile global demand for milk products grew steadily. The big money, the pot of gold, no longer lay in sheep but in cows, and converting sheep farms to dairy became highly profitable.

Dairy herds began covering the land, in every sense. As the old millennium ended their numbers were growing steadily and now there is more than one cow for every person in the land. Between

1994 and 2017, the number of dairy cows in New Zealand as a whole rose by 70 percent, while sheep numbers shrank 44 percent. Dairy farmers were the new rich. In the South Island, dairy cow numbers rose from 0.6 million to 2.6 million, with almost half to be found in a single province, Canterbury.

The Canterbury Plains were formed from sediment that washed down from the Southern Alps and created a great flat apron running out to the coast. Naturally, the plains were largely composed of gravel, sand and clay. They were green in winter, golden dry in summer. Farmers here traditionally grew crops such as wheat, or ran sheep, and groused about Canterbury's arid summers. This was unlikely dairy country, far removed from lush green pastures. The solution was to suck up the groundwater and spray it onto paddocks. Giant irrigators, often kilometres long, rolled across the plains. Sure enough, the grass turned green; well, greenish, for when you could see it between the cows it was of course patched with ordure.

But cows belch and fart greenhouse gases into the atmosphere. And as Sir Tim Shadbolt, then Mayor of Invercargill, declared, they are like freedom campers because 'they love nothing better than pooing in rivers'. (It was difficult to say who was more offended, the farmers or the campers.) Cow faeces and urine pollute lakes, rivers, groundwater and drinking water, and nowhere more so than under the open skies of Canterbury.

It didn't take long for anglers, trampers and other backcountry users to notice something strange: their rivers were shrivelling and streams were disappearing completely. Health authorities chipped in with their own warnings: Cow urine was causing nitrate levels in waterways to rise steadily, raising the risks of cancer.

Swimming holes were declared unswimmable, one after another. Of forty swimming sites in Southland, only six were swimmable. By 2017 two-thirds of Canterbury's rivers were pronounced off limits to swimmers, a roll call of Edens: Pareora, Otaio, Waihi, Opihi, Temuka. Coes Ford in the Selwyn River, one of Christchurch's favourite swimming holes and a place where I swam for much of my life, went from fresh and clear to cloudy and then to a green so toxic it didn't really need the warning signs that were its only thriving feature. At the ford itself, a place where traffic crossed the river, the water looked as if it could take the chrome off a bumper. Some locals referred to it as having been 'Chernobylised'.

Two lakes near the city, Forsyth and Ellesmere, became so bad one environment commissioner described them as toxic puddles. In the 1990s I visited a farm beside Lake Forsyth and walked down to the lake edge. The shingly ground was covered with dead eels. They lay on the shore as dense as a mat. I was both amazed and despairing. New Zealand freshwater eels were tough. They could survive almost anything except commercial overfishing, habitat loss and oxygen depletion caused by pollution. Of the three suspects, only pollution fitted the frame.

Christchurch city once boasted of the cleanest, purest drinking water in the world. No one could make that claim in the twenty-first century. Public health authorities warned that nitrate levels were reaching crisis point: Canterbury's water could become undrinkable. New Zealand went from being a place that could say to visitors that they could drink the water anywhere to one where public authorities were advising that a third of the population were drinking water so unsafe it was making many thousands of people ill every year and, unless it was cleaned up, would start killing them. The tourist marketing campaign slogan was '100% Pure'. One response seemed appropriate: crap.

As bad, or worse, was the nuclear option: treating the water with chemicals. Chlorinating town water supplies, formerly controversial, became common, notably in the Canterbury heartland, from quaintly named Pleasant Point in the south to Springfield in the west.

Dairy cows were not the only cause of tainted freshwater, just the most prominent. And although the burgeoning herds were not good for the environment, they were great for the economy. The government smoothed the cows' way. The regional council responsible for balancing the competing interests of business and local populations was called, ironically, Environment Canterbury or ECan. Its members were elected. The government saw the council as an impediment to progress, sacked it and replaced elected councillors with people it appointed itself, so-called 'puppet commissioners'. Oh, the arguments in favour of suspending democracy for a while. It would only be for a short time, they said. It wasn't, for the suspension lasted almost a decade, the government arguing that restoring elections could jeopardise its grand plan, an argument not unknown in various unsavoury parts of the world.

The soporifics were even harder to swallow: conscientious farmers were becoming more environmentally conscious, streams would be fenced off, protective vegetation planted, Ecan had new rules. Upbeat officials proclaimed a wonderful new world that would fix the mess — setting off alarm bells all over the place, for Canterbury had learned to distrust its officials. At one conference, speakers even predicted climate change would be a good thing: more water would fall in the South Island.

It was hard to spot reality in this sylvan dream. Irrigation schemes still flourished; permissible nitrate levels, already high, were waived despite suspected links between those levels and bowel cancer; and one official answer to the problem of polluted streams and rivers was simply to lower the standards.

Certainly water was being sold off to overseas interests and, sure, some of those were prone to a spot of water poaching, but heavens, it was for the public good. Besides, we'd passed peak cow and numbers were on the way down, even if, like the top falling off Mount Cook, it was not noticeable.

Even when a degree of local democracy was restored, the new council came without guarantees. Too many farming councillors, too few city ones. Allegations of gerrymandering clouded the council chambers.

Canterbury people didn't take all this lying down, of course, especially as the trend seemed certain to enhance the numbers in that prone position. One very cold June day in 2010 they protested their loss of democracy and the polluting of their waters. They waved placards and shouted. One protest filled Cathedral Square, ending with thousands of people writing messages on river stones and building a cairn. The Bishop of Christchurch, Victoria Matthews, then a powerful figure in this Anglican city, lamented the pollution and later resisted efforts to remove the stones from the Square. The cairn, it appeared, was on Anglican land.

A crowd was demonstrating outside ECan's offices one evening when word of a National Party conference rippled through the assembly. The conference was only a few hundred metres from the ECan offices. An even better target for wrath!

Common descriptions of protestors hardly fitted this demonstration. We were middle-class, law-abiding people who loved living in our gentle city. So when one man, a well-known sculptor and artist, passed through the crowd handing out water-filled balloons, I declined. They seemed ... well, unseemly. But the young man next to me took one.

Meanwhile, texts flew around the city. The crowd swelled. So many people poured in that police were forced to close the roads, blocking two of the one-way routes through the city. The police presence swelled too.

Unfortunate party delegates now had to make their way past a demonstration that would have filled a rugby stadium on test day. They crept up the stairs to an accompaniment of hoots, cheers and jeers, looking puzzled, and a little worried too.

The youth beside me cut loose with his water bomb. It was a mighty throw and I admired his style, a kind of cross between a fast bowler and a basketball shooter. It missed. But the ranks of plain-clothes police looking down on the crowd from the ramp of the nearby hotel did not. Before you could say splosh, a couple of them had the bomber by the arms and were marching him off to the pokey.

I knew his parents, and felt some responsibility. After all, he'd taken my bomb. Sally and I went off to the central police station to plead his cause. Anyone who has dealt with police in a situation like this would recognise the subsequent censure of demonstrators generally, the pugnacious disavowal of any knowledge of this culprit's whereabouts, all the while rendering the interested parties (us) powerless. But eventually someone decided we'd all been punished enough and he was released without charge.

Dairying, when last I counted, employed more than 37,000 people, was our top export income earner, and was critical to both heartland economies and national living standards. Did that qualify it as a golden fleece? I just couldn't bring myself to use the word 'golden', although it seemed to me that a lot of Canterbury people were being fleeced, all right.

Much later I travelled back to Christchurch and found, beside the ruined cathedral, the cairn of stones, with my own, cunningly placed on the outside, still readable. The cairn looked a little weathered, a bit worn, and it probably puzzled the earthquake tourists, but it was intact.

CHAPTER FOUR

The Gilded Life

Towards the end of the twentieth century, new worlds opened to New Zealand farmers. Agricultural entrepreneurs studied the heavens and discovered new stars. Ostriches and emus. Alpacas and llamas and water buffaloes. Goats, goats, goats. Dairy sheep and every other creature that might be milked.

The best thing about it all was that you didn't need to own a high-country station, or a dairy farm, or a comfortable spread in the foothills. You could prosper on a much smaller place, according to the revolution's leaders. Even the classic ten-acre block might do at a pinch. It was well within the reach of a modest budget — yes, the very sum an adventurous man or woman might have in the bank just waiting for an opportunity like this.

It was not so much a shift in the nation's agricultural history as a kink in the narrative. In my own experience most of the people who made money were among that mix of hustlers, believers and enthusiasts who were always in at the beginning with something to sell. They offered novices a vision of the golden fleece.

I was one of the neophytes. I'd been writing for a living most of my life. This was a time of change and, by God, I was up for it. There had to be a better, simpler, purer way of living. I liked the idea of deer. They were the future. My dreams filled with stags and hinds. *The Darling Buds of May*, the television series, sang its siren song.

The local polytechnic offered a course on deer farming. There proved to be complexities, the twist and turns of another world, but nothing any of the numerous hopefuls could not handle. Deer were easy to manage, the tutors said. They liked being left alone to fend for themselves, they said. They were well suited to part-time farmers such as myself, they said. Essentially, you piled food into your animals, got the progeny up to a certain weight in time to meet the demand from the German market, and called the stock truck … they said.

Farming started as a notion but it quickly became a passion, for me anyway. Sally, my wife, was a little harder to convince. We lived in an old house in Sumner, in Christchurch, which had taken a lot of effort to restore. She loved her house, but evidently loved me more, for she left her home and friends and followed me over the hill.

We found the remnants of an ancient farm in Denis Glover's iron hills and quiet tides of Port Levy, a deep bay on Banks Peninsula. The bay was known to Ngai Tahu as Koukourarata, the biggest settlement in Canterbury following the sacking of the Kaiapohia pa. The homestead had been built by the Fleming family, who arrived on the First Four Ships, classic Canterbury.

It was two-storeyed, huge, with so many bedrooms I always ventured into one or two of them with a sense of strangeness.

One winter's day we drove through snow over the high pass into the bay, Sally and I, our twin sons, Sam and Simon (who found country life esoteric and soon moved back to the city), and the boys' border collie, Tim. The house was full of people I didn't know, local people there to help. A warm fire burned in the kitchen. Someone lugged furniture, someone emptied cartons. Marina brought pikelets, Pauline brought pork bones. That was how it started.

The property had been set up as a deer farm and I bought deer too. And was confronted with the realities of farming.

*

In Port Levy this day the wind was blustering in from the sea. The trees bent before it, shedding branches, which the deer pounced on, worrying leaves off the boughs like dogs with bones.

The farm was mud. My boots sank to their tops. It should have been depressing, but was not. It was exhilarating. The whole valley floor was moving water, the farm a river.

The next day was worse. Rain and wind battered the house all night. What a desolate scene it was, that morning. Yellow mud-water flowed down the hill. The old wattle, about to flower, was blown over.

I had other worries. A huge log had washed down the stream and taken a fence with it. At that end of the farm, nothing now stood between my deer and the freedom of the hills. I waded a metre into the stream and was immediately swept off my feet. Terrifying.

Neighbours came to help. We made a temporary repair. It was not right but the best we could do. Night fell. I went inside, showered, lit the fire and huddled against it. Sally was not coming home, at my suggestion, for once; she worked in the city but did not drive and I just couldn't spare the time to pick her up from the ferry that ran across Lyttelton Harbour. I called a fencer who promised to come next morning and I felt better for all of ten minutes.

*

Late autumn: it was very cold. I drove home in darkness, half-expecting snow to block the pass into the bay. Come the morning, snow covered the tops, pure white against the sky's cobalt blue. A sharp frost glittered on the paddocks. The deer breathed puffs of steam. No wind. The sun touched the hills with pink and the sea was silver-blue and so still I could see the reflection of a pied oystercatcher as it flew towards breakfast on the flats.

Philip arrived as I was driving weaners, young deer, up the race. Like other farmers in the bay, he kept a kindly eye on me. I walked behind them slowly, talking to them. They didn't say much and I gathered they'd much rather be somewhere else, but they moved on. Very professional, he said. I realised I'd been doing it automatically and must have learned something, at least. The truck arrived, its exhaust sharp in the cold air, the driver huge and friendly. We loaded the weaners and off they went. Next day the agent called: $180 for the stags, he said, but only $90 for the hinds. Disastrous.

*

The vet, Chris, came to cut regrowth off the stags whose newly grown antlers were termed 'velvet' and were harvested, then, for the Korean market. They grew back and needed to be trimmed before they hardened and made the animals armed and dangerous.

The stags did not want to go into the race. Sam and Simon were there. Was it a clash of pheromones? Even when the animals were at last in the shed, they kicked the pens' walls, making the plywood boom like bass drums. The walls were two metres high, yet one stag still managed to get most of the way over one of them, despite there being no room for a run-up. Sam was standing on the other side of the wall and it was even-stevens who was the more surprised. 'Shit,' said Sam, and I think the stag said it too.

Simon came into the pens to give me a hand. He was scared. Don't be, I said. You'll upset them more. I heard the ring of hypocrisy. The stags stamped and clattered. Simon shuffled uneasily but held his ground. Chris cut off the velvet with his usual lack of fuss.

One of the big stags was lying anaesthetised on the floor. The tourniquets around the stumps were always a problem. If you left them on too long, you risked the stag awakening, and while he was still sleepy he'd know he was upset about something. If you took them off too soon, blood poured from the stumps, as it was doing now. It dripped through the slats in the shed floor, onto the ground below.

A little later there came a scream. Tim the dog had appeared. He was a mass of blood. Everyone was convinced he had been in a nasty accident. But Tim had just been under the shed floor, lapping up the drips.

*

Port Levy gathered for its annual residents' meeting in the old school, closed in the early 1970s. David, the president, wearing a maroon jersey, sat at a battered table in front, with Ray, the secretary. The patterned carpet on the floor could have been any colour once. I sat in the front row, because the establishment farmers clustered at the back, like the big kids on the bus.

We went through the agenda and arrived at general business. A young-ish engineer from the council was there to explain why we had the last unsealed roads on the peninsula. He wagged his fingers at us. Evidently we were lucky he was there. We were to take what we were given, and he was indignant at the suggestion that some didn't like it.

Most, though, were grateful for whatever services they got, which, considering they pumped their own water, disposed of their own sewage, took their own rubbish to the depot, ran their own fire brigade and dug their own graves, were few. A sealed road didn't seem too much to ask and the engineer reckoned it was coming, although Lyn pointed out that he'd sat in exactly the same chair this time the previous year and heard a man from the council saying exactly the same thing.

'That was the draft plan,' the official said, as if explaining to infants. The road was in the draft plan again this year, he said. He thought we should be satisfied with the possibility. He wanted to know who had spoken to us last year. 'Wheelbarrow,' replied a farmer, mysteriously to me, but everyone else seemed to know who he was talking about. Evidently Wheelbarrow had also told us we'd be getting a new fire engine. That proved wrong too.

They couldn't find a new one that was old enough for us, so we were stuck with our vintage Land Rover.

Divisions became clear. People on the pa side of the bay wanted their end sealed first. After all, most of the bay's inhabitants lived there and they were smothered by dust in summer. A reasonable point, and they had a majority. But farmers wanted the other side, where I lived, done first. They had the money and the council's ear, they held the power, and they were implacable.

We moved to other business. David wanted us to object to a new cemetery in Diamond Harbour. He read out the law, which said that if a public cemetery was more than thirty-two kilometres away you could be buried at home. He wanted to be buried under his trees. But they were planning a new cemetery at Diamond Harbour, which was just over the hill. That would end his plan. David was taking this personally.

We were pretty cold on the idea, especially when it was explained that the new cemetery would be multipurpose, used for both disposing of corpses and passive recreation. 'Very passive,' said Mary, 'couldn't be passiver.'

Then there was the question of the school itself. The residents' association wanted to buy it. But it was covered by a Waitangi Tribunal claim, which in fact had saved the school from being sold off amid the excesses of the day. It had tennis courts and a swimming pool. I imagined the number of cake stalls and working bees it had taken a tiny community to raise the money for those.

*

THE GILDED LIFE

Weaning. A simple word for a big day.

All was bustle. Bill and Philip arrived, with dogs. I locked Tim in the garden shed, where he howled piteously.

It was the day for getting the fawns in. Oh, we were barbarians. We were going to tag and drench them, and, best of all, count them, for until now they'd been just vague shapes hiding in the long grass and the bush.

One of the problems I'd worried about was how to get the hinds with their fawns off the hill paddock. In the end it was easy. We opened the gate to the hay paddock one day, came home just on dark and found them all feeding happily. Simon sneaked along the stream and closed the gate on them before they could think of escape.

We got the hinds and fawns into the shed, finally. We'd darkened the place and they stood quietly in the gloom. We separated them quickly into pens to stop them crushing. Got the hinds apart, drenched them and identified the dries (hinds which had had no fawns) by examining their udders. 'Don't feel them,' Philip had said, 'they'll kick the shit out of you.' So we looked. The wets had small udders with teats. The dries had none. There were only four dries in my first herd of fifty. Yet I'd counted fewer than thirty fawns in their paddock, so good at camouflage were they. Now I had forty-six fawns. The biggest were large and gangling. They were surprisingly easy to handle on their own. Some lay on the floor, as if they were posing for old masters, too lovely to even be considered as a venison dinner.

The hinds clustered around the fence, although I'd put their fawns as far away from them as I could. They emitted low groans, which they used for calling their fawns; now they sounded like distress signals.

I thought Sam and Simon had been intrigued by the day, despite their reservations about country life. I realised how few city kids knew anything about the country now. Even I knew the basics when I was a kid. Farming was just part of being a New Zealander.

That night everyone was kept awake by the haunting, birdlike calls of the fawns on one side of the house, and the groaning on the other. I felt like a criminal and I pleaded guilty. In another paddock young stags were alternately moaning and roaring. The two elk stags were trumpeting, one varying the note with an ending like a factory horn at knock-off time. The sulphur-crested cockatoos in the poplar trees rasped like old nails being pulled from corrugated iron. The plovers in the sea paddocks took fright over God knew what and screamed blue murder.

Oh, the peace of the countryside.

*

Sometimes I hated agriculture.

I was cutting zucchinis in the garden when I heard screaming. I bolted into the paddock and found it was coming from a hind. She had woven herself into the fence. I grabbed her and immediately started screaming myself: she was wedged into the hot wire and was getting an electric shock every two seconds.

Then I saw the fawn lying in the grass. I asked Sam to carry it in. Poor Sam. Simon told him off for being late. 'Just leave me alone,' he sobbed. Later he told Simon, 'It was terrible. It was crying, not like an animal, like a baby. You don't know what it's like, carrying something that's dying.' He was right. When I checked the fawn an hour later, it was dead. Probably from yersinia, plague of fawns.

Farmers talked in terms of lost dollars, but it was the first of my own I'd lost and I was desolated. The poor creature had died because I'd done something wrong.

*

One Monday my stock agent called. He was fifty and had just stopped playing rugby because of his knees: a former shearer, he needed new ones after being butted by tens of thousands of sheep. He had the habitual shuffle of the shearer, the forward-leaning walk. He also had a ready laugh and his kids had the cheerful look that went with a fair and happy home.

He was a moving university. He pumped out information. It filled my eyeballs, squirted out my ears. After half an hour, I felt dizzy. Somehow, whenever he appeared, I ended up buying, and today was no different. I finished with one more stag and fifty more hinds. 'Everything's looking great,' he said encouragingly, although if that was right, it was despite my ignoring some of his advice. Later he rang and suggested buying another stag.

Two new stags arrived next day. Hungarian deer. 'Hungarians,' snorted a neighbour. 'They look like alligators.' I treated them with respect.

I rang the seller to say they'd arrived. She told me I had her favourite, 'the biggest in the herd, out of my pet hind, a natural leader'. I named him Floyd. (Ex-city farmers always name their animals — a mistake, for it makes it harder to put them on the truck.)

Floyd was a leader all right. As he got older, you approached with caution, then trepidation, then outright fear. Later, after I left, the new owners got a neighbour to run the farm for them. Floyd bailed him up and forced him to hide underneath his Land Rover for a couple of hours. Alas, Floyd shouldn't have done that; everyone had had enough of him by then and he had sounded his own death knell.

But stags were always difficult. Once I rented one. It cost $500 for the season, but I could deduct the fee from the purchase price if I bought him. He was so quiet that he duped me into making a fundamental mistake. I went into the pen with him, but for only a second or two. *Whack!* I was booted right out of the door. For a moment I thought my thigh was broken. It wasn't. It came up in a huge bruise, which changed colours like traffic lights and warned me against foolish escapades for weeks.

After that I wore knee and elbow protectors, a heavy jacket, and a groin guard from a sports shop. I made a heavy plywood shield. I looked like a Transformer.

*

Port Levy wasn't far from Christchurch, not much more than forty kilometres. But it was over high, windy roads. People arrived there like travellers from another land.

The boys found it hard, remote and not much fun. They'd roar over the hills in their old Holden every so often but gradually their absences grew longer. They stayed in town with friends.

They spent more and more time in the city, less and less at home. They wanted to move back and one day they did.

We waved goodbye and went back into a big, empty house. I discovered my cheque account was heavily overdrawn. I was thoroughly depressed. What were we doing sitting in this huge cold pile on our own? Six bedrooms and three living rooms and still my children had nowhere to live. We were broke. I didn't have enough time to do anything. And the television was awful.

We lit a fire and ate leek and kumara soup, which the boys loathed. Later we drove over to Akaroa and drank hot chocolate and returned realising there was nothing we had to do for anyone but ourselves.

I went to a side window. The cherry trees were afire. Flames of bright red, brilliant orange and yellow filled the panes. Could anything be more beautiful? The lime tree was pale yellow. I went outside and sat beneath it, as if in a room full of light. The sycamores, usually pests, filled the little wood beside the house with colour. I stood at the edge of the front paddock. A gentle nor'wester glided down the hill and over the water, warming the twilight. My God, I thought, I hope this works. The awful loss if it didn't.

*

At the beginning of a day's shearing, helping on my neighbour's farm, I was looking forward to it. The sheep moved softly in pens shiny with lanoline, so softly I only slowly became aware of them in the gloom. The woolshed looked like a museum when it was empty. Actually, it was a museum. Ancient pulleys, venerable presses and old butter churns lay beside draught-horse harnesses. Gig seats, old saddles and bikes mingled with mysterious tools that had found their way into this woolshed during the previous century.

The farm was owned by Bill, my neighbour. He had a reputation for never throwing anything away. An old motorbike stood beside a box of sewer pipe bends and a bar from a rugby club lounge. But when the shed was in action, everything that was supposed to work, worked. The order! Everything had a purpose.

The shearers doubled over like hairpins. Pat loved racehorses, and ran a live crayfish transport business. Lou had a shaven head, lots of tatts and guileless blue eyes you'd try not to meet in a bar. Chub was the rousie whose days as a shearer were rumoured to have finished with a gunshot wound. He had a gap in his teeth that made him look dangerous, but he was not. He did the cooking in his house. When Pat found out I cooked in mine, he said, 'You two can swap recipes.' This was a huge joke.

They worked with a rhythm, setting the pace for the supporting cast. The rituals, the towels on hooks, the oiling of combs, the pauses to straighten themselves, like straightening wire. Chub had his son with him, to Pat's disgust: 'No children in the shed!', an old shearing rule.

'What was I supposed to do with him?' complained Chub, who had come all the way from Kekerengu. He was doing up the family home and looking after the kids while his wife worked.

My job was to take the edges and dirty bits off the fleece as Pat stripped it from the sheep, and to keep his pens filled. 'Sheep-o' he'd yell when he got to his last sheep, or maybe he'd just say 'Po', or then perhaps he'd whisper so softly I thought I'd imagined it and risked the sin of allowing him to run out of sheep.

All day the fleeces rolled off, some 500 of them. The soft white wool lay in mountains on the floor. Sometimes Bill came in and loaded it into a press. He was very proud of his press. It worked on a system of pulleys and cables and steel pins and produced a plump bale of more than 200 kilograms. Once, you could buy a car with a few bales; now you needed dozens. We stopped for cheese and relish on toast at smoko and stew for lunch. At the end of the day they sat freshly showered, drinking beer delicately out of small glasses while I sat in the friendly kitchen and looked over the lawn to the pigsty and henhouse. My back was one solid mass of pain. It took me a week to recover. They'd do it all again tomorrow.

*

Sally and I went for a walk down the lane, with the two cats and the dog. We were stopped by a couple in a vintage Model A Ford. Was this the only way out of here? they asked. I looked at the car, thought of the other routes, Wild Cattle Hill and the Western Valley road, neither much more than shingle tracks and said yes. 'You're joking,' they said.

Flat Christchurch could not come to terms with this place. Friends treated it like an expedition, a journey to the end of the earth. The lovely weekends at the farm? Well yes, but we turned more and more to our own community, less and less to the city's. This was hard on Sally. She relied on lifts. Just getting to work in the city involved a winding hill road, a ferry and a bus. She never complained, never regretted.

Autumns always brought a faint sadness. They arrived promptly on 1 March. The air immediately became cool, the sea instantly too cold to swim. But … the poplars were pillars of gold, the willows were turning, the sun was yellow on the hills. We admired the lovely joining of house, hills, paddocks, trees, stream, sea.

Spring arrived on the dot too, 1 September. The trees were wonderful. First the flowering gum, then the bright yellow kowhai and sycamore and the creamy dogwood with the rata blood red in the middle. Soft, ploppy rain bent the fat heads of the old-fashioned daffodils to the ground. The banks of azaleas smelled of hops. The fawns uttered their strange bird-like cries, their mothers groaned on the hillsides, elk stags trumpeted like elephants and the red stag barked back.

Early one spring we took a picnic beside the stream, the water shaded by a wattle, rustling gently to the sea, the air redolent with the scent of the heavy white hawthorn blossom. Gavin the elk stag ambled over curiously, then grazed nearby, beautiful in his shiny spring coat. The vast animal standing so quietly emphasised the peace of the moment, with the dog lying at our feet and the cheep of ducklings from somewhere in the rushes.

*

Bang bang bang on the brass knocker on the side portico no one ever used. Fluoro pink and green through the glass: cyclists. They were Dutch, Rob and Monique, both very tall and beautiful.

They wanted to camp. I said sure, and when I went out later there was a third, Dan from Minnesota. Dan had no food because he couldn't believe he was somewhere where there were no shops, no gas stations. They pitched their tents on a stream terrace by a stone wall, fed the deer through the fences, stroked the dog, and later came in for a drink.

Dan talked a lot. He referred to the bay as 'the lake'. There were 18,000 lakes at home, he said, and went misty for a moment. Then he broke into a nostalgic tale of what he was going to do when he got home: strap on his cross-country skis, get out there, way to go. He liked litres of milk and all the ice cream he could get, he said, inclining at a sharp angle towards the fridge.

He cast an envious eye upstairs. 'Bet you have six bedrooms up there,' he said. 'Only the two of you?' Dan had been away from Minnesota for two weeks. In that time he had travelled much of the most difficult terrain of the South Island and certainly the most beautiful: Central Otago, the southern lakes, Wanaka and the Haast, then over the Otira and so to Banks Peninsula.

What captured his attention most?

His daily average, he said proudly, 156 kilometres.

Next morning Dan was in the lavatory and judging by the noise he was making his digestive system was coping with more than just ice cream. Then he hopped on his bike and disappeared without a word, doubtless intent on his average. Rob and Monique had heard about the rare Hector's dolphins in the bay and wanted to see some. In the evening I took them out in my boat.

The dolphins obliged. Rob and Monique were terribly excited. I heard a splash, rushed out of the wheelhouse and discovered a pile of clothes. 'He's swimming with the dolphins,' Monique said proudly. But the dolphins had disappeared and so had Rob. The light was failing. I spotted him on the crest of a big easterly swell rolling in from the open Pacific and told Monique to climb on the cabin roof and fix her gaze on him while I turned back.

They'd been in New Zealand only three days and had headed directly for the Peninsula's steep, windy roads. It was a hell of an introduction after flat Holland.

They were a bit anxious. Would the rest of the country be like this? Disappointed too. Beautiful, but the tourists! 'We came to the Peninsula because people told us there were not many tourists here,' said Monique. They gazed sadly at a helicopter-load of Japanese clattering in to the neighbouring horse-trekking business, then went back to telling me how beautiful the country was, how friendly its people.

I drove them over Wild Cattle Hill, then up Middle Road, so steep the truck ground to a halt on the loose shingle and I had to use four-wheel drive to get moving. They were silent. What if the rest of the country really was like this? From the top they gazed down onto blue Akaroa Harbour, shimmering slightly in the morning heat with its picture-book town and boats moored all around. They cheered up and departed on their bikes next morning with renewed zeal.

The pears were fat yellow globules dripping from the tree. I bit through tough skin into the grainy white flesh. The fruit sent a thrill of pleasure through my body.

Sally and I picked walnuts from the ground. It was always a race between us, the deer and the rats. The nuts had burst from their soft green coverings and lay clean brown in the race, on the shed roof, in the paddocks. Sally climbed onto the roof and we filled bins and spread the nuts on the loft floor to dry.

THE GILDED LIFE

*

It was the worst day of my farming life.

I drove Max, my beautifully made, expensive but irascible elk stag into the old bailing race I'd converted from its original purpose for handling cattle. Max hated it. He tried to climb out, failed, fell and broke his velvet.

The vet anaesthetised him while he was down, knocking him out with a shot through his hide. We took the remaining velvet from him and left him to recover.

I heard him throughout the day. He was snoring. Tiny moans came between the snores, like a child whimpering in its sleep. By 8.30 at night he was still not on his feet. When I went into the race, his ears pointed to the ground and he snarled, the very image of the stag at bay, but in a horizontal position.

He tried to stagger to his feet, slumped back to the ground. I called the vet, who said he'd given him a heavy shot.

He sounded reassuring. I went to bed and slept badly.

Very early next morning, while the grey light sneaked into the creaking macrocarpas, I looked through the window and knew immediately something was wrong. The five other stags were at the railing, looking into Max's race. They had the anxious stance of hospital visitors. With a dreadful lump in my stomach, I joined them.

Max was dead.

My beautiful stag was on his side, flies already buzzing around his eyes. Oh my God, what had I done? I'd killed this lovely beast.

I called the vet. He was silent, even for an unusually silent man. I sensed his horror. I called Bill. He sorrowed with me. I called Roddy. He came over. Later, he began dismembering Max for dog food. He performed a rough autopsy too. Max had a broken thigh. He must have broken it attempting to turn around in the race, which I now wanted to attack with an axe. Roddy tried to comfort me. He would have been fired up on adrenaline, he said. He wouldn't have felt a thing. But I knew the truth. It was simply bad farming. I'd lost a prize stag, and a lot of money. But worse, I'd killed an animal through sheer malpractice.

*

There was a knock on the door. It was Edward, a neighbour's child: Dad says to tell you the deer are getting out.

Cold panic. I called Bill to help. He was unperturbed, possibly because he had only six hinds in my paddock, whereas I had $20,000 worth. 'Look,' he said, 'I don't think they'll go far. They might even go back in by tomorrow morning. Other Peninsula farmers have this trouble. That's farming!'

The expression was the universal panacea. But it was dark now, and nothing could be done anyway.

I watched the weather forecast morosely. Heavy rain, it said. My mood went blacker than the night outside. I defined gloom as feeling that $20,000 was slipping through the cracks and you couldn't do a thing about it.

Before first light the next morning, I was out on the farm. The rain had stopped. The deer were still there. They showed no interest in leaving. That was farming.

*

Ah, the delights of the big vege garden you could have on a farm! The rich brown earth, the shovel whose handle seemed worn smooth by honest toil. I wrestled with both, usually in the very early morning when the purity of the task shed a light that easily outstripped the dawn. I dreamed of fresh veg and pitied those forced to go to the supermarket for their greens.

I planted potatoes and courgettes and runner beans. The garden seemed intent on its own purpose, the mass production of weeds. For a while they succumbed to guerrilla warfare, the raid on fat-hen, the quick snatch at chickweed. But as spring went on they brought in reinforcements: nettles, dandelion, dock, twitch. Soon it was a jungle out there.

Underneath it, however, lay potatoes. Sacks of the things. We couldn't eat them. Half a plant a night was maximum and even then we were inclined to lie about afterwards, like pythons after they've eaten something several sizes bigger than themselves.

We gave them away, but our friends paled when they saw us advancing with a bag: oh God, not more spuds! In fact, several told us firmly to bring no more courgettes onto their properties. Nor could we blame them. How could such small seeds do this? Triffids were trifles by comparison. If I didn't cut them quickly they grew into marrows. Go on holiday for a week and they'd take over the world. Only the runner beans were not a problem. Gavin the stag stuck his head through the fence and ate them.

It was almost a frost one morning. The paddock across the creek glinted silver in the early sunshine. I dug the garden and debated whether it was too late to plant broccoli, or too early to plant onions. In the end I did neither. February, still summer, felt like autumn.

The next year, the built-up beds and composted rows lay in ruins. I let them lie. Deadly nightshade sprouted triumphantly above the corpses.

*

The handwritten *Koukourarata Mercury* used the Maori name for the bay, much more enticing than the obscure Sydney trader the British named it for. Its motto was *Quorum stupefactae carmine lynces*, 'At whose song the lynxes stood spellbound.' This issue said:

> The dumbfounding song we think of and hear, however, is not that of this humble little broadsheet, but the song of our hills and streams, bush and bays, and the songs, rough-hewn perhaps, but sturdy and sincere, with their own integrity and grace, of those who live here ...
>
> As many of you will know, a motion was passed at the last annual general meeting of the Resident's Association, prohibiting smoking in the school. To a considerable extent this merely formalised the practice of some years, for local smokers have, by and large, courteously smoked outside the building should anyone's health or comfort be threatened inside. Nevertheless, this formal prohibition has excited a certain amount of feeling among those smokers who regret that what was once a courteous neighbourly understanding has now become a matter of bans and rules.
>
> We are a small and pretty harmonious community. We all have a good sense of our responsibilities to each other and

we know that living together successfully calls for restraint and compromise on everyone's part ... The committee is gravely conscious that even mentioning this matter could perhaps be construed as some sort of undermining of an annual general meeting's motion. It is not intended to be. It is a request for goodwill on the part of all concerned. Next year the matter will, it seems, inevitably be raised again at our next AGM. Until that time, let us all display that consideration for each other's wishes which has characterised our life in the past. It would be very sad if a quarrel over a matter such as this were to damage the good-neighbourliness and easy-going mutual tolerance and respect which are one of the most pleasant and important aspects of Port Levy life.

In the evening we had a committee meeting in David's house, another Fleming mansion, which was being painted white with yellow trim (the colour was gorse or broom, he explained). We sat around an oak table in the small panelled room near the kitchen, which had hooks where sides of mutton used to hang. Scenes of David's family at Port Levy, watercolours and photographs of moments abroad hung on the walls. A good fire burned in the grate. We drank sherry and ginger wine and discussed the issues of the day, the road (we didn't believe it would be done that year), the new toilets on the waterfront (could we plant around them to soften the shape?) the 'no dogs' sign (how should it read?) and the smoking ban (all right, we knew the AGM voted for it, but was it fair?).

*

Tim the border collie had become indispensable. Some kind of border collie instinct guided him. He was a heading dog and didn't bark and he could move deer without upsetting them.

I took him into the cattle paddock while I attacked thistles with the mattock. Suddenly a great rumble of hoofs. One of the cows was charging — at me, I thought at first. But no, it was Tim she wanted. She chased him over to the fence. Cornered, he turned on her and growled, then took advantage of her pause to flee. The entire herd of cows and calves joined the chase. Tim slid under the gate like an oil slick then ran back along the fence on the other side to gaze at me with sad eyes.

On the last day of autumn, a soft warm day when the sycamore created a golden room, Tim died. He'd been a Christmas present for our twin sons as a pup. Surprisingly, he'd proved a good working dog for one that had never previously set foot outside the 'burbs. We loved him.

He'd been listless for some time. He seemed uncomfortable and sometimes in pain. We'd stopped at the top of the hill on the way to the vet's. Tim lay tiredly, looking down the valley. Smoke from our chimney drifted across the paddocks. The bay was perfectly still.

When Chris the vet opened the car door, Tim watched us both with his gentle eyes, then lay back on his blanket. He didn't move again, even as Chris declared him beyond hope and slipped the needle into his leg. I didn't know when he died.

I drove him home over the narrow road and we buried him under the cabbage tree. Sally planted a russet hydrangea over him. Then she went down the drive to collect the mail and for the first time in the years we'd been on the farm, no Tim followed her.

*

Everyone belonged to the fire brigade. We were supposed to practise once a month and often we did. Today, Roy turned on the fire alarm. *Whirrr!* A cloud of straw and feathers shot out of it. An indignant sparrow appeared on the roof, although not as indignant as Bill, the fire chief. 'Didn't you LOOK at the siren first?' he demanded. 'I said not to turn it on.'

'Oh,' said Roy. 'I thought you said to turn it on.'

'I said not to,' repeated Bill. I searched the ground for bits of baby sparrow, but there were only a few feathers. The outraged sparrow chirruped from the gable.

We went down to Pa Creek. Bill wanted a show of force to impress locals and holidaymakers. 'A public relations exercise,' he called it. Bill was wearing his white overalls and the yellow fire chief's helmet with the visor. He'd made us wear helmets too. Otherwise, we were in the rags we'd worn picking up hay bales shortly before. Roy was in his shorts. Steve had brought his family, who thought it all very entertaining.

The poor fire engine, a fifty-year-old Land Rover laden with ladders, pumps and hoses, could barely get us all over the hill.

A silver car pulled up and a well-tended head in designer shades leaned out of it. 'My,' said Marina, 'I'm very impressed. And how smart you all look.'

Bill looked dour. Before he could object, she was out of the car with a camera. 'Now, line up. Oh, where are those funny things ... nozzles? Yes, those. Come on Bill, strike a pose ... Oh, I am impressed. Now is there a red light and a siren on that thing? Would you escort me home?'

Bill drew the line at that.

Later I went to his place and bought eggs. A car went by. Helen's, he said, without looking. How could he tell? It was just a swish of gravel. But, he puzzled, it was too early for her, for a Tuesday. I told him she'd changed jobs. He took note. He missed nothing.

*

Peg, in his late seventies, had an easy, graceful lope, a direct stare below a mysterious dent in his forehead. A burn? A bash from a flying block in his days as a seaman? He said he was dying and a year or two later, he did.

Sally and I went around to see his wife, Dot. A New Zealand flag flew at half-mast from the flagpole by the back door. Dot said she thought Peg had been coming right. Then he'd died.

The men gathered in the churchyard next morning. Port Levy people did everything for themselves, and that included digging each other's graves. I always thought the hard ground was a great incentive to look after our health.

The legend was that people were buried as deep as they could get by lunchtime, when they knocked off and drank home brew. But Dot wanted to be buried in the same grave, so the hole had to be seven feet deep. We worked and worried away at the stony ground with shovels and crowbars, one down the hole at a time.

Peg's relatives dropped by. One was an All Black halfback. Everyone watched intently as he climbed into the hole with his shovel. He chipped and battered the ground mightily and came out sweating without any significant advance.

I knew how he felt. I'd beaten away at the stones several times already for no discernible result. But Ted, and Philip, and Richard, and Coopy and Spider, all lean men, simply dropped into the hole and, with the easy economy farmers brought to everything, each dug a few inches. If they'd been left to themselves, it would have taken half the time.

Then the surrounding ground was covered in green cloth and as Peg was lowered into the ground I knew from the sudden concentration that each of the farmers was calculating the width: would the coffin stick? Of course not, and as Peg rested safely on the bottom we sang 'Abide with Me'. Then we went down to the old school and drank his home brew.

*

Neil, one of four farmers in his valley, told me he expected to be the only one left in five years. He made it in three. The other farms had been cut up for forestry or dismembered as grazing blocks. Farming had become harder and meaner. Only the stalwarts remained, and their children found something more profitable to do.

I thought of the old joke about the farmer who won Lotto. When he was asked what he'd do with the money, he shrugged: 'I suppose I'll just go on farming until it's all gone.'

Despite all attempts to develop a clever economy, a huge chunk of our fortunes remained in the hands of a dwindling number of the increasingly disillusioned, isolated by our determination to become the only nation in the world that didn't nurture its farmers. In only six years I watched a community full of hope and life retrench. It wasn't so much that anything collapsed, or vanished; more an ebbing of spirit, a retreat to farmhouses, a reluctance to take on anything more, a growing conviction that 'farming is stuffed'.

It was a bad time for farming, but farmers are probably best described as resilient pessimists. Even when they're down and all but out, they come back for more. Farmers are people who stay. They hope the fleece will be golden again, some day, and from time to time, it is. In between those times they look around for new crops and new animals, for experience has taught them that first in gets the prize, even if in the longer term the project is a fizzler. Quite often, it is not: fortunes were made in deer, then lost, then the industry settled into an equilibrium. This makes farmers both innovative and imaginative or, at least, enough of them to make a difference. As for the golden fleece itself: 'Sheep are rubbish,' a neighbour remarked to me one Sunday afternoon as we were talking over a back fence. They were too, then, but soon they were not. The shades of gold vary, but the fleece endures.

*

Pauline, who became my friend, died one summer. Her husband, known in the bay as Russian Bob, even though he was a Latvian forced from home as a young man, wept for her still. We built a low concrete wall around her grave and Bob made a wrought-iron fence of hearts and sun.

Later, at dusk, I sat on the small balcony of Bob's house. The smell of a thousand dinners, smoked fish and roast mutton, drifted from the kitchen. Outside the air was sweet and fresh. We had a glass flagon of Bob's home brew on the table and our feet on the rail. I watched the island through the bubbles in the golden liquid. Neither of us said much.

The nor'wester blew the sea into spiky rows growling on the stony beach at the bottom of the garden. The evening sky was iron-grey. The sun setting behind the far Alps tinged the clouds and cast a shaft of metallic light onto a rocky peak called The Monument. The hills across the bay vanished into purple.

I could hear the farm sounds over the water: a dog's melancholy bark, sheep, a stag's rutting cough. The air, neither warm nor cold, was heavy with sadness.

Bob had lost his love and his life. I didn't know then how much I'd lost. I knew only that my farm was sold and in a few days I would have to leave this place where I'd known so much contentment and peace. I knew I'd never be a good farmer. The best I could hope was to be an all right one. Good farmers were born to it, and I could never absorb several generations of learning in a few years. That realisation accompanied a huge respect for them. They were very good at what they did, and what they did was part knowledge, part experience, part understanding and mainly that overworked word, passion.

I didn't know any more why I'd been so anxious to get away from the city. It no longer seemed important. You just lived your life as best you could. But there was where it ended, on Bob's veranda, surrounded by life and ghosts, watching the yellow light fade from the hills with a warm nor'wester caressing the darkening sea and thinking how lucky I was, how much better for those years.

CHAPTER FIVE

The New Argonauts

The walls of the ancient caldera forming Akaroa Harbour reflected shards of sun on that autumnal morning. The water was smooth, the breeze from the east. The easterly wind, meteorologists said kindly, was cool. The easterly wind, said people who lived in its craw, was bloody freezing. It flowed through Christchurch's streets like tap water at Scott Base, Antarctica. But Akaroa Harbour didn't get the easterly. It sheltered beneath the hills of Banks Peninsula, nicely out of that wind at least, though the southerly was a different story: that one blew right up Akaroa's harbour and whacked the town in the face.

Canterbury always argued over its winds, about which was worse: the easterly (which chilled), the southerly (which froze), or the nor'westerly (which was warm but was said to drive people mad and vastly increase the divorce and suicide rates).

Today, emergency services took a breather, for the easterly puffed happily through Akaroa's little streets, although no one in those streets took very much notice of it. For today was cruise ship day. Some time around the dawn of the day the *Celebrity Solstice* had crept up the harbour, anchored in its waist off French Bay, and settled there, as tall, solid and still as an apartment building.

Passengers aboard the *Celebrity Solstice* probably did not know, or care, which way the wind was blowing. I hadn't talked to many of them before finding they didn't know much about anything at all. They didn't know that they were here in Akaroa because the Christchurch earthquakes had wrecked the usual tourist port, the port of Lyttelton, and destroyed many of its best buildings. Lyttelton was not expected to be open to cruise ships for another year, but they didn't know that either.

They didn't know these things because they were tourists. At the same time the following year they might be puzzling over Ha Long Bay, or the earthquake-riven Grimsey Island off Iceland, or just beating the hell out of whatever part of Venice remained above water.

That day the tourists had got out of bed in staterooms redesigned by five women known, the shipping line boasted, as the Leading Ladies (although there seemed to be more leading ladies in design than ever appeared in cast lists). They'd worked out in the ship's gymnasiums or even, perhaps, in the Canyon Ranch Spa ('soothes body and mind') or pumped iron with one of the ship's fitness instructors, or done none of the above (which seemed more likely as I observed them shuffling through Akaroa's streets).

No doubt they'd had breakfast in one of the ship's many cafés and restaurants, perhaps the Grand Epernay ('world and continental cuisine, famed European-style service'). 'If only life on land were as good as life on board this exceptional vessel,' the shipping people said. Well, Akaroa might be second class, being on land, but lots of tourists were going to give it a go. They piled into the ship's lifeboats and chugged over to the Akaroa wharf, to be hoisted deftly onto terra firma and head for town for the full French experience.

They'd been told that Akaroa had a rich French history, and that Akaroa was the most French town in New Zealand (true, although many more French people could be found in any of the cities). The town's European history was Franglais, or more accurately frAnglais, for it was English with just a dash of French. You could buy a baguette there, but in my own view Akaroa's contribution to international cuisine lay in its excellent, very British, steak pies.

The French element was injected by one Capitaine Langlois. (His surname, appropriately, given his role in Akaroa's history, was a verson of *l'Anglais,* the French word for Englishman). I could not find a picture of him, but *le capitaine* seems to have been an unusual figure, a mixture of brawn and brash and a quick eye for a deal.

Langlois was one of a number of French captains hunting whales around the New Zealand coast in the 1830s. He based himself in what was then Port Cooper (now Lyttelton Harbour). It was named for Cooper and Levy, a Sydney whaling and trading firm. The historically insignificant Levy left his name on the neighbouring inlet, which became Port Levy. The Australian traders ousted the original Maori names, the more musical Te Whakaraupo and Kokourarata, respectively. Ah, the arrogance of it.

There were several accounts of what followed. The more authoritative came from the Waitangi Tribunal's investigations into the Ngai Tahu land claims. The more colourful came from other sources. The Maori population of Banks Peninsula then was probably under 200. The European population was even smaller. The first four ships bringing immigrants to the Canterbury Association's new settlement, Christchurch, were more than a decade away.

According to a deed dated 2 August 1838, Langlois bought the entire Banks Peninsula from Maori for 150 francs down, with the balance of 1000 francs to be paid on possession. Even by the standards of the day, *c'était de l'arnaque* — it was a rip-off. Moreover, the deed was in French and, even worse, Maori had signed blank sheets of paper, leaving Langlois to fill in the details. It was safe to conclude the Maori signatories didn't have a clue what they were signing, even if they had the right to sell, which the Waitangi Tribunal concluded they did not.

Langlois then went home to France and sold his Banks Peninsula land rights to a group of French businessmen. Together they formed Nanto-Bordelais, the French-New Zealand Company, whose aim was to buy and colonise the whole of the South Island. The French Government supported them and provided a ship, the *Comte de Paris*, to take fifty-seven French and German prospective colonists off to their new southern outpost, and threw in a warship, *L'Aube*, for good measure.

At about this point, I prefer an older, more entertaining and probably apocryphal tale. It was not plain sailing for the *Comte de Paris*. As it departed it got stuck in mud. The ship was dreadfully slow, lost some of its sails, a mast and rigging in a storm near Tasmania, managed to reach Banks Peninsula, buried a couple of unfortunate would-be immigrants in Pigeon Bay, narrowly escaped being wrecked at the Akaroa heads, and in 1840, at last, reached the site of the future town where the surviving immigrants hastily debouched.

Meanwhile the British had got wind of the voyage. William Hobson, the first governor of New Zealand and a man with land ambitions of his own, entertained the commander of *L'Aube*, Capitaine Lavaud, in the Bay of Islands and got him, well, just a little *merde*-faced.

Lavaud spilled the beans. Hobson hastily claimed the South Island for Britain and dispatched a British warship, the *Britomart*, to Akaroa, with a couple of magistrates to hold courts and prove 'effective occupation' by British subjects. The ship's company were to hoist the British flag right smartly while the jolly French viewed the New World through the bottoms of their wine glasses and danced the night away.

So the Union Jack was already fluttering when four days later *L'Aube* arrived, followed by the *Comte de Paris* with its fifty-seven immigrants all set to grab their allotted acreage and leave their stamp on their new *quartier*.

Langlois quickly discovered that the Treaty of Waitangi had been signed and the kybosh firmly placed upon his dream of a *petite France là-bas*, down there. The new arrivals must have landed on the little beach and looked around in both wonder and apprehension, rather as the arrivals from the *Celebrity Solstice* were doing today, if for different reasons: the earlier passengers wondered how they'd survive in this strange land, the later ones where they'd have lunch.

The French colonists were allotted sections, and they built houses on them. The Germans went a little further up the bay to a place called German Bay, now Takamatua. The French laid out streets. They built houses of a particular character, with steep, hipped roofs and small dormer windows, sometimes featuring a fronton, a triangular feature on the upper-storey frontage, often copied in local architecture since but seldom matched.

By 1844 the population count was sixty French, twenty Germans and forty British. There were also ninety-seven Maori, but that did not stop historians from proclaiming the town as definitely French at that time. French was spoken in the town, the buildings had a French character, there were French officials and even a de facto French mayor.

But *la vie française*, such a tiny pocket of it in a rapidly growing land of *les Anglais*, didn't have *l'exposition de chien*, loosely translated as 'a dog's show'. Of all the houses and shops and other buildings put up by the French, only a couple survive. A few French names endure: Duvauchelle, Petit Carenage Bay, L'Aube Hill. But the rest of it, really, comes down to streets named *Rue* ..., a few berets and some striped T-shirts and aprons worn on occasions such as today's cruise ship visit.

On those lovely, special days when I was taken to Akaroa as a child, we climbed over the Britomart Cannon, said to have been placed on the foreshore by the ship's company to warn any future parvenus of the folly of taking on the might of the British Empire. Even the cannon proved false. The weapon was real enough, and it was the same sort of cannon found on the *Britomart*, but it arrived more than half a century after the ship did, being sent out from Britain for display at the 1906–07 International Exhibition in Christchurch.

Akaroa derives much more of its character from its British history. It's a charming town, carefully preserved, at least by New Zealand standards. Many of its oldest, British, houses and buildings survive. Old houses and tiny cottages still dot the townscape. As I climbed the narrow staircase of one of them and emerged into a tiny room whose ceiling was too low to stand under, I thought two things: first, the town must have been home to a population of dwarfs; and second, what a marvellous feat of preservation this little town was, for people were prepared to put up with its limitations for the sake of its beauty. Oh, and to avoid falling foul of the town planners, of course.

The biggest surviving house from the era is the nineteenth-century Oinako, built in 1896 for a family named Le Lievre. The family name lived on in Akaroa, a place where a French-sounding surname carried a good deal of *le prestige*.

Historic houses, shops, commercial buildings and even the old Criterion Hotel survive. You might find the same number of colonial buildings in other towns around the country. The difference here is that Akaroa is a very small town, little enough for the survivors to give it character. It might no longer be French, and the French influence may be, largely, *la connerie*, crap, but who cares? It's very pretty.

Character sets the tone and Akaroa has carefully and sometimes painfully preserved that tone. A few years previously the authorities had produced an environmental plan masterminded by the (usually) revered architect Peter Beaven, whereby anyone planning to build a new house had to run it through a 'design and appearance committee' on the basis that holiday homes were doing what holiday homes did, going from bad to horrible and threatening the town's charm. Unease over its changing nature became accusations of bad taste, of tilt-slab, pseudo, stuccoed, dull, ill-suited houses despoiling the townscape.

Insults flew, and new developments ran the gauntlet. Some of the most controversial were designed by architects who were prominent in the town. True, they gave the town's French village reputation a terrible beating, or what Gallic pedigree there was left to beat. A report prepared for the Christchurch City Council in 2009 contained the sentence: 'The reinvention of Akaroa as a little piece of France … needs to be recognised for what it is — faux.'

At cruise ship time, however, the town's *histoire* climbs off the canvas, is fanned and watered and helped back into its corner ready to come out fighting once more. Mass tourism has not just fed off the alleged French character, it has nurtured it, promoted it, hosed it down and buffed it up.

Cruise ships have pushed local tourism from a cottage industry to something better accommodated in *un château*. They have rewritten the script, redesigned the set and filled it with a cast of actors.

Akaroa doesn't really need the French touch; the New Zealand one is enough. It is an excellent little town in Akaroa Harbour, one of the two harbours formed when the sea cut an entrance into the craters of the two biggest volcanos that formed most of Banks Peninsula. Akaroa town nestles in a deep bay, French Bay, well into the harbour. Behind it the hills rise to the crater rim in a gentle, rolling sort of way and when the highway brings you over the rim of the crater on the other side of the harbour the township seems to lie in its vale far below like a flower unfurling in the sun, which, of course, is always shining here.

Though it's bent, broken and still a construction site, Christchurch retains its own magnetic field. As I drove over that hilly road into Akaroa Harbour, I passed a flotilla of tour buses. Tours to Christchurch are popular among cruise ship passengers and by the time I reached the Akaroa wharf most of them had been booked out. I wondered which the tourists preferred, a fake French town or a disaster zone? Plenty of passengers remained in town.

Tourism had underpinned this economy for as long as anyone could remember. Before the cruise ships there were the buses, and any fine weekend, or any good day, saw a stream of traffic pouring over the hill from Christchurch. You went to Akaroa when you wanted to cheer up, or get away for the afternoon, or escape the eternal, infernal easterly, or watch the harbour's rhythm.

The *Celebrity Solstice* can carry almost 3000 passengers. The previous Census had produced a population of 624 in Akaroa (which, incidentally, was only a hundred or so more than its population at the turn of the twentieth century). The ship multiplied the town's population nearly five times. Akaroa's French-ness does better out of the cruise ships than it ever did out of Peter Beaven.

These were of course the kinds of twists and turns common in any small town, if exaggerated here in Akaroa. The town never seemed fake to me, just charming and comfortable. But that was without 3000 tourists marching through it eating takeaways, buying stuff and trying to find a place to pee. That particular worry seemed to have been addressed by setting up Portaloos, themselves a subject of curiosity. Did they work? How? Would they be locked in? Would they tip over? (This from someone of a build making him quite right to be anxious.)

Locals seemed a bit thin on the ground that day. I imagined those without some sort of tourist business stayed indoors until the coast was clear, and holiday home owners remained on the other side of the hill.

Stalls lined the streets. They sold everything, and anything, although their view of what the average tourist needed was sometimes puzzling. The visitors were invited, for example, to buy 'superior underwear' — no riding-up, no panty line. They were offered possum socks. They were urged to imbibe potions for beating off psoriasis, eczema and dermatitis. They could buy an Akaroa passport stamp ($2).

The tourists clustered around real estate agents' windows. 'A million bucks? Phew!' They queued to ride on such uniquely French attractions as a London double-decker bus, or a hot-rod trike, or a vintage Ford or an old Dodge. The stand-up paddleboard hire didn't seem to be doing so well, this being a cold spring day when no one really wanted to take their clothes off, even if the bodies underneath had been up to the challenge.

The tourists wandered through St Peter's historic church, made of the totara that covered Banks Peninsula before the forests were destroyed. Did they know anything about this, or anything else that mattered? None of those I spoke to did. Did they care? Not a bit. They munched their croissants and gave the architecture the twenty-second look.

They weren't uncaring, or indifferent, or pushy, or confronting: they were only people, doing what people do. They were allowed to be older and not so active and take a cruise. It was just that there were so many of them. They crowded the cafés and the souvenir shops and the supermarket and assured each other that the pharmacy was out of everything they needed. They spoke in the tourist tongue:

'Where are you from?'

'Sydney. You?'

'Hawke's Bay.'

'Where's that?'

'Up north.'

'Have you lost your wife?'

'Yeah, purposefully.'

All right, I only heard that one once.

I talked to a woman who was raised in Hawaii and now lived in Ohio. She was travelling with her daughter, son-in-law (who was watching me suspiciously) and two grandchildren. Within a sentence I had learned that 1. She was a Republican; 2. She admired Donald Trump; and 3. She just wished the Democrats and the Republicans would stop fighting and accept her hero as the winner.

She was awaiting the return of fellow passengers who'd taken a tour to Christchurch. They'd had earthquakes in Christchurch, I ventured. She looked surprised. 'Did they?' I decided to leave before I fell unconscious.

What might Jason have thought of this modern boatload of heroes? Well, the numbers said Akaroa definitely accommodated the Golden Fleece. Come cruise ship time, the town was awash with money. When the accountants totted it all up (in June 2018) they found that shipboard tourists had spent $35 million in Akaroa in the previous year and another $29 million in Christchurch.

In the beginning, Akaroa saw this as a Good Thing. A survey showed that locals mainly approved of cruise ships. They benefitted the area, the locals said, or more than half of them did. Of the others, half were neutral. They reacted as most small towns did in the first flush of an exciting adventure, describing the cruise ship industry as 'a new chapter in Akaroa's history as a tourist destination'.

Yes, there were strains on resources, overcrowding, environmental threats. They were worrying, and those concerned about these matters were absolutely right, although perhaps not in the way they intended, for it was not long before the debit side of the balance sheet started turning red. Only a few years later, Akaroa was counting the cost. By 2019, oh, the crowds, the strain on roads and footpaths, the packed, overflowing public toilets (the town had enough for a visiting football team but that was about all). The tour touts, the flotillas of boats cluttering their once-pristine harbour. Locals couldn't get a coffee. They had to queue in the supermarket. Better, if you had the option (this was a town where census-takers found far more than half the houses unoccupied because most were holiday homes) to stay out of town on cruise ship days. And when two ships at a time came into the harbour …

Even the beach was running out of sand, and roads out of gravel. The little town looked so … untidy (a very Canterbury complaint). Residents were going from sanguine to angry in a hop. Some wanted cruise ship visits limited, some had simply had enough of the whole business. They'd come to Akaroa for its peace and tranquillity after all.

Akaroa has just one road in and the same number out again, except for a few narrow routes, some hardly more than tracks, leading to nearby bays. Those bays are entrancing places, wild, rocky, standing in the teeth of southern gales like ancient fortresses themselves. Fortunately they were too difficult, too ponderous, too savage for tourists.

But in the town it was only going to get worse. Oh, the poor wharf, which on a calm sunny day, or even a cloudy one, was always one of my favourite places to sit with the seagulls and look at the fleet of unpretentious boats nuzzling their moorings and admire the patterns of hills and valleys and bush and farms and sky and absorb the peace and contemplate the world in the company of a few kindred spirits. All of that was still there, but divided between a thousand people at a time. Only the seagulls were pleased.

Even when Lyttelton opened its new cruise ship berth, the ships would keep coming to Akaroa. Residents hoped, though, that re-opening Lyttelton would ease the pressure on Akaroa. One of them told Radio New Zealand news: 'We're going to have to survive next season with 120 ships. When there's hope that things are going to change, people will find ways of adapting. If we thought there's going to be ten years like this ... I think you'd find a lot of people packing up and moving out.'

Tourism had set its pattern, and it was one the townspeople were increasingly failing to admire. Some drove too fast and too close, threatening visitors on the narrow streets, and I observed a readiness to sneak up on people crossing the road, honk at the last moment and sit with a righteous expression as the victim (in this case, me) took to the air. No one had told the locals about mass tourism. The vision was appealing — to some — but the reality was not. What's more, it was self-defeating. People came to Akaroa for its charm, and the charm was vanishing down the maw of this voracious new industry. Locals said to me, with that confiding note that tips off a much-used line, that they were calling this town 'Tackaroa'.

Akaroa was a blatant example of overtourism, well past any happy balance point if it was defined as numbers of tourists versus what the town could handle. And if the town expanded to meet the demand by building more public toilets, more bus-friendly streets, better access-ways, would that be Akaroa plus? Or minus? What would changes to accommodate the passing parade do for local people who were not part of the tourist trade but instead just wanted to live good lives in a peaceful place? Would they declare their town no longer inhabitable and leave?

They might have said the same about Milford Sound, if enough people had lived there to say it. The sight of a giant tourist ship anchored in that deep green sea of tranquillity seemed to suck the air out of my body. Milford is a UNESCO World Heritage site, one of the great natural areas of the world, a place whose flora and fauna date back to the time when New Zealand was part of the vast continent of Gondwana. Was it still a place of 'untouched beauty?' Not when a huge white ship sat square in the frame.

Yes, Akaroa struck back, in a rather limp way. Sternly, it banned freedom camping in most parts of the town, except for a few campervans and only those with on-board toilets. And

Akaroa townspeople began looking at places like Barcelona and Venice. Cruise ships were said to be eroding Venice's foundations, even as the ancient city state was already slipping beneath the waves of climate change and the impact of 36 million tourists a year. Its permanent population, little more than Invercargill's, doubled every day. Barcelona attracted similar numbers, the growing fleet of cruise ships riding the wave. Soaring rents were chasing permanent residents from the city. Tourism there was actually increasing poverty as the rich got richer and the poor were forced into arid, low-paid jobs.

Tourists were not only pounding parts of those cities to bits, they were swamping their characters, overwhelming their treasures, destroying their ambience, chasing out their residents and creating urban deserts. And these were cities built to withstand punishment, to endure. Akaroa, well, not so much. Those European cities were built of stone by master architects and craftspeople centuries ago; Akaroa was a little wooden town that, centuries-wise, was still well short of two. Those cities had endured aeons of wars, revolutions, invasions, sieges, vandals, billionaires, fools. If they were suffering, quivering under a worse invasion than any others in their histories, namely twenty-first century tourism, then what chance did Akaroa have?

Then something awful happened. Something no one had predicted, or even imagined might happen. Something that instantly changed the way people viewed tourism. It was called coronavirus, or Covid-19, and it spread around the world in a flash.

Cruise ships packed with thousands of passengers were immediately seen as floating Petri dishes, places where the virus could flourish. Three cruise ship passengers were tested for it while their ship was in Akaroa. No one was allowed to leave the vessel. The virus became a modern-day Siren, one of those legendary beings who lured ships onto rocks. The government promptly halted cruise ship visits to New Zealand.

Akaroa was devastated. Overtourism suddenly became not so much a problem as a lovely memory. Previous grizzling was now drowned by howls of anguish. The town had become dependent on tourism, and without tourists its businesspeople wondered how they would survive.

It was New Zealand in miniature. We were great travellers, but we didn't like tourists so much. They choked little towns and their rental cars crossed white lines. Their buses blocked roads. Their campervans crowded the scenery and the occupants peed in the trees.

We needed them though. Tourism had become essential to the New Zealand economy. It made up around 6 percent of the gross domestic product and another 4 percent counting supporting industries, and those figures were growing steadily. It employed 8–9 percent of the national workforce.

The rest of the world was confronting exactly the same issue. The boring, under-paid jobs in Barcelona were better than no jobs at all. Venice went from protesting about 'hit and run' tourists who descended from the cruise liners towering over their delicate buildings, to rejecting a solution whereby the ships would be re-routed, to outright horror when Covid-19 settled the issue by scaring the tourists away. Covid-19 had changed world tourism in a flash. Barcelona emptied. The Louvre, Notre Dame, the Great Wall, the Vatican, Venice and St Patrick's, Akaroa, were all deserted. Hands were wrung.

Well, it was in the nature of a crisis to pass, but this one at least demonstrated the modern dilemma: you might abhor the jabbering mobs, but, essentially, you were either stuck with them, or stuck without them. Turns out that the only thing worse than having too many tourists is having too few.

*

In the beginning there was the OE, the overseas journey young New Zealanders took to gain experience: around two years of scraping, saving, living in dumps and waiting on tables. You went, you saw, you marvelled and you came home again.

Then came the guided tour. You climbed on a plane, then a bus, and you followed a prescribed route, which usually had little to do with the country you were visiting. In Rome you saw the Vatican, in London the Tower, in Rome the Colosseum.

Cruise ships were the logical development. You saw fewer sights and more sea. The journey itself became the reward. Better to travel hopefully than to arrive, especially when you hoped for a big dinner. So they invented the floating city, with cafés, restaurants, bars, swimming pools, gymnasiums, cinemas, shopping malls. The places you stopped at — the towns, cities, sights and wonders — all became incidental to the main event, the Ship. You got off it rarely and when you did you wondered where you were and what was for lunch. Welcome to Akaroa.

The cruise ships, if not their passengers, were growing ever more adventurous. The Marlborough Sounds had become a regular destination, despite the *Mikhail Lermontov*'s fate in 1986. The Russian cruise ship, carrying mainly elderly Australians, hit rocks and sank near the Tory Channel, the entrance to Queen Charlotte Sound, in circumstances that are still mysterious. One crew member died. The ship lay in thirty-eight metres of water, safely out of sight from the decks of its much bigger successors, although it had created a tourist industry of its own: it was popular with visiting scuba divers. Disaster tourism was an international phenomenon, but the South Island of New Zealand had produced a new twist, tourism feeding on its own disasters.

Another cruise ship, the *Azamara Quest,* also hit a rock near Tory Channel, in 2016. It stayed afloat and all 652 passengers lived to tell the tale, undoubtedly over and over again. Including a shipwreck in the price could become a star attraction for Marlborough Sounds cruises. Picton and nearby Blenheim counted the revenue. The costs could always be totted up later.

Even Stewart Island joined the queue. Its tourist industry had been, well, cosy, served by a smallish ferry and light aircraft. Now it had squeezed into cruise ship schedules. These ships could increase the island's 400-odd population ten-fold, and did very little for the peaceful ambience valued by natives such as myself (well, I once worked down there), but these were tiny places where dollars were hard to come by and horror stories were not appreciated.

Overtourism, too many tourists in other words, was easy for people in larger urban areas to decry. By the standards of very small town New Zealand, city folk were flush. Small towns were lean, and quite capable of becoming mean. But could you look at the juxtaposition of the deep, cool green Milford Sound or peaceful Akaroa Harbour or the remote (even for Aucklanders) Great Barrier Island, and an anchored, huge white cruise ship, and not shudder?

Thailand's Maya Bay, for example, was a place of tranquillity and wonder in the 2000 film *The Beach*, starring Leonardo di Caprio. The resulting wave of tourists destroyed the coral, wrecked the beach and buried its surrounds under litter, ruined the mangroves, polluted the ocean and even scared away the fish. On the credit side, tourism there brought in $20 million a year or, borrowing an expression I heard from an Akaroa cynic, thirty pieces of silver. Thailand's tourist industry had ruined the place, on the cheap. Even an environmentally calloused government had to do something. It closed the bay for a few years in the hope it would recover.

Equally remote places in New Zealand are not beyond the reach of the burgeoning tourist industry, including those lonely places most New Zealanders have never been to but like to think of as uniquely theirs, the ones whose solitude could light the most miserable soul. I climbed Mount Fyffe near Kaikoura one crisp day when snow lay in patches under a clear blue sky. The mountain wasn't high: I could look across gorges and ravines to the Inland Kaikouras and see real mountains, austere and lonely. Fyffe, though, was a perfect little mountain with shoulders and a neat pointy top. It hunkered beside the town and defined it almost as much as the sea did.

Robert Fyffe, a rough Scot, set up a whaling station on the Kaikoura Peninsula in the early 1840s and became patriarch of the first European family to settle there. His cottage had become a tourist attraction, like the whales he'd once hunted. He'd killed them so efficiently that he'd had to seek alternative employment, thereby becoming, perhaps, New Zealand's very first redundancy. Fortunately the whales came back, and Kaikoura discovered they were worth much more alive than dead. Despite this near disaster, Fyffe's name was literally set in stone, and the rocky flanks of Mount Fyffe could be seen rising above the river plain from any point in the town.

I'd set out with a small company of trampers on the walk of about eight hours return, depending not so much on endurance as determination. It's not one of the nation's Great Walks, even if it features in tourist literature of the '20 out-of-the-way places to go in New Zealand' kind. The track plods up the mountain on a steady gradient and passes a hut a little over halfway to the top (where on this occasion four lonely young Germans huddled, looking down on the town below and wondering whether they'd really made the right choice for a night out). Despite the grandeur of the ranges — the Seaward Kaikouras and the mighty Inland ones — the walk itself is a little boring, the kind where you look down at your feet — left boot, right boot, left … (is that one getting a little worn around the top?) — and follow another bend, then another and another, each one revealing, yes, another bend, until you get to the top.

But then you explode with a barrage of clichés that could collectively make up a fine tourist brochure. The beauty, the view of the sea, Kaikoura below in the sun, everything sparkling away like mad, and there you are alone in this perfect universe, except for half a dozen kindred spirits. And then …

Chop chop chop chop … As we stood there a helicopter rose above a nearby ridge, just like one of those thrillers where someone in the chopper shoots you, or you shoot them. Instead, this one clattered up to where we were standing on the rather small summit and landed beside us. Three tourists climbed out.

We could tell they were tourists because they were neat and tidy and their gear was expensive. Our own style was, well, New Zealand tramper: good boots and packs and parkas, everything else well used.

They'd been to see the whales, said the pilot, and they'd thought they'd pop up here for a look. I asked one of his passengers how long it had taken them, and he said quite a long time because the pilot had taken them into a valley, a spectacular one, and they'd probably been, oh, ten or fifteen minutes getting up here. They were decent enough, pleasant, but I couldn't help thinking of our four-hour trudge. All of those things the tourists missed out on! The sweat, the aches. I bet one of my companions that they'd have so much energy left they could even stay up past nine o'clock.

All the same, I was a little, well, troubled. I'd earned my stripes and they hadn't. Tourists, in this far-off place? What did you have to do in this country to get away from them? Once, you only had to drive over your city or town boundary and there it was, New Zealand, yours for the taking. I hated to say it but (in times of stress you fall back on clichés), we didn't know what we had until … well, you know the rest.

It's true though that we'd always had that New Zealand thing about our country: it was beautiful but not as beautiful as other countries. Their places always seemed so much better than ours. That's why we went Overseas, in droves, on the great New Zealand OE. We were the world's most enduring, persistent, intrusive (and possibly ignorant) tourists. Now the world had discovered us and we were startled. We (well, many of us) had had to be told of our home attractions in tourist campaigns of the 'don't leave home 'til you've seen the country' type.

Tourists! We didn't understand them. Who'd have thought they'd like this place? Or that thing? There was simply no accounting for them. We could cope as long as the tourist industry stuck to the honeypot principle: the tourists went to a few overrated, overpriced and tarted-up places like Queenstown, where no real Kiwis would ever go unless they were from Auckland. They travelled to Rotorua and Taupo and Aoraki Mount Cook and the glaciers and Queenstown. Stayed in hotels, for God's sake.

That was fine. If they liked that sort of thing they could have it, as long as they left the rest of the country alone.

They did not, of course. Tourists became younger and more adventurous, and if they weren't, they journeyed on cruise ships. They started going to places which we considered uniquely our own, places where we could find tranquillity and most of all, solitude. Alas. I don't know how many of the tourists who come here every year go off-piste, but when I travel to some of my own favourite out-of-the-way spots, I encounter an awful lot of them.

For those searching for the new golden fleece, the statistics were entrancing: around four million people were visiting our country every year, almost doubling New Zealand's population. Most were from Australia, followed by China, the United States and Britain. The tourist hotspots were Canterbury and Queenstown.

South Islanders are, however, inclined to look this particular gift horse in the mouth, and find more than a few teeth. The smaller the place, the more prominent tourists are, and you run across them in some quite odd spots. Once I was walking high above the sea on an obscure track, invisible from the road far below. I hadn't known it existed. It was very quiet — until we rounded a bend and there, admiring the view, was a cluster of tourists. They were not noisy, or offensive, just some young people doing exactly what we were doing: taking a walk and enjoying the silence and the feeling that they were far away. They were even dressed as we were, with shorts, thermal gear, boots, day packs. It was just so … odd to see them. Oh, and somehow annoying. This was my place. How dare they?

*

Officially the West Coast is delighted with tourism. Unofficially, not so much. It's not in the nature of a region both physically and philosophically barricaded from the rest of New Zealand to welcome such an intrusion. Despite the Coast's reputation for friendliness, I've always found people there wary of strangers. The reverse side of that is that if you are a Coaster — that is, you were born there — you are a Coaster for life and always welcome.

Most wear the badge proudly no matter where they live, but it's a sad fact that they are more likely to live over the hill (Christchurch or Dunedin) or up north (anywhere else) than on the thin strip of land squeezed between mountains and sea that they call home.

For much of the twentieth century, Coasters worked to the motto, 'If it grows, cut it down; if it doesn't, dig it up.' Gold gave way to coal and timber and the rainforests were felled, to the dismay of an increasingly conservation-conscious New Zealand public. Logging native forest on the Coast slowed in the 1980s but ended only in the new millennium. By then attitudes had changed: the then prime minister, Helen Clark, became notorious (on the Coast) for calling the pro-logging lobby 'feral', although what she actually said was: 'Attitudes of some on the West Coast could be fairly feral.' I thought it an understatement. What was left of the rainforest was saved but greens and conservationists were, by and large, despised.

Yet the forests are now part of the West Coast's new economy. People come from all over New Zealand and the world to walk, bike and drive through them. Or just to stop in a clearing and soak in the silence, be awed by their nobility. On a good day tourists far outnumber the 33,000-odd locals. They spend sums approaching $600 million a year and rising steadily — until Covid-19 stopped tourism dead.

Tourism is, or was, the most important sector of the West Coast economy. Only agriculture, forestry and fishing come close and coal mining is now far down the list. Once, working on an article on the West Coast economy for the *New Zealand Listener*, I was assured that far from being properly laid to rest on environmental grounds, coal mining was resurgent. I was given the new Pike River mine as an example. Ah, well. This was a region of lost dreams, but that particular nightmare didn't vanish with the dawn.

None of that meant Coasters welcomed their new economy with open arms. A quality-of-life survey by one local council revealed a good deal of resentment towards both international and national tourists, all of them perceived to be so much wealthier than many Coasters (a fifth of respondents had no disposable income at all). It was just that needs must.

In 2018 I was trapped on the Coast by a cyclone named Gita, which meant 'song' or perhaps 'good'. Gita was neither. It didn't sing, it howled. It was a badly behaved lady. The highway south of Whataroa leading to the glaciers and the Haast Pass was blocked by slips and fallen trees and power lines. Hundreds of tourists were trapped, more than a hundred of them on the high rocky passes to the glaciers.

I was among a crowd of them stopped by a roadblock at Whataroa. The predominant emotion, other than indignation, was amazement. Blocked? A main highway? There must be another way? No? How could this be? What were they to do? Where were they to stay?

The tourists became an attraction themselves: a small crowd of locals gathered, themselves amazed, but more by the general consternation. A few trees and slips? What was the fuss about? It would be fixed in a day or two. It might be quite a bite from a tight schedule, but this was the Coast, and these things happened well, quite often. They didn't quite say so, but I interpreted the body language as 'suck it up'.

I found myself, ironically, in an ancient loggers' accommodation block. I was carting my gear inside when a van-load of Asian tourists pulled in, asking the same question: where could they stay? No room at this inn, the owner replied, but she'd contact someone in a town further along the road. Which she did, and they had space for the tourists, rather to my own host's surprise: 'She doesn't like overseas tourists.'

The West Coast has an insoluble problem. It's not environmentalism or greenies or an indifferent government or climate change or any of the bogies that haunt dreams. It is, simply, rain. The Coast has far too much of it. The nor'westers rush in from the Tasman Sea to be wrung out by the Main Divide, saturating the Coast. The heavy rain makes the Coasters stoical and the rainforests grow. And it regularly washes away bridges.

Just before Christmas 2019, a thousand tourists were once more stranded in Franz Josef when a bridge near the wonderfully named Mount Hercules was washed out in a flood. Whoever could afford it simply abandoned their rental cars and escaped by helicopter. The Coast was always a wonderful source of travel stories along the lines of 'I went there, and I lived.'

The curious thing about the West Coast is that most of its tourists are New Zealanders. We've always loved the Coast legend, the characters, the odd little towns, the difference of the place. Though mostly we like it with either the Southern Alps or Cook Strait between us and them.

We like the pubs too, or thought we did. Once I stayed at the Empire Hotel in Kumara before a Coast to Coast race. The pub sat beside the road. Its floors were so uneven that you felt unsteady even before you went into the bar. It was not luxurious. It was not even comfortable. I was kept awake by shrieking frogs. Later the pub was converted into rental accommodation and someone attacked it with a Molotov cocktail. I was nowhere near, I swear.

Well, things changed. As cities spread and native forest disappeared, taking the wilderness with it, the West Coast seemed to hold the line. Coasters stopped felling the forests and started selling them to the tourists. It was more profitable and less controversial. The region's tramping and cycling tracks became world famous, especially within New Zealand. They were tracks through Coast history, really.

Lyell, inland from Westport, was once the biggest goldfield in the region, and also the most difficult, as access at first was by way of the notorious Buller River. The town was named after a British geologist who died without knowing it existed. The place grew steadily from the 1860s. Eventually it had a newspaper, school, two churches, police station, brewery and lots and lots of gold, which of course slowly ran out. It was razed by a huge fire soon after the turn of the twentieth century and isolated by the 1929 Murchison earthquake so effectively that some in the town died for want of help. In the end only the pub remained and it burned down in 1963, taking a fine collection of the town's artefacts with it.

Lyell was only a sign beside the road and a bush track leading to an old cemetery until someone had a very good idea and connected the old dray road used by miners to a track running alongside the Mohikinui River and called it the Old Ghost Road. Meridian Energy had wanted to use the Mohikinui for a power scheme, to the great detriment of both the river and some 330 hectares of native forest, which would be inundated. Environmentalists protested. I didn't give them a dog's show and took a sentimental last walk along the river, discovering that the Department of Conservation evidently agreed with me because track maintenance seemed to have been given up as a lost cause. Yet the scheme was abandoned, to the delight of nature lovers and the despair of vested interests on the Coast, who claimed that greenies were both locking them up and closing them down. This had been their constant refrain for decades: 'their' forests, 'their' rivers, their right to cut them down, dam them up and dig for gold in whatever modern form it existed.

You do not hear so much from them now, though, because the Old Ghost Road has been an outstanding success. It hauls in tourists, and consequently money. The West Coast Wilderness Trail is doing the same. This four-day cycle track departs from Greymouth, runs down the coast, turns inland to Kumara then heads into the mountains and over the Kawhaka Pass to a place named Cowboy Paradise, a replica Wild West Town that more or less sums up the tourist paradox. Then it goes to Hokitika, where it dithers on the town streets before setting off for a treetop walkway inland from Lake Mahinapua, whose pub was immortalised in a television cheese commercial ('I've never seen them so excited'). The trail continues to Ross, home of the Honourable Roddy gold nugget, which weighed 3.1 kilograms, and is worth around $226,000 at today's prices plus a margin of who-knows-what for being a nugget. In the end, however, that's not very much compared with the tourist dollar, proving, again, that all that glitters is not gold.

The West Coast economy, battered by the Pike River mine tragedy, mine closures and the lack of enthusiasm for coal worldwide due to its contribution to climate change, is grateful to tourism. But climate change, boosted to an unknown extent by coal from the West Coast mines, is doing the glacier towns, Franz Josef and Fox, even more damage. The two glaciers, ironically, represent the high point of West Coast tourism; 'ironically' because current projections estimate they'll have about the same lifespan as a Coast gold-mining boom town.

The glacier towns are not unlike those eighteenth-century villages: more solid but with the same air of haste and transience, of inhabitants urgently in search of a dollar. I've been through them every year or two for a lifetime and always found it hard to get so much as a good cup of coffee. Even the glaciers themselves are out of reach, at least the reach of a casual visitor. To get a decent look at them you need to get into one of the helicopters that swarm around the towns like flies around a … well, honeypot.

The noise they make can be tremendous. The most enthusiastic glacier tourists are the Chinese, from one of the most polluting and polluted nations in the world, possibly keen to see their handiwork before it vanishes. The glaciers' terminal faces jog back and forth along their valleys but are losing the race. Astonishingly, the local council refused to sign the climate change declaration circulating among councils nationwide, on the grounds that more evidence of climate change was needed.

Nevertheless, Franz Josef and Fox remain the anchor points of the West Coast tourist industry. They are by far the most popular of the many attractions running the length of the Coast. Tourist-wise, the circuit runs from the Oparara Arches, one of the remarkable limestone formations near Karamea in the north, down to the Haast world heritage area in the south. It's a huge area, covering almost a tenth of New Zealand, the nation's least populated 10 percent, with less than 1 percent of the population. And it was a wild and lonely place until the tourist influx, which, on any good day, can far outnumber locals.

Despite the revenue and the tourist industry's efforts to convince locals of the benefits in terms of employment and income, many Coasters remain unconvinced. They feel they are being swamped, that tourists are poking into every corner of their domain. The old ghost town of Waiuta lies in the hills between Reefton and Greymouth, and was once reached only by a very difficult road. In the past I'd fossicked around the old swimming pool and the mine manager's house, which contained a huge safe whose door had been hacked open (nothing, apparently was found). A last, lonely hermit chatted to the occasional visitor and posed for a photograph with a practised air. But now even this high, lonely, cold place was scheduled for tourist development. The Department of Conservation was masterminding a plan to restore the town as a tourist attraction. A series of signs indicated the main sites and the road was smooth as silk. But by the time they blocked off all the holes and the tunnels so people couldn't fall into them, took away most of the machinery so people couldn't break bones on it, and fenced off everything else, you were left with something that had absolutely nothing to do with the exciting, boozy, frantic place it once was.

Environmentalists — and it must be said that in a toss-up here between tourists and conservationists, the greenies would come a dismal second — fret about the loss of peace and tranquillity and threats to the environment, ranging from damage to the huge cave spiders of Honeycomb Hill in the north, to the theft of moa bones, to tourists piddling in the Haast River in the south.

The Department of Conservation controls most — around 85 percent — of the Coast, but in truth, squeezed between its duty to conserve on one side and pressure from industry and sometimes government on the other, it has sometimes been a dodgy steward. It teamed up with the Ministry of Business, Innovation and Employment and the tourist industry to turn the Oparara Basin, with its caves and arches, into a bizarre theme park with walkways, light shows, huge fake moas and equally extinct Haast eagles. They even wanted to rename Karamea 'Moa Town'. Environmentalists truly spat the latte and, in the end, the plan, like its subjects, didn't fly.

Coasters have to make a living in a place where a living is hard to make. Chainsaws have been evicted from native forests, miners from their shafts. The modern gold-miners have moved out of Reefton, the cement works in Westport has closed. Hospitality workers do not earn much money, but at least they are paid.

Tourism has become so critical that a bridge collapse can bring the local economy to its knees. When the bridge over the Waiho River, fed by Franz Josef Glacier meltwater, was swept away by floodwaters in March 2019, it took tourist traffic with it. The damage to the local economy was variously estimated at between $1 million and $3 million a day, and it took eighteen days to repair the bridge.

*

This is the essence of the south's problem. Southerners don't like their streets clogged with tourists, their spectacular landscapes effectively fitted out with turnstiles. No one who doesn't need the money is enraptured by tourism. It has been the golden fleece for the West Coast, but that doesn't mean the Coast has to like it.

When I'd met Greymouth's mayor Tony Kokshoorn, on his last day in office, he'd told me, 'Tourism is a massive contributor to our [West Coast] economy.' And it is, accounting for an eighth of all jobs, with the numbers steadily growing, especially south of Greymouth, and spending going up and up. All the graphs the West Coast has mourned over, especially falling employment and failing businesses, are heading heavenwards instead of diving into the abyss. New cycleways, new tramping tracks, new attractions.

Tourism pays good wages, gives enterprising locals a chance to own their own businesses, keeps people in the district.

But, as it turned out, the departing mayor was conflicted. 'The other side of the coin is, with tourism comes busier roads, rental cars driven by people who drift to the right-hand side of the road and drive slowly, campers who park anywhere and pee in the bush.' Mayor Kokshoorn reflected the views of many Coasters. Pouring coffee and making beds wasn't a proper way of making a living, not for people reared in a tradition of tunnelling, digging, milling and generally wrestling a living from a tough country. It might turn a dollar, but it wasn't coal, or timber. It wasn't Coastly.

The rental car argument echoed up and down the coast. It was true enough. In my travels over the years I'd seen some truly astonishing feats. One rental car I was following south of Timaru suddenly stopped dead in the middle of its lane on State Highway 1, just before a blind bend, while its two occupants pored over a map, oblivious to the crescendo of screeching tyres as drivers behind braked desperately. They turned left, evidently mistaking a farm track for a road, and I could say with certainty that no one in the traffic chaos they'd caused was going to go after them to put them right.

Another time, in the North Island near Taupo, I watched a rental car travelling on State Highway 1, with its open speed limit, make a right turn into the Turangi supermarket car park, across the path of an oncoming car driven by a woman with several children. Smoke poured from all four corners of her vehicle as she braked desperately, managing to squeeze around the back of the rental and past the parade of horror-stricken drivers who'd been jammed behind the tourists. Again, the rental's occupants seemed unaware of the near-tragedy.

This isn't prejudice. According to the Ministry of Transport, 43 percent of crashes on the West Coast involved foreign drivers, and 33 percent in Queenstown and 23 percent in Southland. I usually drive a rental car labelled with the company's name on the back window or, put another way, branded with the curse. Its disadvantage is that I am blamed for every indignity ever committed by a rental car driver if I so much as brake at a give-way sign. The advantage is that I am given a wide berth.

Well, said Tony Kokshoorn, never a man to kick the golden fleece into touch, 'If we want jobs for our kids, that's the trade-off. If there are no cars on the road, that's when you start worrying.' In other words, no point in grizzling, you're better off looking for a place to pass, and the point was being made at that very moment.

By 2020, it was not only glaciers that were shrinking. The upward curve in the tourism charts was faltering. It was Brexit. It was Trump. It was the Chinese and the trade war. Mainly it was the coronavirus. The industry might be disappearing like the red in raspberry ripple. Was the market 'correcting' or was it on its bum on a downhill run? Tourism's critics rapidly faded out of the frame. Akaroa, and Queenstown, and the entire West Coast studied the tea leaves. How bad could it be? Oh no, really?

What could be done? New Zealand's clean, green image had taken such a thumping it scarcely existed outside the deluded minds and desperate imaginings around boardroom tables. Beads of sweat could be seen on the '100% Pure' slogan. A tourist who'd been told to be careful about drinking the water just wasn't going to buy it.

Even as I sat there with Tony, the cityscape outside the mayor's office scarcely reflected a booming city. Greymouth looked, well, there was no kind way of saying it, shabby. Depressing. It had only been a couple of years since I was last there, but they seemed to be dog years: there were fourteen years of decline packed into that time. The town's main attraction now seemed to be the notorious bar at the entrance to its harbour, where on any bad day you could watch fishing boats ploughing in from the Tasman Sea on waves that a good surfer would drool over.

Had Greymouth missed out on the tourist boom sweeping the West Coast? Instead of finding the golden fleece, had it simply been shorn?

Yet new attractions were opening up all over the place. Gently rotting old towns, like Kumara, or Blackball, where the New Zealand Labour Party had been born, were now springing back to life (I'd stayed in both places, lulled to sleep by those thousands of singing frogs in Kumara's old Empire Hotel and by Saturday night drunks in the Formerly the Blackball Hilton, whose singing made me wish they *were* frogs.) The tourist traffic was pouring over the Alps, but it turned left on the Coast side, heading for Hokitika and Westland. Greymouth lies to the right.

Franchises and cafés were deserting the town. The bars were going and, most devastating of all, the famed West Coast pubs. The city had gone from forty-seven hotels to six. Driving in, I'd been greeted by the empty Revingtons Hotel, once the smartest in Greymouth and grand even by national standards. Why, the Queen had once stayed there, after driving into town on a road that the local council had tar-sealed specially for the occasion. But being short of money, they had only sealed one side, known from then on as 'the Queen's side'. When I stayed in the hotel with my father, the royal rooms were sealed off and labelled, like museum pieces.

Now Revingtons was a decaying old building with its railings cut off. As it happened, the mayor had wielded the saw. With the building becoming derelict and a danger to the public, he had spent a whole day helping a contractor cut off the rusting balconies, then, with his own money, had paid a friend to paint the ruin.

Mayor Kokshoorn had been fifteen years in office, the West Coast's longest serving mayor. Yet he was in the unusual position, mayors being generally boastful creatures, of being unable to claim that the town was a better place now than when he'd taken office. And now, on this, his last day, here was some smart alec having a crack at the land of his birth. Did I see a glint in his eye?

'I've had to work hard,' he ground out, 'but yes, at the same time the place is declining. My hard work has been just to stand still, let alone go ahead. We have a town of two halves and we've had a perfect storm. That perfect main street full of hotels and activities hit the perfect storm over the last ten years.'

First, the central business district sits on leasehold land owned by the Mawhera Incorporation, in turn owned by Poutini Ngai Tahu Maori, the original landowners on the West Coast. Various hurdles lay in the way of redevelopment, not the least of them a consequence of the Christchurch earthquakes, and that was Tony Kokshoorn's second half of the storm: all those fine 1920s and 30s buildings had to be earthquake-strengthened. Who was going to spend that money on an old building standing on land they didn't own? Who would lend the money? So poor Greymouth's centre was slowly crumbling.

Hmm, I thought. Greymouth was missing out on some of the tourist stream to the south, but there were still plenty of travellers left over. Every day Greymouth had a market all of its own: the TranzAlpine express from Christchurch, said to be one of the world's great train journeys (rightly, based on my own experience) pulled into its station and disgorged hundreds of tourists who then wandered around the city centre looking for something to do. It didn't take much to set up a café, which didn't care very much about who owned its building, much less about earthquake strengthening, as long as the rent was right. There was plenty of business being done outside the CBD, but who came to Greymouth to visit a warehouse? Or a supermarket? Or to buy a car, even one from Tony Kokshoorn's own car yard?

My own opinion, which I might not have mentioned to the mayor (for he could be formidable), was that the town was disappearing into a vortex of depression, whatever its cause, and no one was going to pay to be depressed.

As usual, no one could be certain of what the future held. Tourism was far beyond the control of anyone in New Zealand; the best they could do was to create conditions they thought tourists might like — price, accommodation, standard — and hope for the best. Tourism might bring the golden fleece, but the beast was flighty.

*

Much further south, on the road to Milford Sound and just before the Homer Tunnel, a sign indicates a track up to a mountain feature called the Gertrude Saddle. It's not a long walk, around seven kilometres, but it takes six hours, which might give the odd tramper pause.

It is described as a multiple hazard area. You can go there only in summer, because snow and rain make it truly death-defying. Even in summer you face a steep climb over loose rock, through rivers, and up a good deal of mountain granite, which really and truly does frown. In places, the path is so steep that steel cables have been installed. You deal with all of this for the same two reasons people climb, say, Everest: for the adventure, and the view from the top, the Gertrude Saddle.

The saddle is not just an unlikely tourist attraction, it's impossible for many. People have died there, at least half a dozen of them. An Israeli man and a French woman both lost their way, missed a stream crossing, and found themselves in deadly terrain. Both fell to their deaths. A German man took the route but slipped, fell and died two days later. It's one of those places I only need to look at to decide that if I want to scare myself, the Homer Tunnel will do it nicely and much more safely. Yet a good summer day, and even a not-so-good one, fills the little car park to the point where you'd assume a popular café lay in there, somewhere. Social media has made it a tourist attraction.

All over Fiordland, tourists seek out danger. A Czech woman spent a month in a remote mountain hut after her partner slipped and fell to his death on the Routeburn Track. It was mid-winter, when no one tramped on that track, and they were ill-prepared, and she was lucky to be found: otherwise, she'd either have frozen to death or starved.

The Mountain Safety Council produced a publication called, with classic understatement, *A Walk in the Park*. It showed that the highest number of deaths by misadventure had occurred in Otago and Southland. Fiordland, which has four times as many international visitors as homegrown ones, was the biggest killer. In other words, tourists are finding the most remote and the most dangerous spots in New Zealand and killing and injuring themselves in rising numbers. According to the statistics, international visitors died more often in winter than New Zealanders, and they usually died in the South Island. When ignoring signs was a cause of the fatality, all of those who died were international tourists (possibly, I suppose, because some couldn't read the signs).

Those awful figures said two things to me: firstly, that the aging, overweight people who filled the streets of every major city and a rising number of remote places whenever a cruise ship called might be a nuisance, but at least they were not as expensive as their younger, more daring and certainly more attractive counterparts who required teams of rescuers and helicopters and boats to get them out of trouble.

Secondly, that we should not be surprised when they turn up in all sorts of weird, out-of-the-way places that many New Zealanders would never go near, because that is the nature of tourism.

Oh, and thirdly, I admired the native tolerance. At one end of the spectrum New Zealanders made way and spoke politely. At the other end, they risked their own lives to pull out the dead and wounded from some truly horrible places, without complaint.

I went to Whakaari, White Island, once, travelling the forty-eight kilometres in a tourist boat. I found it spectacularly terrifying. At the time of my visit the risk of danger was officially at

Level One: minor volcanic unrest. Level Two indicated moderate to heightened volcanic unrest and the potential for eruption. The only thing anyone needed to know about Level Three was that they did not want to know about it. There was one more thing: scientists were doing their best to predict the unpredictable.

The guides were excellent. They warned of the dangers, told people to keep to the narrow tracks between seething pools, to walk in their footsteps. We listened, we obeyed. The stench, the toxic, bubbling craters, the hellish colours — mauve, and purple, and pink, and red, and violent yellow — all shrieked peril. We walked as gently as we possibly could around mounds so fragile that a human body could break through them and boil to the consistency of cabbage in a nanosecond. After all, it had happened: when the place had a sulphur works in the early twentieth century, a fireman named Donald Pye disappeared one night and all they found of him were his boots.

One art of adventure tourism was making people think they were living dangerously while keeping them well away from trouble. Briefings were part of the process. By explaining the perils, and telling people how to cope, you were juicing up the enterprise, making the clients all the more eager. They were already imagining going home and telling people (travel stories being the curse of dinner parties) about the risks they'd run, and triumphed over.

I knew that, but standing there amid the boiling and the stench, I listened intently. We were warned about an eruption: should it happen while you were on the island you should run, and hide behind something solid. I hoped, fervently, that it wouldn't happen: running past molten pools seemed exceedingly dangerous to me, and finding somewhere to hide might be tricky when even rock was melting. That proved more premonition than worry, for a couple of years later, in 2019, Whakaari did erupt, when there were forty-seven people on the island. The risk for the day had been rated at Level Two. Twenty-one people were killed and the rest injured, some suffering severe burns.

Why would I want to visit this smoking, stinking pile? Because where else in the world could you see a live volcano, from the inside. And I was writing a book at the time. I wrote that it was a beautiful, evil place, like Dalí's *Vision of Hell*: steam billowed, vents hissed, everyone coughed and sneezed, and even the sea foam was streaked with brown scum. Oh, and because I had become a tourist.

Tourists suspend judgement. They allow other people to make decisions for them. They *want* other people to make decisions for them. After all, you don't go on holiday to make any choices more important than what you'll have for dinner.

'Why were tourists allowed to visit an active New Zealand volcano?' asked a headline in the *New York Times*. The newspaper only needed to look across country to Washington State for an answer. There, Mount St Helens was a popular peak until it erupted in 1980, killing 57 people, destroying 250 houses and doing vast damage. Now, only some forty years later, despite constant eruption warnings, people can walk around it, climb it and even descend into its crater.

George Mallory, the celebrated mountaineer, might have answered the *Times* question with his famous quote on why he climbed a mountain, 'Because it's there.' But I was from a later, less heroic generation. My answer would have been, because I am a tourist.

*

Mount Cook was not always visible from the main road through the Mackenzie Country. The view depended on the season, for it was often covered by cloud at the head of its valley. On a good day, when it shouldered through the mist and revealed itself at the head of Lake Pukaki, it was the most perfect sight. It made me feel lucky. It was transforming. If I stood there and gazed at it, I felt anything could happen and I was always inclined to buy a lottery ticket.

A big car park was laid out on the lakeside so people could sit and watch the mountain. The view never palled. Once, the car park was pretty much empty for most of the year but now it is just about full all year round. Campervans and rental cars crowd the asphalt. People line the lake edge, selfie sticks out. If you stand close to the lake, you can just about block out the vans and the selfies and the crowds.

The Mackenzie Country was always aloof, a sparse empty land. In the past it seemed arid, suitable only for rabbits. Tekapo stood at its edge, a sentinel at the last outpost of civilisation. Twizel down the road had started life as a construction town for the upper Waitaki hydro-electric scheme and editorial writers had a lot of fun with its name. How did you pronounce it — *twizzle*? What did it mean? (It came from a bridge crossed by the English army in an ancient battle).

It was a sterile town, laid out on hierarchical lines. Single, male workers got the meanest houses; families, schoolteachers and so on got better ones; the best were occupied by the town's aristocracy: engineers and Ministry of Works brass. Everything was joined up by curly streets, which only added to the derision. A barren town in a desert.

As the twentieth century wore on, the emperor donned his robes. The hydro scheme finished. Some Twizel houses were sold, but the decision was made to keep the town intact. After all, it sat beautifully amid mountains and lakes (three of them hydro lakes, but picturesque nonetheless.) A fine ski field lay just down the road at Lake Ohau, and the Alps2Ocean Cycle Trail progressed from a gleam in a planner's eye to a thriving industry. Turquoise canals ran through the landscape. Irrigation greened the scenery. People took a second look at the surroundings. Barren? Why, they were outstanding! (In my own view, for what it's worth, it's among the best country in the entire, beautiful, South Island.)

Holiday homes began appearing. Twizel sprouted cafés. Locals began fighting preservation battles. Conservationists fought to protect the natural heritage, to save for example the critically endangered black stilt, whose only breeding population resided in the Mackenzie Country.

Then something entirely new in tourism was proposed. The Mackenzie Country was renowned worldwide for its clear skies, allowing what many claimed was the world's best view of the universe. In fact, the place had been declared a Dark Sky Reserve, where lights are strictly controlled. The few remaining smokers in the territory could hardly light a cigarette without someone slapping a ticket on them.

A whole new tourist industry sprang up in Tekapo, capital of the Mackenzie Country, complete with a massive headquarters. Tourists were bussed in to look at — and here was the novelty of it — absolutely nothing. They gazed through an empty night sky, free of particles, pollution and anything else that might block their view of the planets.

The good news was that it was in the region's best interest to keep its environment exactly as it was. The bad news was that it wasn't possible. Tourists need transport, things to do, places to stay. Tekapo began growing. Up to then tourists had gone to the Church of the Good Shepherd and its neighbouring bronze sheepdog sculpture, taken a few selfies and moved on. Now they were staying. Soon, Tekapo town was booming. A new commercial zone, playgrounds, a supermarket. Plans for a five-star hotel appalled locals. What next? Putting greens? Condos? New lakefront developments blocking views? Why, the place would be just like Wanaka in no time at all, and no one wanted that, did they?

Well, that was the trouble with tourism. What local people wanted was of little account. Locals usually start off believing their place needs that ambiguous treatment, a shot in the arm. What sort of shot? Heroin? Pentobarbital? Let's assume it's some civic equivalent of anabolic steroids. Like athletes, the townspeople soon began to regret the dose. They'd believed their place would be full of happy, appreciative tourists who would shower them with money. Instead they got crowds of people blocking the streets, trampling the scenery, clogging the sights, shopping in pop-up shops, living in vans and, according to many a local legend, pooing in the woods. The locals liked the good bits, the merry ringing of tills. The bad bits, not so much.

Errant campers were guaranteed to get them hissing. Never mind that collectively, they spent quite a lot of money, or even that the term 'freedom' was rapidly becoming a misnomer, as they were herded hither and thither and coralled into a decreasing number of increasingly regulated spots, while tourist hotels, malls and cafés blotted the landscape.

No place in the south is too small or too remote to remain aloof, even if it wants to be, and that's rare among the island's struggling towns. Tourists are bussed along the sands of Farewell Spit, shipped around South Cape, and infiltrate everywhere between the two.

Most New Zealanders have never seen Doubtful Sound. I've been there only twice, both times crossing Lake Manapouri by launch to the lake's West Arm and going over the Wilmot Pass into Deep Cove by bus. It's a superb trip into the heart of Fiordland National Park, through deep bush and peaks and waterfalls, but too remote for most Kiwis. Yet it appears on the list of international tourist attractions. Fiordland itself, however pristine and far off and difficult to reach, is increasingly popular. Tour operators call it 'the place of silence' and so it is, between tours.

Even the least likely corners are not immune to the tourist invasion. According to the *Guinness Book of Records*, Baldwin Street in Dunedin is the steepest street in the world. In the way of early planners, no one checked the terrain before the street was laid out: it was on the plan, so it became a street. But it was so steep that tar would run off it, hence its concrete surface. The usual footpath was replaced by stairs, which must have been cursed by generations of residents struggling uphill with their groceries. They once rolled truckloads of jaffas down here for fun, during the Cadbury chocolate carnival, until the Cadbury chocolate factory (which had been turning out chocolate since 1884) was sold, then closed. A thousand or so people used to run a race to the top of the street, called the Gutbuster (one winner complained that the street would be the better for fewer tourists), but the race went too, along with adventures by every kind of wheeled vehicle from supermarket trolleys to the wheelie bin that killed one of its two student occupants in the early hours. Though it's an otherwise quite nondescript thoroughfare, its fame spread around the globe. Then its title was pinched in 2019 by the Welsh village of Ffordd Pen Llech.

The reaction was, well, mixed. Yes, there'd be fewer tourists but, as one city leader remarked, that could be a blessing in disguise for residents fed up with crowds, trampled gardens and bad driving. The very dilemma of tourism, in fact. A year later the *Guinness Book of Records* revisited the matter and decided that, yes, Baldwin Street was indeed the world's steepest. Crowds rule: ruined gardens, wheelies and all.

On the other side of the city Tunnel Beach soldiers on as one of the country's less likely tourist attractions. It was built by Edward Cargill, son of the city's autocratic first superintendent and dedicated Scot, William. Edward had built a grand Italianate house that locals dubbed Cargill's Castle, then allowed it to fall to ruins. God knows why Cargill's family wanted to get down to the inaccessible and rather forbidding Tunnel Beach, because it was an easy walk from the castle to the lovely St Clair beach, where I lived for a time — the water was cold enough to put goose pimples on the sandstone. But they did, and to get there while staying dry they built a tunnel. This tunnel still leads to the beach and is now on every adventurous tourist's list.

For nowhere is unknown or unexplored. Tourists troop up Castle Hill near Arthur's Pass in Canterbury to see the weird rocks on top. They journey into deep bush near Murchison to see the Natural Flames, fires fuelled by natural gas that seeps out of the ground. They travel to Springfield, a tiny town on the edge of the Canterbury Plains — and in my opinion a fine little place for a cup of coffee on the way into the mountains — to see some native art: a six-tonne doughnut created to reference Homer Simpson's hometown of Springfield and his love of doughnuts, all in one go.

They trek on the precipitous path to Nugget Point. They walk a track to Blue Lake in the Nelson Lakes National Park, two days minimum. The attraction here, apart from bush, mountains, etc, etc, is a lake certified by the National Institute of Water and Atmospheric Research, no less, as containing the world's clearest water, although as it climbs up the tourists' lists I wouldn't bet on it staying that way.

Freedom camping has become an epithet the entire length of the South Island. Local councillors either gloom over it or rage. The subject occupied far more of their time than lesser matters such as global warming or environmental destruction. In Golden Bay, campers jammed themselves into a spot behind the Takaka library, no less; locals had no time for their new literary set. In Marlborough freedom campers were accused of trashing the environment. Banks Peninsula simply barred them from the top spots. In Tekapo, people complained that freedom camping was out of control and even when tickets were issued, fines — surprise! — were not paid.

Old gold-mining sites further south, Bendigo, Jacksons, Lowburn, even those fitted with flash new solar-powered toilets and self-compacting rubbish bins, were being overrun. On the

West Coast, residents blockaded a bridge over the appropriately named Squatters Creek leading to the little town of Kakapotahi south of Ross, and turned the modern squatters away. It wasn't clear what they disliked more: the tourists' discovery of a little place so remote I'd never noticed it, or the overcrowding of their pride and joy, a new camping ground, developed, ironically, with money from the government's tourism infrastructure fund.

Up and down the South Island, towns hang out the signs: tourists with fat wallets welcome, freeloaders keep out. When freedom campers make up something like 20 percent of tourists, it's not an easy distinction to make. Freedom campers were accused of bad behaviour, including littering and of course urinating and defecating in public places, though most probably did that for the same reason wealthier cruise ship passengers were caught short: the shortage of public lavatories. The campers suffered the fate of the powerless and the poor, and became the whipping boys and girls for resentment towards tourists and the industry. Never mind that many New Zealanders had been freedom campers as they bargained and bludged their way around Europe and the world and, decades later, were still boasting about it. Cynics said that the main difference between cruise ship passengers and freedom campers was that the seaborne tourists spent a whole lot more money.

*

So, is there any form of 'good' tourism? That is, tourism that might be measured by anything except receipts? Yes, possibly. These places are little known and remote, but nothing compared with the secrets unlocked by *The Lord of the Rings* film trilogy. *LOTR* opened the doors to a new world for tourists.

The location for Hobbiton was a farm near Matamata, once a quiet little country town in the Waikato. It became a middling town in Middle Earth. The tourist industry here started with a man in a van doing a few trips a day with a stop at the dairy, then it got big. The *LOTR* films turned it into New Zealand's third-largest tourist attraction. The usual grizzles arose, about noise and congestion on Matamata's quiet streets, for instance, but when I last visited the town seemed to have taken the money and stayed much as it was.

The difference was the spread: *LOTR* tourism is year-round, whereas Akaroa's, for example, is seasonal. And there's a second difference. *LOTR* turned real places into imaginary ones, whereas tourism turns imaginary places, a so-called French village for example, into reality.

Real or not, Sauron's eye fixed on many a hidden spot beneath the Long White Cloud. In Golden Bay I swam with family and friends high in the Aorere River where gold-miners once picked and dug. We lay on pale rocks sculpted into fantastic curves and angles below Salisbury Falls and dived into the cold water, a very long way from anything. Yet here Tauriel and Legolas met.

A little further downriver at a place called Bainham, the Langford Store and Post Office sits where it has been for most of a century, alone in this magical landscape. Could it disappear under a flood far worse than the Aorere ever produced? When I last visited, *LOTR* pilgrims had passed through, but it seemed unchanged. I kept my fingers crossed. I watched the film and fancied I saw the swimming hole fleetingly. Locals insisted it did show their patch; at least, the few dozen who made a living up there did. They were still hoping for a new gold rush, this time tourism.

Deep in the upper Rangitata Valley, in a place almost as remote as Salisbury Falls, lies Mount Sunday. It's not a mountain at all, more a rocky outcrop on the valley floor. The Department of Conservation describes it as a small hill where boundary riders from surrounding high-country stations met on Sundays. It became far more than that in *LOTR*, of course. Construction crews took months to convert it into the set for Edoras, the capital of Rohan, and months to tear everything down again and restore Mount Sunday to its original state. That doesn't deter the people who call themselves Tolkienites, or, in this country, Tolkies or Ringies. Even if Edoras has departed, they are quite happy to see Mount Sunday *au naturel*. They have to be determined to get there: they need to drive up a rough station access road, then take a walking track. I once wrote a book about a nearby high-country station and found surrounding farmers more curious than irritated by the pilgrims: 'Silly buggers,' they said.

Far to the south, the Mavora Lakes lie jammed between two mountain ranges, between Lakes Wakatipu and Te Anau. I lived most of my life in the South Island, but only discovered them a few years ago. The lakes are to be found along a shingle road running up the kind of valley where you could stop in perfect silence and gaze at a landscape of mountains rising from golden flats dotted with farms looking as if they'd been there for centuries. You turn off that road to two thin lakes and drive through bush only metres from the water, with the hills on the other side that particularly wonderful shade of southern umber. The lakes are still, and quiet, and very beautiful, and you can camp in bush running down to their edge; but only camp, for there are no motels or hotels or cafés, nor any sort of tourist clutter. There's not even much of a road, for it gives up all pretensions after a short distance and becomes a track. I've only been there in autumn and winter, and have always felt alone, and proud.

Several *LOTR* scenes were set at and around Mavora Lakes. Aragorn, Legolas and Gimli trekked through the area, following the trail of Merry and Pippin escaping the orcs on the edge of Fangorn Forest. The Fellowship ended their journey on the Anduin River at North Mavora Lake, and Merry and Pippin hid in its forest. At the end of South Mavora Lake, there was a swing bridge where the Fellowship left Lothlorien.

No hobbits or orcs nor any trace of their passing marks the ground here now. They exist only in the route maps followed by the Ringies. Perhaps Peter Jackson lit the path for a perfect form of tourism. His followers are inspired by literature or at least, the film of the book. They travel simply and have a vested interest in leaving the places they've come to see unspoiled or even unchanged. Pilgrims, after all, don't want to mess up their shrines. A phenomenon in literary history and all of its disciples have passed over this land without littering or spoiling or soiling it. You can go to any one of these places and imagine yourself the first person to see it. They haven't been overrun, polluted or degraded. They haven't been scarred by a mishmash of kiosks and pop-ups.

Nor has the *LOTR* phenomenon battered other places featured in the movies, such as Kawarau Gorge, aka the Anduin River; Skippers Canyon, where Arwen summoned a flood to wash away the pursuing Ringwraiths; Kepler Mire near Te Anau, aka the Dead Marshes; or Snowdon Forest running beside Lake Te Anau, known to every devotee of *LOTR* as Fangorn Forest.

All these places have one advantage over Akaroa and the other remote secrets of New Zealand that tourists have discovered. They don't have anywhere cruise ships or fleets of buses can park; they don't even have much space for cars. Moreover, they are permeable. People, any number of them, can lock in and out again. Compare this with, say, the Milford Track, once claimed to be the finest walk in the world and now inundated with tramping tourists marching ahead with their headphones clamped tight.

As for the rest, I thought of that old advice to the soon-to-be ravished: lie back, close your eyes and think of the gross national product.

*

I contemplated all of this over a glass of wine in a waterside bar in Queenstown. It was a mediocre red, although it was hard to tell for it barely covered the bottom of the glass; it cost $20, and it was served by an asexual hodophile with no apparent interest in anything at all. Beside me a tourist had his picture taken next to a row of four rubbish bins while behind him (and out of frame) the last of the snow on the Remarkables twinkled like mad. Truly, I thought, there's no second-guessing a tourist.

New Zealanders love Queenstown, and hate it. They like the beauty and the narrow streets and the cosy atmosphere and the charm and the mountains and lake. And that feeling of being in another land. But now they hate that too. Although it still is their land, actually, most of them can't afford to go there and when they do, they are at the end of the queue. Queenstown is chequebook tourism and New Zealanders are the small change.

Multinationals have built hotels there, and rich foreigners own those lovely mountainsides and valleys. New Zealanders don't like that: the arrogance, the crowds, the feeling of not belonging. So most take their holidays somewhere else. That's perfectly all right with Queenstown. New Zealanders don't tip, for a start.

Pre-Covid there was no question about overtourism in Queenstown. It's stuffed with tourists, and you can use that word any way you like. The people who run the town — the vested interests, the councillors, the hangers-on — love it. New Zealanders increasingly do not. Queenstown is the diamond in New Zealand's tourist crown. Everything it possesses — mountains, lakes, ski fields, hotels — is measured in carats. Plus it's quite small, it sparkles, and hardly anyone can afford it.

International tourists spend more money in Queenstown than anywhere else in New Zealand except Auckland. But where domestic tourists are concerned, Queenstown is well down the list.

Even Queenstown people are not overjoyed about Queenstown. They can't afford to live there, for a start. Locals complain Queenstown is in danger of becoming worse than Auckland. I have news for them, as a nouveau Aucklander: it's *already* worse.

I stayed in Frankton, in a small apartment which I could afford for two reasons: first, it was in Frankton, at the lake's elbow, too far from Queenstown for the average earthbound tourist. Second, it was October, a lower point in the tourist year, although down times in this tourist mecca are entirely relative. At that time, shortly before the Covid-19 disaster, Queenstown was packed with tourists. If October was once a shoulder season, the town now has shoulders like an All Black forward, for there is no slack in the modern calendar at all, really. The clamour goes on year-round.

In Frankton I had the feeling of being in the middle of a shift. Property reports were saying that prices had shoved not only local people along the lake but also small businesses and shops. It didn't seem much of a penalty. Frankton is still lakeside, after all. It sits contentedly at the end of its own little arm. It has its own ski field, the Remarkables, within easy reach. The surviving gorge, the Kawarau (Cromwell Gorge has been lost to hydroelectricity) is nearby. It takes you through to Cromwell and Alexandra and the full splendour of Central Otago. Or you can nip over the Crown Range to Wanaka. Or head south to Kingston and Lake Te Anau. It's a very fine place indeed.

A big new commercial development was rising up on Frankton Flats, a local high school had moved into town. There were hotels and supermarkets and the big chain stores. Frankton lacks Queenstown's charm, but, as they say, needs must. Besides, charm is increasingly at a premium up the lake as new hotels and retail developments rise into the blue sky without, locals complain, anyone asking them.

In Frankton tracts of new housing were spreading up the valley towards Arrowtown and if they looked like new suburbs anywhere in the country, well, at least people could afford them; for the moment anyway.

Little affordable housing remains in Queenstown. One of my favourite areas there has always been the village by the municipal camping ground above Queenstown Bay, which is made up of pretty, council-owned cottages, most rented to low-income earners. A great deal of style and, oh, millions of dollars separate them from the stone facades and blank windows and stainless steel of their neighbours. Amid the concrete, this place has character. Its homes look eccentric and homely; neither adjective is usually applied to Queenstown. The village lies along Cemetery Road, one step from the grave and looking down on the town's statue of William Gilbert Rees, said to be the founder of Queenstown, a place he picked up for a song and sold for a handsome profit, thereby setting the stage for the town's preoccupation with property speculation.

Queenstown always looks to me like a town that has been taken by surprise. Whoa, all these tourists! Where can we put them? In the upstairs room, and we can turn the downstairs into a café, or a junk shop (they don't call them that, of course; they sell brand clothes or jewellery, or wool, and tourists shamble dutifully through). In turn, tourism businesses have appealed to homeowners to rent spare bedrooms to seasonal and service workers, the poorly paid, who in the evenings gather on the foreshore, playing guitars and singing, and themselves becoming an attraction for envious tourists.

Some of them lived in the village. They were the lucky ones, I thought. The cottages were unique. They were a slice of mid-century New Zealand. The two things they had in common were their size — small — and their colours: red, blue, green and all shades in between. They seemed to have sucked the colour out of Queenstown, which was brown. I could not think why they were not a tourist attraction themselves. They escaped that fate, but fell victim to another: the axis of business and the town council.

I talked to a woman who said, 'It's a great shame.' She was one of several who had been relocated from the cottages to another place, the only similarity being uncertain tenure. All the tenants had been moved a fortnight previously, including some forty families. They had left behind their signatures: a brick veneer, a patio table, the frosted glass window portraying the tree and the dog, the little rock wall at the edge of a garden now in spring bloom. Wrought-iron veranda posts supported a kaka beak bush. A framed living-room sign invited visitors to live as if this were heaven on earth, which of course it had been. One cottage had dream-catchers on its walls to ward off evil. They hadn't worked.

She looked around her. 'It's a great shame,' she said again, and I wondered if she was still talking about the cottages. It's hard for any New Zealanders who feel they are being pushed out of their own town, but it's much worse if you are poor.

The local council had fretted over the lack of affordable housing for the workers essential to its tourist industry, for house prices had risen by 75 percent in just five years and it now cost more than $1 million for an average home. It was the highest such price in the country, and one that poorly paid service workers could not afford. But that hadn't stopped the town from getting rid of the camping ground houses. The council had weighed up the options: protect this rare piece of community-owned land for future generations, or adhere to the Queenstown ethic, which in a word was development. If you wanted to double the word count, you could add 'money'. The land was 'under-utilised'.

The council decided to develop part of the land and offer the community a choice, although not on whether to sell or keep it all, which some might consider the main issue; instead, the council kept part of the land for the community and then gave the community two options as to what to do with the rest: lease it or sell it. That seemed to me a uniquely Queenstown solution.

They handed the business end of the deal over to a consortium of Australian and Auckland developers promising the Queenstown staples of hotels, cafés and shops, and even some houses, although not the kind the evicted workers could afford. Where would they live? Well, there was the traditional Auckland alternative, which was to live in their cars, but the council had banned overnight camping, so that was not an option.

The evictees, some of whom had been in their cottages for many years, couldn't even move down to Frankton, because the 110 permanent residents of the council-owned camping ground there were getting the boot too. Their prospects were not good, and their chances of a sympathetic groundswell were well illustrated by Queenstown's first beggar. He'd come down from Auckland and he was happy with his move, telling a reporter that people in the town were more generous than Aucklanders, and he could make $100 a day. That let the dogs out. The online gallery flew into a frenzy. How could he afford to come down here? And $100 a day tax-free? This in a town whose vital statistics undoubtedly included an ample proportion of tax avoiders. And which, incidentally, had no emergency housing or refuge. Reading all these messages, you might conclude that Queenstown took its milk of human kindness lite.

Tourism was indeed the golden fleece here, but at the same time it had rendered the town untenable for any but the rich and, possibly, indifferent.

The coronavirus epidemic turned off the tap. The town emptied. Rents dropped as workers were made redundant and left. House prices fell. The accommodation industry dusted off its vacancy signs. Businesspeople predicted years of decline. They even gave me a new name. I was no longer the old Jafa — 'just another f...ing Aucklander'. Now I was the new version, 'just another fabulous Aucklander', one of the northerners who, if spoken to nicely, might come down and fill the hotels. The golden goose might not have been killed, but it was not the perky chap it had been.

*

Before Covid-19 changed everything, I sat at the edge of the little peninsula that juts out beside Queenstown bay. It was full of action and colour. People dangled from parachutes towed by speedboats. People drove speedboats. Speedboats pulled strange craft that looked like dolphins and even dived underneath the water. Tourist launches pinched through the melee. The *Earnslaw*, the lake's venerable steamer, matriarch of the water, steamed sedately through the lower orders and berthed at its wharf.

The water looked inviting. I might have taken a dip if the faecal coliform bacteria *E.coli* hadn't been found there quite so often. Where could it have come from? I asked. Take your pick was the answer, more or less. It could have been high rainfall washing contaminants off the land and streets. Or birds. Or sheep and cattle poop. Or campers, always a popular choice. In all, an unlovely soup in a once-pristine lake.

When tourist numbers were shooting upwards even the mayor was upset. He'd been to Edinburgh Castle in Scotland and had hotfooted out of there after half an hour, decrying a sea of people. Queenstown only had a lake-full. Now the numbers were falling, and people were even more upset. No one expects the reversal to be permanent, but who knows for sure?

Three million people visited Queenstown each year, and before the pandemic those numbers were expected to go on rising. Covid-19, ironically enough, gave the town some breathing room. Queenstown was not just at capacity, but full to burping. It needed new infrastructure and it couldn't afford it. Town councillors were talking about putting a limit on numbers until the pandemic did it for them.

The airport had to be expanded, but what about the noise? Lake Wakatipu and the Kawarau Gorge essentially share a deep hole in the mountains, a natural amphitheatre. Would the nearby new town of Frankton, the locals' escape chute, itself become untenable?

The airport terminal was already too small. I sat in it for several hours waiting to fly back home, which were several hours past its use-by time. The seats were uncomfortable and there were not enough of them, the food was abysmal, and all of that was eclipsed by the public address system, which, when things were not going right (and they were not that day), was incomprehensible. Passengers were clearly surprised when they found themselves boarding. I was surprised too, and more than glad to get out of the place. This town had sold its soul. Now its people were wringing their hands over the loss of tourists to the pandemic and my reaction to that was, 'Tough.'

Despite moving north I was still a South Islander at heart, and I'd always loved Queenstown. It is so beautiful. But it just didn't seem to have anything to do with me any more. Tourism might be the golden fleece. Or it might be some other part of the sheep.

CHAPTER SIX

A Silver Lining?

Very early on the morning of 4 September 2010, I was woken by a strange sound, a buzz, a chatter. The house appeared quite still, but it was murmuring, rustling in the dark. It wasn't threatening, not at first, and we lay in bed just wondering, my wife Sally and I.

Then the air seemed to die, leaving a vacuum. Slowly the prattle became a rattle, then a soft vibration, then a shudder, then a shaking, then a growing roar and a rocking, lifting, pulsing; then things started to break and vases fell off the table and books flew out of the bookshelves and crockery shot out of the cupboards and pictures dropped from the walls and we seemed hopelessly lost in a hell of noise and violence.

'It's the Big One,' someone said. Perhaps it was me. We'd been warned often enough: the Alpine Fault snakes through the mountains we could see from our windows, and seismologists had long been telling us that we were due for a serious earthquake. Or overdue.

We didn't take much notice of the caution, of course. We were always being warned about something: wildfires, rising sea levels, tsunamis, pollution, epidemics of the sickness du jour, moral collapse. When it was something that might happen only every 500 years or so, well, you were probably going to push it down the list and worry about something more pressing, like the power bill.

Now the house seemed to roll, dipping its cantilevered front. We were at the top of a hill with a long drop to the bottom of it and, at 4.35 in the morning, in that peculiar darkness before the dawn, I imagined us flying off the edge in a great shower of concrete and glass.

What did you do in a situation like this?

The government's agencies described an ideal situation. You should move no more than a few steps. Then, you should drop, cover, hold and stay inside until the shaking stopped.

In practice, this was what happened: you dropped under the blankets; you held onto each other; you stayed inside until you, your body, your mind, stopped shaking. Then, in that treacherous calm that followed an earthquake, you shuffled out of the bedroom and through the rubble of broken china and glass and books and furniture and everything else you'd nurtured and admired over your many years of life and you realised that none of it counted for very much.

You didn't come upon that truth right at that moment, of course, because you were too concerned about what was happening, and whether you were going to survive. Nor did you have very much time to think about that either, for just at the moment when you were starting to breathe again, you felt the first aftershock. And after the aftershock, another. Then another.

A SILVER LINING?

You turned to National Radio's all-night programme, whose presenter was getting scattered reports of a calamitous event in your city, then more reports, and she knew something awful was happening, and she became the only outside voice in the entire world, the only person who could give you some idea of what was going on outside your house, and it was so dreadful that even years later when I was writing this, tears dripped onto my keyboard.

Aftershock followed aftershock until dawn's light played on the wreckage of a past life and you knew nothing would be the same again. Outside, your city was broken. You rang your family, and your friends, and there was nothing to say except that you were all right, and they were all right, and it was horrible, and what about the city, for you were being advised to stay in your house, and information was thin, and on television reporters were only now starting to move through shattered streets covered in dust and rubble and they could tell you little more than you already knew, that tragedy had struck your quiet, graceful city in the south.

You felt betrayal too, for until this unsuspected fault zone cracked, the city had thought itself largely immune to earthquakes. With Auckland, Christchurch was regarded as being relatively safe. Disaster was always supposed to hit Wellington first. The capital straddled the main fault line and when people talked of the Big One, they usually had Wellington in mind. The Big One had no business visiting Christchurch first. When history was revisited later, this in itself proved a shaky proposition, like so many other things Christchurch people held dear. Twenty years previously the Earthquake Commission (EQC) had predicted earthquakes, and even liquefaction, in Christchurch.

And on this morning something had triggered a movement in a farm paddock lying over the web of faults in the gravels beneath the Canterbury Plains west of Christchurch, and it sped through the farms and the towns into the veins of the city.

A few days later, just as we were getting used to the aftershocks, a far-off thunder became a roar and the trembling grew into violent shaking, as a quake attacked in broad daylight, clubbing us without warning as we ate our breakfast, striking so fiercely that for the second time in a week I imagined my hilltop home must be ripped from its site and turned into a huge wood-and-concrete toboggan.

Our 1950s modernist house had floor-to-ceiling glass windows overlooking the plains and mountains. They were to break so often that our glazier, who marvelled at the way he'd morphed from tradesman to saviour ('Everyone loves me, I'm their friend'), became such a familiar figure that when he announced his daughter's forthcoming wedding we fully expected to be invited. He replaced our windows three times.

As the earthquakes went on and they were inundated with claims, the insurance companies instituted some rather basic investigations. A woman telephoned after our second claim. These glass pieces, she said (Sally collected them), how were they to know that this truly expensive vase had in fact been broken?

I sent her before and after photographs. The first were pictures of the main room in the house, complete with pottery and glass. The second showed the same room after the quakes. It looked as if it had been showered with confetti. The earthquakes broke plates, bowls, sculptures and vases into tiny pieces lying thick on the floor. See those little blue-green bits? That was the vase.

(Funny, Sally said, what happens when things you love get broken. Suddenly they are just stuff.)

The woman seemed satisfied; in any event, the insurance company paid out, not for the last time. This was the trivia of the first earthquake, when we learned about the relationship between the Earthquake Commission and the insurance companies and who would pay what and how much and expressions such as 'over-cap' and 'under-cap', never before heard in the city, became part of every conversation.

Over-cap meant the damage to your property would cost more than the $100,000 per earthquake the government, through the EQC, would pay. After that you depended on your insurance company. You had to attribute damage to each earthquake, and there were dozens upon dozens of them.

One of the most damaging to our own home (yes, all of those windows broke again) was an aftershock that the assessors hadn't even recorded on their list. Oh well, they said, and put a mark somewhere on the bales of paper they brought with them.

So many earthquakes, so much uncertainty, so many dejected people sitting amid the ruins of their lives, for owning your own home was one of New Zealanders' favourite boasts. Years later, a sorry train of litigants was still arguing before tribunals, committees, courts.

The city was damaged, but there was a note of relief in the chorus from engineers and politicians that September: it was serious, but not that serious. It could be fixed. Life would go on. My own house, and my neighbours' and friends' houses, were relatively undamaged, although their contents had taken a beating.

In the weeks following the earthquake, we developed almost a feeling of relief. We were sure we'd had the Big One, and we'd lived to tell the tale. We became experts on the aftershocks: that one was bruising, around 4.1 we guessed; this one was routine, maybe 3.2 — as if the quality of our lives could be measured in decimal points.

The most important statistic was almost a relief: amid all that noise and damage and fear, only one person had died, from a heart attack. That death was sometimes attributed to the earthquake, sometimes not, which must have been hard for a family knowing only that they'd lost someone they loved.

Everyone became quite upbeat. We could pay for it. Money was available, announced the Prime Minister, John Key, declaring that Gerry Brownlee, a resident of Fendalton and Member of Parliament for Ilam, would become the Earthquake Recovery Minister. Rather than leading the multitude from the wilderness with banner held high, the unfortunate minister would ride from one disaster to the next until his charger took on the appearance of a truly exhausted nag.

Could there be some benefit, a silver lining, some subdued tint of the golden fleece in this tragedy? Economically, the earthquakes would not hurt us much, the authorities insisted. Think of all the money that would now come pouring into Christchurch, whose economy had been gracefully declining, rather like the city itself. Moreover, much of that money would not be our own; a chunk of it would be coming from overseas, because the EQC had invested in reinsurance, which, in short, meant insurers buying cover from other, international insurers. (In 2017 the EQC would report it had paid about $1.9 billion to international insurance companies and got more than $4.2 billion back in claims.) That was good news, wasn't it? All those fat suits in London and New York forking out for our earthquakes?

*

Any sense of peace, any confidence in the future was destroyed four and a half months later, at 12.51 pm on 22 February 2011. Five kilometres beneath the surface, only ten kilometres from the city, near its Port Hills, another fault ruptured. The earthquake was magnitude 6.3, less than the September quake's 7.1, but much more damaging.

In the weeks that followed we learned about something called 'ground acceleration', the upward forces exerted on the earth and anything standing upon it. The ground acceleration of this earthquake was much higher than the previous one, in fact among the greatest the world had ever seen, mighty enough to throw people and buildings into the air, and it was closer to the surface and closer to the city, and this evil concoction laid waste the city of Christchurch.

But we didn't know any of that, at the time, not Sally and I nor anyone else. We were in a fourth-floor apartment in the city centre and we struggled to stand, to find handholds on its smooth white walls. All I remember of those minutes was the two of us clinging to each other as the rumbling became trembling then a shaking that struck a savage rhythm with our own bodies. The apartments were built of concrete block, not good in an earthquake, but neither of us was scared. Fear came later. We simply held on and hoped.

The shaking stopped. But we knew all about aftershocks by then. We also knew the fragility of concrete and concrete blocks. We weren't going to stay there and be entombed. We went out the door and down four flights of stairs faster than I would have thought possible.

We raced across the neatly kept quadrangle that had given the apartments a collegial atmosphere but now looked to us like a killing-ground surrounded by cliffs of crumbling rock, then through a cloistered entrance and out onto Colombo Street, central Christchurch. Just a few hundred metres down the road a huge pall of dust rose out of the city like smoke, a few tower blocks rearing out of its top. It looked evil, and lethal. We gathered across the street, where there was some open space with nothing to fall on us. Sure enough, in the next ten minutes there were ten aftershocks of magnitude 4 or more.

We were quite a large group by then: inner-city residents, tenants, passersby. No one said very much. We weren't stunned, or terrified. We knew what had happened and we were appalled. We waited, because there didn't seem to be anything else to do.

Then a single woman emerged from that dark cloud. She was carrying a briefcase, and she might have been on her way home from work if she hadn't been covered in dust, white from hair to shoes. She looked like a ghost, except that one of her legs was muddy and bloodied. She seemed dazed. She walked past in silence, looking straight ahead. We were silent too, mourners at a tragedy.

Someone else followed, then another, until there was a procession trudging out of the city. Most said nothing or at most offered a few words. 'Cathedral's down,' said one. 'I saw bodies,' said another.

A SILVER LINING?

Buildings along the street were cracked and damaged. We walked closer to the city centre. People were dazed and mostly silent. Ambulances and fire engines and police cars were crowding in, barriers going up. We moved into the city centre with the vague, useless notion that we might be able to help. In the way of tragedies, this one was compounding: an epicentre close to the city, a shallower and more damaging quake striking at lunchtime when there were a lot of people in the streets.

Now, people were being moved out. An Asian tourist stood outside her hotel, sobbing. When I spoke to her she collapsed into my arms and we stood there, both of us desperate.

Just looking, even being there, seemed an affront. We returned to where we'd come from, where bystanders at least had a common interest, and we all gazed over the street at the apartment building, still standing and, as it proved later, undamaged, and beside me a voice said, 'It's designed for worse.' It was Peter Beaven, the venerable architect whose buildings and houses both graced Christchurch and reflected its character: solid, neat as much as stylish. He'd designed the apartment building and lived on its ground floor. Now he said he'd planned for just such an event, which was the way architects described disasters.

'It's perfectly safe,' he said. As an architect, Beaven was often described as a breath of fresh air, and he certainly fitted the description this day. (He died the following year of a cancer caused by asbestos.)

I took him at his word and dived into the building's basement car park, for the city was filled with cars that had been parked on the street in the September earthquake and were there still, trapped in the rubble or squashed by it or abandoned because their owners weren't allowed to retrieve them. I had no clear idea of what we'd do, but I knew we needed that car to do it. The strange thing is that I'm both easily frightened and claustrophobic, but the horror of what was happening seemed to banish fear. I went into that dark, shaky cave, climbed into my car, drove onto the street, collected Sally and one or two others who needed a ride, and that was the last we saw of the city centre for months.

We went to a friend's house in the suburbs and for the first time, but not the last, saw the phenomenon of liquefaction: liquid earth pouring out of the ground in volcano-like cones, silent and menacing, covering the city with a revolting brew of mud and filling homes and schools with silt. Buildings sank into it. Roads collapsed into giant holes filled with mud awaiting cars like primitive traps. The city's swampy pedigree was inescapable.

We didn't know it then, but the real horror lay in the rubble: 185 people had died and another 164 were severely injured. Three men had died as they worked to save an old organ in the Durham Street Methodist Church. The church and organ were equally venerable: the building was Canterbury's first stone church, opening on Christmas Day 1864, the organ a very fine one installed in 1902 and valued at $1 million. The church had been badly damaged in the first earthquake and was destroyed by the second.

Several people had died walking on the Port Hills. They were out in the open, and the terrain seemed safe and solid, but those hills were made of volcanic rock and the earthquake had sent boulders shooting through the air like cannonballs.

People died in crushed buses and cars, in tattoo parlours and fish shops. They died picking raspberries and building retaining walls to contain, yes, rockfalls, and they died as wives and friends and relatives struggled to keep them alive.

Most, 115 people, died in a poorly constructed seven-floor building in the city centre. They were crushed, burned and choked to death, and some may even have drowned beneath the fire hoses. The building was a hotch-potch of flawed techniques, a product of shonky bureaucracy, supervised by a fake engineer.

I challenge anyone to read the coroners' court reports of those deaths without sobbing. I read them several times and the accounts of courage, and sacrifice and love and endurance, were as raw as ever. As moving were the questions that friends and relatives of victims put to the coroner. Did they die immediately? Quickly? Painlessly? Where did they die, exactly? In which seats on the bus? If someone had managed to get my loved one to hospital, would they have survived? Did a mother and her five-week-old baby die together? The coroner did his best to answer every question, but all he could say, often, was that he just did not know.

As for us, we decided that a couple more displaced, useless citizens were what the city did not need. A huge exodus had begun and every petrol station in the city was already out of gas. We found one on a lesser road where the city's fringes faded into the country, joined a very long queue and made it to the pump just as the owner was putting up an 'out of gas' sign. The hose gurgled and grunted but produced enough petrol to get us well up the coast and we crept out of town for a while with a guilty feeling of escape.

*

Two days later, the prime minister, John Key, stood in front of the Christchurch Art Gallery and its great glass curtain. Could buildings withstand such a quake? Of course they could. He waved towards the curtain. Not a pane was smashed. Key was right, in a way. Its curtain might have survived, but the art gallery remained closed for the next five years and, even so, was one of the lucky ones.

Christchurch lost so much that day. Some 100,000 buildings were damaged and 10,000 of them were demolished. The city I'd grown up in and loved all my life was gone. Many — most — of the buildings I admired most seemed beyond repair.

A few days after Key's visit, an ancient Sydenham church was demolished without its owner, a heritage trust, being told, or those responsible seeking any formal consent. It was a bellwether. Some wondered whether we should be joining hands around the Anglican cathedral in the Square.

George Bernard Shaw visited Christchurch in 1934 and talked of its beautiful cathedral. Most thought he meant the one in the Square, of course. But he was talking about the Catholic cathedral. 'You have produced a New Zealand Brunelleschi,' he declared. 'The ... cathedral is original and powerfully drawn.' Nonetheless, a few years after the earthquake the church announced (to the horror of the heritage lobby) that, restoration being vastly expensive, it would tear down the old cathedral and build a new one. Meanwhile, Christchurch Cathedral, that symbol of the city, lay shattered in its centre, along with many more of the city's best churches.

The Arts Centre was once the Gothic, stone University of Canterbury. As a student I climbed a winding staircase there to a narrow lecture room high above the basement in which Ernest Rutherford had conducted the early work that led, eventually, to his splitting the nucleus of an atom. The lecture room, too, seemed far more removed from the earth than a mere three flights. The Arts Centre was badly beaten up but restorable.

Not so lucky were the fine old Canterbury Provincial Council Buildings; the brick Central Library, with its wonderful wooden New Zealand room high in the rafters; a thousand, maybe ten thousand houses, shops and pubs; and even Queen Elizabeth II Park, with its tracks and swimming pools and gymnasium built for the Commonwealth Games.

Even Shag Rock, the distinctive pillar of stone jutting from the tide at Sumner beach, the boundary peg of my own turf, had crumbled into, well, a pile of rock.

We were told the damage would cost $4 billion to repair. That estimate proved as unreal as pretty much everything else about the earthquakes. At last count, which certainly will not be the last, the price had gone up to $40 billion, and was rising steadily. Alone, the cost of repairing repairs that had been poorly done would be $1 billion.

But the good thing about the money everyone said, again, was that it all came from overseas. Oh, and another good thing, we were going to get a lovely new city out of it.

We were invited to look at Napier, ruined by its 1931 earthquake, a destructive disaster whose impact was compounded by the Great Depression. A beautiful Art Deco city had risen quickly from the ashes, and is still a place of pilgrimage. The reconstruction had been achieved by a couple of commissioners, who within only a few years were celebrating progress, and the job was pretty much wrapped up by the outbreak of war eight years later. The twenty-first century should be able to better that by far — shouldn't it?

Yes, yes, everyone cried. Groups of architects, engineers and officials formed around briefs to shape a new Christchurch. Visions appeared like holographs. Business leaders talked of a new centre they claimed to be already on the drawing-board, a low-rise central business district based around a series of parks. City leaders talked of 'the most beautiful city in the world'.

The wider public was swept up in the 'Share an Idea' campaign, in which we all — well, more than a quarter of the population, 106,000 people — told the council how we'd like the city to look: new public buildings, libraries, swimming pools, squares, European styles, Asian patterns, the odd drop of the South Pacific, wonderful public transport on the new streets, buses, light rail. It was a lovely idea to share ideas. Where else in history, certainly New Zealand history, had the women, men and children who lived in a city had much of a say in how that city should be?

I wrote at the time that 'our hopes and dreams, our lives, hang on the outcome [of those ideas]'. We hoped and dreamed for the best, until the government stepped in, binned our ideas (assuring us, of course, that they'd be taken into account) and announced that the whole thing would be swallowed up by the official recovery blueprint (gulp!), and that the rebuild was now under the administration and control of the Canterbury Earthquake Recovery Authority (CERA). Any writing not on the wall you could certainly find in that blueprint. Officials insisted, however, that 'a number' of the public's ideas had been implemented, including the Margaret Mahy Playground on the banks of the Avon. If a city's progress could be measured by a playground, Christchurch was doing quite well: the kids loved it, at least.

Many of us had wanted to save as much of the city's built heritage as possible. Of course we did. People who grew up in Christchurch, and stayed, loved the graceful old city. We much preferred things as they were, pre-earthquake. We might not have subscribed wholly to the pre-earthquake model: a city founded along lines well established by a clutch of Englishmen without regard for climate or topography, much less for anyone already living there. It wasn't that they scorned the Ngai Tahu so much as that tangata whenua were beneath notice, ranking somewhere in the bottom layer of the society they imported lock, stock and barrel from old England. That model was the private property of people who carried on those traditions, building houses behind high fences which they claimed provided shelter from the omnipresent easterly. Those people shopped at particular shops, sent their children to schools roughly modelled on a tight society half a world away, and spoke with an accent any true Pom could pick a kilometre away. The rest of us were more enlightened, we believed, but nevertheless we felt at home with those lovely old buildings — the churches, old government buildings, courts, follies, private houses.

As it turned out, the fundamental error the city's founders had made was not trying to set up a little England halfway round the world; it was misjudging the weather, the climate, the terrain. They'd plonked the city down on a flat piece of land just over the hill from the only decent harbour in the vicinity, without any apparent regard for the fact that land had been a swamp and was in fact still a swamp in many parts. Only 7000 years before, the city would have been below sea level, and it was still full of water trying to get out. Still, it allowed them to use the stock city plan they'd brought with them: all straight roads, except where the Avon River rudely intruded.

The earthquake was a great leveller in more ways than one. It knocked over the statue of William Rolleston, once superintendent of Canterbury and such a staunch advocate of provincialism he certainly would have been given a corporate box at any Crusaders' ground. The earthquake also knocked off his head, and someone wrote on the stump of the neck that the head might be found at Christ's College (where might also be found his heart). The earthquake wrecked the statue of John Robert Godley, 'the founder of Canterbury'. Sir Bob Parker, the former mayor, insisted that putting Godley back on his plinth was 'the first thing we will do'. Godley stood upright again in February 2015, four years after he fell, while the cathedral still lay ruined behind him.

The city founders in fact needed no monuments. Their legacy lay all around. The swamp they'd built the city on rose triumphantly as liquefaction, squirting from roads, filling houses with mud and slime, creeping through the city and slurping foundations like some ghastly sci-fi production.

Gerry Brownlee, Earthquake Recovery Minister and inner Christchurch resident, had this to say about Christchurch's architectural heritage: 'My absolutely strong position is that the old dungers, no matter what their condition, are going under the hammer.' The irony was that the most dangerous building in the city had been constructed in 1987, that grand era of economic enlightenment.

Nevertheless, under the hammer the old dungers went. Heritage people noted not long after the earthquakes that 43 percent of the best old buildings in the city centre, even those listed by Heritage New Zealand, or buildings protected by the city itself, had been pulled down. Some 240 listed heritage buildings simply vanished into the maws of the demolition machines.

One of the first and most significant was a heritage-listed house in Colombo Street, the old thoroughfare running dead straight south to north, right through Cathedral Square. The house looked mysterious, with pointy turrets and lacy verandas and big bay windows and curly woodwork. It carried an enticing mantle of intrigue, for it had been built very early in the twentieth century by a wealthy bookie. What had gone on there?

After the earthquake, the new government body CERA ordered it demolished. Its owner demurred. He wanted to restore it. He took CERA to court. It was the first time the agency's powers had been challenged, and it proved to be omnipotent. The judge threw out the case and the house was demolished the following day.

This proved an early sign of a martial note in Christchurch's new governance, and building followed house followed building to the dumps. The Ministry for Culture and Heritage eventually produced a heritage recovery programme which became part of government policy, but only in 2014 when much of the damage had already been done.

Meanwhile, the intricate old Central Library, superb blocks of flats, movie theatres, halls and churches were demolished, every one of them carrying a little bit of Christchurch's story. The CERA clerk churning out the demolition orders had to take sick leave for writers' cramp. (Yes, I'm making that up.) Even Christchurch Cathedral, long the city's most recognisable symbol, would have followed them to the dumps had not Christchurch pulled out its practised strategy, prolonged argument.

Now you can visit the city and see what replaced many of these buildings: barren patches of ground, some of them pressed into service as parking areas (parking for God knows what, for there seems little enough to do). Sometimes, the city swapped like for like, or not quite like, or sometimes nothing like. The beautiful Millers Building, a Bauhaus masterpiece dating from 1939 and loved by children for the first escalator in the South Island ('the moving stairs') was demolished. The gloriously Art Deco Majestic Theatre nearby went with it, over the objections of both the City Council and Historic Places Canterbury, not to mention a wider public who loved its eccentricities, such as its orchestra pit and a service whereby you could register for urgent calls and telegrams, which, if they arrived while you were watching a film, would be brought to you by one of the staff. The theatre was last used by a Christian church, which must have fretted over its Moorish features. Why was it demolished? Because CERA wanted to widen the road. A spokesperson explained the philosophy of demolition: 'Our aim is to keep the pace up and really enable the rebuild.'

The pace was, indeed, kept up. A bus exchange rose in place of the Millers Building and it said much about the pace of the rebuild that the exchange was for a while one of the best new buildings in the city.

Some old buildings were saved, at great expense: The Arts Centre, the Theatre Royal, the more modern but still badly damaged Christchurch Town Hall. But much of Christchurch's architectural history turned to dust, with the cathedral sitting at its centre like a rotten tooth, watching public affection transferred to its allegedly temporary replacement, dubbed the Cardboard Cathedral.

By then, 70,000 people had left the city. Sally and I were two of them. It was not an easy decision. But to reach the city from our house on the hill, where the only public road was blocked by slips and debris, we had to take an old military road. We splashed and slid through mud that got worse day by day and was fast becoming the world's most challenging commute. En route, we had to pass through the property of a nice Christian couple who'd lived a gentle life for decades, growing vegetables and selling them at the gate and bothering no one, and who now did their best to fulfil their civic duty by leaving their gates open and their backyard clear for a daily, noisy cavalcade, out in the morning, back in the evening, to which they invariably smiled and waved. From there we'd climb to the Summit Road, drive around the rim of the extinct volcano that comprised this part of Banks Peninsula, and drop down onto one of the roads leading into the city. It was an adventurous journey, but the novelty wore off quite quickly.

In the city nothing worked properly, understandably, since everything had been entangled in a catastrophe now rated among the world's worst natural disasters.

All the while aftershocks rolled through, some of them as terrifying as the original quake. Once, as we were walking along the Sumner seawall, the concrete path beneath us seemed to curl and the great boulders anchoring the wall rattled like marbles in a bag. Builders working on the roof of a house opposite clung to the framework like possums in a tree then, as the shaking lessened, rose to their feet and pointed out to sea in amazement. A cloud of red dust was rolling across the waves, thick as fog. The red rock of the beautiful Scarborough Cliffs was crumbling into the sea.

It was an earthquake too far. It felt like the betrayal of everything: our faith in the city, even the earth we stood on. When the solid things in your life, including the rock on which the wise man builds his house, crumble into dust, you experience a loss of trust that seems to empty your soul. The world we'd built our life on was gone.

Sally and I had both grown up in Christchurch, both of us living near the sea all our lives and revelling in the city's long beaches and huge skies and windy ocean. Christchurch had raised us and our family from childhood, nourished and nurtured us through good education, health and housing, given us heart and strength. To us it was the best place in the world to live, and this was a city where people genuinely did work to live rather than the other way round. But a low-rise, cheaply built urban desert would mean the end for us and, we guessed, for many of our fellow citizens too. The pressures of having our twin sons living in Auckland, with children and lives which it took a lot of effort to be part of, were starting to tell. Plus, we had already lived in other places around New Zealand — in Dunedin, in Wellington and sometimes in Auckland — and I could work from anywhere.

The city centre was cordoned off (and would stay that way for 858 days). Vast areas designated collectively as the Red Zone were being cleared. They included some of the suburbs near my childhood home, places as familiar to me as my backyard, and it was like having a hole excavated in my life's memory.

Still, it was not an easy decision. All of our oldest friends lived in Christchurch, and most of our closest ones too. Leaving them was the most difficult part, and we were diffident about telling them, almost ashamed; it felt like a betrayal. Yet they were all supportive. We'd had some 9000 earthquakes by then, including, of course, the worst of them.

We bought a house on Waiheke Island. Our Auckland friends regarded our plan in a sympathetic but rather complacent way. Yes, Auckland was the second-safest place to be, earthquakes wise, and since Christchurch had just dropped out of the rankings, Auckland was now number one.

We packed the car and drove out, sniffling like anything. As we left we pondered the same question everyone was asking: how many of us would go back? We wanted to be among them.

*

A new city would emerge, we told each other. Well, that was true enough. The question was, where would the new city be?

We drove out through the northwestern suburbs, the area least affected by the earthquakes. It was another world. People sat in cafés, washed their cars, mowed their verges. Only a few kilometres from the worst of the carnage, life as we'd once known it went on. Had we imagined it all? Had all of those people died? Had we lost half of our homes and most of our city? Out here the sun still shone and the grass grew and people smiled.

We weren't the only people to notice that life on the city's outskirts was largely unaffected. Soon Christchurch began to bulge to the north and west. It seemed to me its alter ego had taken over: this city had always, metaphorically, turned its back on the sea and now it was doing that in earnest, spreading towards the mountains in the west and upwards to the north. In the wake of the earthquakes, people saw these areas as the safest places to live.

How this would work out in the future was anyone's guess. My own was that Christchurch would become even more of a suburban city, for you could not recreate a city centre with all its life and history in a decade or two or three. It took — had taken — generations, lifetimes, a century and a half even to get as far as it had.

But what of all that reconstruction money pouring into the city, the government funds, the insurance settlements, the enterprise, hope, imagination, that heady feeling of a community rising to meet disaster?

Was it some awful new kind of golden fleece?

As it turned out, Canterbury was not short of fault lines. They lay under the city and Plains in webs, and to a seismic ingenue like me, the mystery was why they hadn't fluttered before. The worst of the quakes had a magnitude of 6.3, a once in 2000 years, 16,000 years or 85,000 years event, depending on who was totting it up. We were then, allegedly, safe for another 1000 years, at least.

*

A SILVER LINING?

We hadn't been on Waiheke Island very long when, one fine day, we felt a familiar tremble, heard that terrible death-rattle of doors and windows and loose objects, sensed that a monster deep in the earth was loose. Our neighbours were on their deck. 'What was that?'

'An earthquake,' I said. They looked unconvinced. Then the shaking started again, stronger this time, and there was no doubt. An earthquake, a small one by Christchurch standards but a quake, definitely.

Not long after it died away, the telephone rang. It was our son. He said, 'One of our friends is suggesting that perhaps you should go back down south.'

*

I went back to Christchurch as often as I could. We were full of hope for the city then, and many of my friends there still are. The signs of recovery were good. The great surge in building — the new homes, office blocks, shops — the rumbling and the hammering, had quietened, a little. In December 2014 ready-mix concrete hit a new record for a quarter: in layperson's terms, we were told, it equalled one hundred Olympic-sized swimming pools' worth. As a layperson, I had no idea what that meant, except that it was an awful lot of driveways, and I wouldn't want to mix it myself. The ready-mix didn't reach that point again; the number of new homes being built to replace the damaged and ruined peaked in 2015.

Employment shot up. Incomes grew faster than anywhere else in the country. But people quit. They continued to leave the city in droves: 20,000 people. Many of them didn't go far, however. This was an oddly drawn city. The neighbouring districts, Waimakariri to the north and Selwyn in the southwest, were once 'the country', given over to farms and, later, lifestyle blocks. Now they were, geographically, part of a great, sprawling city but still not part of its statistical area. People continued to move north and further west, too, away from the danger zone. So, as the old city shrank, new ones grew. The statistics faithfully recorded the changes without ever reflecting what was really happening in Christchurch. Which wasn't nearly as rosy.

Many of the city's best-known restaurants were going broke. Well-established bars were struggling. Fledgling businesses rushed into the new buildings, shopping complexes, multiplexes and office buildings, fitting the gaps without filling them: they were places to eat, without the atmosphere. The business was changing in any event: a new clientele was not so much there to eat as to photograph what they'd ordered and put it on Instagram. The term 'ghost restaurants' was already gaining traction: restaurants without tables or waiters, only phones and computers to take orders, cooks to fill them and send them off.

Some of those were national trends, but Christchurch was facing further problems of its own. People just weren't coming into the city centre any longer. In an attempt to rectify this, one promotion agency produced, with the help of quite a lot of public money, a campaign featuring twins having a fine time in the CBD to the tune of the 1970s hit, 'Baby Come Back'.

Ten years after the first quake the inner city was still 6000 people short of its pre-quake population, and new apartment blocks, built in the hope that the Garden City would change the habits of a lifetime and give up the roses for concrete blocks and shared pools, were selling only sluggishly. The city council and the government were pouring money into a convention centre and sports stadium and all sorts of other bouncy projects that were all very well if you were a literate businessperson who liked rugby, but Mum, Dad and the kids had business elsewhere.

Many people in that forlorn idea-sharing campaign had wanted a pedestrian-friendly city, with more sheltered walkways and covered malls to match the booming but dull suburban malls, but when the cheering and stamping died down the easterly was as unchecked, as rampant as ever. Now, when I visited and stayed in the aptly named dead centre of the city for a few days (albeit in winter), it was, well, quiet, even in nicely restored places such as the eccentric New Regent Street, aka 'New Zealand's most beautiful street'.

A new city was rising, low-rise. After all, given the often-terrifying rescues of 2010 and 2011, who would work any higher than six storeys? Some of the buildings were good, some modest, some dull. There just weren't enough of any of them. A rather modest visitor centre and café in the city's cherished Botanic Gardens was one of the best new buildings in the city. An entrancing new public library took pride of place in Cathedral Square. The higher you went inside it, the quieter it was. There was lots of wood, huge windows and even books (I didn't agree with critics who complained that the new library lacked them).

The city was said to need 100,000 more people over the following ten years. A shapely convention centre was going up across the street from the library, which, if the city ever got around to building its much-delayed sports stadium a few streets away, would probably guarantee a transient inner-city population, at least. Promising? So far, I thought the North Korean capital, Pyongyang, more imaginative and worse, given that grey state, more colourful.

Cathedral Square remained dominated by the grim remains of the Gothic Revival cathedral, slowly filling with pigeon shit, a horrible metaphor for the city. The light-filled 'temporary' replacement, the Cardboard Cathedral around the corner, was much more popular. The Anglican Bishop of Christchurch, Victoria Matthews, a Canadian, wanted to demolish the old cathedral and build a new one. Restoration would cost too much, she said, and the money would be better spent on the city's needy. The city's Anglican establishment lumbered to its feet. Over their dead body, they said. Or, as it turned out, over Bishop Matthews', for she quit and the cathedral was to be restored. You didn't mess with the Garden City's Anglicans. They ruled the roost, like the pigeons.

Christchurch seemed uncertain of what it wanted. It saw itself as both adventurous and tasteful. But the earthquake had damaged the city's soul. I thought it went like this: when your water had been cut off and you couldn't get to the supermarket and when you did it was closed and your car fell into potholes and your whole life had moved somewhere you could not fathom, you wanted to reduce your world to simple practicalities. You wanted to return to plain, understandable, comforting ordinariness. You didn't have the time or the patience for optional extras, although if ever there was a time for them, this was it. So Christchurch became torn between the imaginative and the curmudgeonly, and it seemed to me for quite a while that the deadweight was winning.

A SILVER LINING?

Anthony Gormley, the celebrated sculptor whose world-famous sculpture Angel of the North stood outside Gateshead in the north of England, produced for the city a work consisting of two figures in raw iron, each promising renaissance, a reassembling of parts, building the new persons within. They were superb works, one peeping from behind a pillar in the restored Arts Centre, the other looking diffidently from the Avon River. These two masterpieces were called *Stay*, and were made for the broken city by Gormley for $800,000, a heavily discounted price.

Even so they stood accused of costing far too much, of catching weeds in the river, and of being graffiti magnets. (That didn't happen, although one was dressed first in one of the city's ubiquitous hi-viz jackets, which I'm sure would have cheered Gormley, and later an All Black jersey, cheering him perhaps not so much.)

A sculpture on an overbridge over the main road into the city now greeted visitors from the airport. Its twin arches rose triumphantly (and controversially) into the sky, evoking the Southern Alps and Canterbury's braided rivers. I first saw them from the taxi carrying me into the city and thought them beautiful. 'Hmm,' the driver said. 'Three million for that? It looks like McDonald's.'

One of the more credible projects post-earthquake was an inner-city housing complex sponsored by 300-odd citizens wanting something new in city living, something sustainable, attractive and 'socially interactive'. The citizens included a potent brew of prominent architects, developers and consultants. They held a competition, judged by the Grand Designs impresario Kevin McCloud. It attracted entries from all over New Zealand and around the world. The judges settled on one that had everything: natural materials, self-sufficiency, sociability, affordability. And that was the last we heard of that, really. Like many a vision of a new world, it sank without trace.

I'd believed Christchurch would always come up with something new and original, and that notion had been shaken, but it wasn't reduced to rubble until the matter of the bridge. It was to have been both a footbridge and a work of art, crossing the Avon River into Hagley Park, which was as deep as you could get into the Christchurch soul. Otakaro, the latest incarnation of the Crown's rebuild company, invited artists to submit designs with a budget of $3 million. Several of the city's best artists and architects duly did. They ranged from one inspired by an eel trap, or hinaki, to a cloud bridge shrouded by mist. Otakaro then scrapped them all and settled for a straight concrete span.

Christchurch's reaction was hardly outraged. I'd sum it up as: 'It's only a bridge, just build the damn thing and stop wasting our money.' But I thought then, have all the grand designs, the hopes and dreams for a beautiful new city, come to this? Yes, earthquakes were a renewable resource and they'd certainly happen again somewhere in the South Island, which, if it hadn't cornered the market, was certainly the market leader. The earthquakes had given us the chance to have a fine new city all fixed up with everything the old one lacked. But for me the balance sheet was showing lots of red and very little black. I found myself lost in the city I'd grown up in. Most of the landmark buildings had gone and I couldn't walk around without that sense of grief that every Christchurch citizen had come to know, and worse, disorientation: often, I lost my way.

A SILVER LINING?

All of those huge sums pouring into this city on one side. On the other, the tragedy, the sadness, the loss. The golden fleece? Some were coining it. But for most it simply remained a disaster.

Yet the city was slowly renewing itself, restoring its best old buildings such as the Arts Centre, the old university. Some good new buildings were appearing in the city centre. From just outside the Square I looked down High Street at a promising new streetscape filled with odd angles and colour. A whole new precinct was taking shape along the Avon River, with new bars, restaurants, a popular market full of artisan bakers and butchers and interesting cafés and best of all, people. Each new development, civic leaders insisted, was bringing more people back to the city centre, even if many of them didn't want to live there. One academic inquiry into this phenomenon concluded that people preferred the outer suburbs because they could buy bigger properties, sometimes for less money.

The city gave away its target of 20,000 inner city residents by 2024 and settled on the same number by 2028. Popular reaction was sardonic, and mine was too. When you woke up on a Saturday morning the suburbs were throbbing. People were walking, clipping their roses, drinking coffee in cafés, piling kids in sports gear into SUVs, pedalling through the streets, strolling in the parks, putting up the umbrellas on the deck, chatting, and smiling, smiling, smiling. This was where Christchurch lived, what the city was all about.

I'd always loved the eccentricity of the city and here it was, exposed. People argued for years over what to do with the wrecked cathedral and held the whole thing in limbo for a decade, but hardly ever went to the CBD. They preferred the suburbs.

I decided it was time to go and have a look at those fast-growing areas.

*

Rolleston, to the southwest, was once a little village in a parade you passed through on your way south: Islington, Templeton, Rolleston, Burnham, Dunsandel, freedom. Hard to distinguish one from the next. Each had a café (née tearooms), a limited speed zone, a pub. I never stopped at any of them except Burnham, where I was incarcerated for military service. And there never seemed to be any good reason for Rolleston. It was just ... there.

In the early 1970s a Labour prime minister, Norman (Big Norm) Kirk, crowned Rolleston an heir to Christchurch, which was seen as growing out of its shorts. When he gazed into his crystal ball he saw 80,000 people living there. But despite his grand plan nothing very much happened to 'Rolleston, town of the future', and one day the sign just disappeared.

The earthquakes were Rolleston's golden fleece. The flat little town became a flat big town. People poured into it. Developers piled one subdivision onto the next. People moved in at such a rate that you could almost hear Big Norm chortling in his grave.

I hadn't been there for a few years and expected to be stupefied by its sudden growth but, essentially, I wasn't. The new town was simply a lot bigger than it had been, but more or less the same. Neat little gardens among new houses, where the fences went in first, then the concrete driveways were poured, followed by the double garage; the pool could wait till later. A shopping centre in the middle of the town seemed to me a good place to get bored in, if you hadn't succeeded already. Yes, yes, these were peoples' homes, but I was glad they were other peoples'.

Heading north from Christchurch, Northwood was the gem, the kind of place many in the city aspired to. You entered the place through an archway, its own version of the pearly gates, which I thought appropriate for not very much was moving the last time I went there. Oh, it was attractive enough, filled with middle-priced to expensive homes in those various shades of brown New Zealanders love. The differences seemed to lie mainly in the size of the garages.

On out to Pegasus Town, further to the north, the brainchild of a southern property developer who envisaged lakes and waterways and yachting courses and bars and cafés and shopping malls and an equestrian centre and a retirement village and an international hotel and swimmers in a lake edged with golden sand and people lounging in cafés all over the place. The developer was a man named Bob Robertson and I talked to him early in the new millennium, when his grand plan was not just a gleam in his eye but in everyone else's too. He was a man with a dream and a promise and he believed every bit of both. He believed so devoutly that I put my reservations about his semitropical paradise and my own knowledge of Pegasus Bay (wild, sometimes bleak) aside.

Bob spent $7 million on a model of his paradise, opened the doors to a rapturous audience and sold $122 million of property in a day. It was sensational. Pegasus Town was born, skipped its childhood and went straight to adolescence. Then the development went into receivership and Bob died and Pegasus had new owners whose intent, they said, was to do their best to follow the dream. Well, some 2500 of the 7000 people Bob

Roberston envisaged living in town actually lived there when I last visited. There was no hotel, no big retail precinct, although the planned retirement village seemed redundant, for many of the residents I saw were of a certain age. I passed a golf course on the way in and the lake was there, if missing the golden sand and the Mediterranean terraces of Bob's vision. The houses were nice, generally modest but suffering from a certain … sameness.

Pegasus survived the earthquakes pretty much intact, but the quakes had hardly supercharged development there either. The golden fleece was more a shade of beige.

*

There were two ways of going north from Christchurch. You could drive up the centre of the South Island, past Hanmer Springs, or more likely into the Springs, for the siren call of its hot pools was usually irresistible. Then you'd travel over Lewis Pass to more hot pools at Maruia Springs, go through Murchison, turn at the Nelson Lakes and travel along the Wairau Valley to Blenheim and Picton. This was the longer of the two routes, beautiful, and less used. But that changed after the quakes.

For the other way went up the coast. It was faster, and even more beautiful, and it passed through Kaikoura. I knew Kaikoura almost as well as Christchurch, for my family went there every holiday for years. The road ran through the vineyards filling the valleys and flats of North Canterbury which once grew only sheep and cows, low ranges to the west screening the blue Pacific Ocean beating on a gaunt coast. From Cheviot it slowly rose into the Hundalees then descended between ridges and through valleys covered in gold when the kowhai bloomed, a grand entrance to the magical Kaikoura coast. Generations of parents and carloads of children would give a happy sigh at Oaro: nearly there, the summer holiday had begun.

Offshore, amid the kelp, seals raised a languid flipper in salute, black against the turquoise sea. Rocks, home to countless generations of seabirds, rose pure white from the swell. The road ran beside a foreshore pitted with pools and inlets filled with bright green and red and yellow seaweed and small fish and shrimp-like creatures and, once, the long feelers of crayfish, the delight of generations of kids until they vanished.

Two sets of road tunnels carried honking traffic through spurs running down from bushy ranges that fell, often nearly vertically, to railway lines so close to the road that when a train came through — oh joy! — you felt you could just lean out of the car window and touch it. In the hills high above, Ngai Tahu had sheltered for generations, and here lay Omihi, whose mighty pa was sacked by the invading Ngati Toa.

The sea changed from aqua to indigo, for the Kaikoura Canyon lay only 500 metres offshore, a highway for migrating sperm whales, which fed in its depths. Baches clung to the hillsides, many unchanged by their generations of owners. Thin strips of land between the road and the sea had been camping grounds for a century or so. Every summer, campers, vans, caravans and tents all jammed themselves into impossible spaces and formed communities tighter than the neighbourhoods they came from.

Our family camped near the Kowhai River bridge in a huge square tent with a green top and sides that lifted to make extra rooms. Gnarly willows drooped over our heads and the smell of the blue borage remains in my memory forever. Nearby was a long beach of shingle covered with driftwood, where my father fished for moki, casting far out to sea with a long rod. When he caught one he danced with glee on the silver stones.

The place reeked of contentment and continuity until just after midnight on 14 November 2016, when a fault line near Culverden ruptured and rippled northeastwards, growing steadily as it triggered a web of faults (one of them previously unknown), travelling at two kilometres a second for 200 kilometres. Two people died. The best guess was that the quake would end up costing the government about $3 billion, with $1.8 billion in insurance claims. (As I said, there's a great deal of money in earthquakes.)

If you lived in Christchurch, the Kaikoura earthquake hurt nearly as much as your own. First, there was the unfairness of it. The odds, we'd been told, were entirely against another massive earthquake. Second, it happened just as we were starting to feel safe.

I'd spent a week in Kaikoura before the quake, staying just across the road from the old New Commercial Hotel, eating dinner under the verandas of the Pier Hotel, whose public bar looked over the bay and its fishing boats to the snow-tipped Kaikouras, and wondering why anyone would bother with Queenstown.

For me, Kaikoura was always its foreshore. Those rocks, the sea you first met at Oaro. They accompanied you all the way to Kekerengu. That shore was perfect, every small piece of it forming a composition so incredibly detailed that you came across each metre of it anew, different from the metre before, a living wonder. The rock walls and tunnels and pools and towers of the coast south of Kaikoura gave way to shingle beaches and the peninsula itself jutting into the Pacific Ocean, snoozing seals giving an annoyed huff as you passed, the rocks coloured by the apricot heads of thousands of gannets, the sea poking around archipelagos of tiny islands.

A little to the north of the town lay Mangamaunu, where the great Australian bush poet Henry Lawson once taught Maori kids, still a mecca for surfers who loved its long even breaks rolling off the point. Then came bays where fishing boats were launched down slipways over the rocks to set pots for crayfish sold in kiosks and caravans. I cannot remember a better lunch than a crayfish on that shore.

All my life I'd stopped at Ohau Point, where seals snoozed on the rocks below the road and smelled to high heaven and seal pups slid over and around each other in a pool below a waterfall at the end of a short track in the bush and stayed there even after their nursery had been discovered by a wider public with kids and cameras and reverent expressions.

Kekerengu lay near the end of that magical road, a tiny settlement hidden in the valley behind the reef stretching out to sea, seals silhouetted on its rocks, a tearoom at its base famous for its afghans and brownies morphing into an even more famous café that became a compulsory stop along this largely unpopulated piece of coast.

Everything changed that night of 14 November.

Of the many faults in the web that ruptured, the Kekerengu Fault was possibly the most gymnastic, rending the countryside, shoving it aside by up to ten metres and throwing it a couple of metres into the air. For a time Kaikoura was cut off as huge rocks tumbled down from the tops onto that thin lifeline of a road wedged into the coast. The town was badly damaged, but an even greater tragedy struck the ancient coastal civilisation when the seabed was hoisted into the air. For a hundred kilometres sea life lay exposed. Colonies of crayfish, whole cities of paua lay suffocating, an impromptu rescue by divers and fishermen and concerned citizens returning as many to the sea as they could.

A huge rolling smell of rotting and death enveloped that magical foreshore. Roads disappeared under thousands of tonnes of rock, railway lines tied themselves into knots. Tremendous forces shoved Christchurch southwards and Wellington northwards, and Kaikoura was cut off.

Lifelines were set up. Visiting American and Australian warships joined the pride of the New Zealand Navy, delivering supplies and evacuating people from the ruined coast. A comparatively little-used route called the Inland Kaikoura Road running from the little town of Waiau to the coast was repaired and pushed into service as an emergency route, a slow and difficult one. Teams of abseilers and road construction crews pinned unstable hillsides, cleared rocks, made tracks through the desolation. Great earth-shifting machines toiled. Engineers moved mountains.

To me, and to any unskilled observer, it seemed an impossible task. That opinion wasn't uncommon in living rooms and public bars. Was Kaikoura worth saving? Were the roads and tunnels and railway lines worth fixing? A thought cloud drifted above suburbs the length of the country: perhaps not. Too much damage, too much money, too many earthquakes, too hard. Perhaps the Kaikoura coast should just be abandoned. But the decision-makers persevered with their task, which, one day just before Christmas, 2017, they proved was possible after all. The road was opened for part of the day then, and, on Waitangi weekend 2018, for the whole day.

I flew down from Auckland for the occasion. I owed it to Christchurch, Kaikoura, Canterbury, to my parents, everyone and everything who'd made that glorious golden pathway of my youth. Oh, and the curiosity which was my own tool-of-trade. The main north road had always been as much a symbol as a highway. It stood for holidays and road trips and escape to the playgrounds of the north, not just Kaikoura but the Marlborough Sounds, Nelson, Golden Bay, the holiday places which tinkled the bells inside everyone's heads.

With State Highway 1 blocked at Kaikoura, the road north wasn't just diverted, it was devious. Not long before, the drive north to Picton, usually a four-hour journey, had taken me eight and a half by way of the diversion. By then truck drivers had dubbed the detour the 'white-knuckle highway' and some had quit their jobs for safer ones, for that road traversed remote country.

Hanmer Springs had taken on the role of civilisation's last outpost. From there I crossed the Lewis Pass, one of those feared routes through the mountains. On a good day it's beautiful, except for the sandflies: they are uniquely large, black creatures, the Rottweilers of the insect world, and they can reduce a forearm to the bone in ten seconds — or at least that's what it feels like. In winter the Lewis can become impassable in barely enough snow to decorate a Christmas tree.

Between the weather, and the overturned trucks, and the slips, and traffic which either proceeded as if it had been caught between two funerals and was undecided which to join, or was alternating between high speed and low flying, the Lewis was now as much a raffle as a drive. After the earthquake, driving through there had become the kind of epic adventure where you expected Bruce Willis to rip out of the Junction tearooms, throw down his gun and plead for mercy.

For 150 kilometres of the inland detour there were hardly any houses and you could take nothing for granted. At the height of the crisis the New Zealand Transport Agency installed both extended cellphone coverage and portable dunnies, an entirely new interpretation of the call of nature. I'd driven through Murchison and on to Kawatiri Junction, where the Nelson railway line had finally fizzled out, an experience not unfamiliar to post-earthquake traffic. Here I'd turned right, driven past Nelson Lakes National Park, the country's least known national park, and headed down the Wairau Valley, the car bumping and grinding like a striptease dancer and even more expensively, for the road had been ripped up by traffic it was never designed for, emergency earthquake routes not having been part of the Transport Agency's grand design. When the traffic had rejoined State Highway 1 at Renwick near Blenheim it had been a joyful reunion, like meeting someone from your family who'd been gone a very long time.

So I was not going to miss the grand reopening of State Highway 1. All the same, I was unprepared for what the earthquake had done to it.

The road was open between 7 a.m. and 8.30 p.m. and motorists were almost as happy about it as Kaikoura residents: drivers were back on their favourite road trip and Kaikoura once more had customers for its whales, and superb cheese.

Near the Hundalees the cavalcade was halted by a man standing outside what looked like a sentry box. We sat in the sun, engines running. We didn't mind. This wasn't a catastrophe, after all. We weren't disaster tourists, we were just happy to be there. Besides, the Transport Agency had kindly provided amusements: all along the road these sentry-boxes stood guard, and beside them stood men and women trained in the finest stop-go schools in the land. They weren't like other stop-go people who merely turned signs around. They were entertainers. They laughed, they waved, they chatted.

We were happy for them to stop us for ten or twenty minutes, even half an hour. The stops were diversions, and we needed them, for our road lay in ruins, cracked, slipping, crumbling. Over the four humps of the Hundalees we crawled then down the other side to the blue sea, where the sun always shined, although we were taken aback by what it was shining on. The seafloor lay white in the air, exposed like the ruins of an ancient civilisation. We couldn't get out of our cars to check, but I dare say the place stank, for the fronds and plants and kelp trees that lived under the water lay dead and dying above it, along with resident colonies of whatever sea creatures had not been rescued (sea life being like creatures everywhere: the better looking, the better treated). Crayfish and paua and kina might have been returned lovingly to the deep, but many others — the twirly ones, the squat and the doughy and the spiky — died clinging to their rocks. Only God understood the carnage here.

All the stop-go troupes in the world, all the new land uplifted high, all the repairs and the rebuilding couldn't disguise the damage. It was massive. The mountainsides above the road and the railway line running next to it had been stripped. Anything that could be loosed upon the earth had been shot downwards with far more force than gravity alone could muster. Great rocks and huge piles of rubble lay everywhere. This road had been blocked for months and to the eyes of an ingenue such as myself it was a miracle it had been re-opened.

The road tunnels where generations of kids had begged their mums and dads to honk their horns had disappeared under newly minted mountains. Flotillas of machines and armies of men and women toiled over the wreckage. Abseilers hung from ropes stabilising the raw cliffs, looking incredibly fragile in their work. It was both the bravest and most desolate human endeavour I'd ever seen and it stretched along the road for eighty kilometres.

Ohau Point, where the seals had once slumbered, lay raw and bleeding. A giant rock that had landed on the baby seals' pathway and lain there like a full stop had been broken up and taken away, but I could not imagine the seals ever returning. (They did.)

What of Kaikoura itself? The town had been bombarded too. The New Commercial Hotel had disappeared, first ruined by the earthquake then destroyed in a mysterious fire. The Adelphi Hotel, where I'd once stayed with my dad and thought it the most luxurious, extravagant, poshest place in the world, had disappeared completely. The damage was awful, but, even if the shop verandas were now propped up, we celebrated its survival, applauded it as we would a once-famous star returning to the stage. Besides, the town's beach, once rather narrow, stony and mediocre as beaches go, was now a wide and welcoming strand.

*

But apparently it could have been worse. The Big One is still biding its time in the mountains, backstage, dressing up, working its muscles for a grand appearance.

The Alpine Fault is the boundary between two colossal plates, the Australian and Pacific plates, which are steadily grinding against each other as they move in opposite directions. Each hiccup in this process produces a giant disturbance in this long, thin island: the earth moves upwards and outwards; the South Island grows longer, the Southern Alps rise higher.

The fault runs northeast from the northern side of the entrance to Milford Sound, under Lake McKerrow, through the mountains behind Martins Bay, along the coast beneath the Southern Alps to Hokitika, its route marked by escarpments so clearly that in winter the snow seems to have painted it with a brush. Turning inland, the Alpine Fault runs to a point near the Lewis Pass, travels northwards then frays into four main faults that extend to the east coast, three of them cramming into the space in Cloudy Bay between Cape Campbell and Port Underwood near Blenheim, the fourth exiting a little to the north of Kaikoura.

On a map that cluster of fault lines looks rather like a bed of snakes that, when poked, turn deadly. They move at a speed of thirty-eight millimetres a year, which to a seismologist is like the speed of a Ferrari Testarossa on a test track. This makes them extremely dangerous.

The Alpine Fault last got seriously testy in 1717 or thereabouts and before that, in descending order, 1620, 1430 and 1100. Those dates were shifting as scientists re-calculated, the average interval between them reducing to an average of less than 300 years, which in terms of simple arithmetic means that New Zealand is due for something very dangerous right about, well, now. Seismologists expect the Big One to dwarf all opening acts.

The Fault's fractured pattern threw up the Murchison earthquake in 1929, the Inangahua earthquake in 1968, the Kaikoura earthquake in 2016, and early in the new millennium two major quakes in Fiordland where, fortunately, hardly anyone lives.

I decided to take a closer look at that deadly lattice-work.

The Wairau Fault runs along the Wairau Valley from Renwick near Blenheim to the Nelson Lakes. This time, I was travelling south from Cloudy Bay, and I went down it with my fingers crossed. I'd endured thousands of earthquakes in Christchurch and didn't trust whatever celestial bean counter was keeping tally. Torn up by the traffic diverted from the coastal route, the road through the valley was rough and lonely. The only place of note along it, called, of course, Wairau Valley, was the centre of civilisation here. I came upon on it quite suddenly, with its school, memorial hall, church, fire station, golf course and a pub that had served travellers for more than a century and a half. I was an early-morning traveller, and the pub was closed.

So was the town, apparently. Very little happens here and, given its dangerous location, locals like it that way. When the main street got a footpath a few years back, the story made the newspapers. Down the road a little, what looked like a concrete watering trough turned out to be a historic place, although it was, indeed, a concrete watering trough.

A power company had wanted to divert the Wairau River through canals to generate electricity, ignoring the assassin in the closet: this was the tail end of the main fault line after all. The plan was approved by the Environment Court then put on hold.

The valley itself was quite dynamic. Vineyards were spreading steadily along it, and the local council thought its growth prospects bright.

Escarpments here rise vertically from the valley floor. To the passing driver they are merely spectacular; they don't look like clues at all. Yet in the 1855 Wairarapa earthquake, the valley's eastern end dropped by a metre.

Following the fault line for one hundred kilometres, I reached Lake Rotoiti, that perfect, narrow little lake squeezed between mountains with St Arnaud at its head. Once I followed the Pinchgut Track up Pourangahau/Mount Robert near the old ski field here and looked across Lake Rotoiti to the point where the Alpine Fault left the lake and cut through the range into the Wairau Valley, and I thought the town of St Arnaud lay perilously close. I was wrong. In fact, like Franz Josef far to the south, St Arnaud actually straddles the fault line, possibly one reason why it is New Zealand's least known alpine resort, though it is otherwise perfectly positioned.

A strong quake here would not only sever this poor, hard-pressed road, it would cut every surrounding road and cause landslides that would likely lift the lake itself, flooding the shoreline and possibly the town, and sending a wall of water down the Buller River. That's speculation, of course, though the lakebed apparently hides evidence of a huge landslide, very old now but probably caused by an earthquake.

Now, in the early twenty-first century, life here seemed too settled for an earthquake, even if the entire landscape had been created by such forces. A few kilometres north of Murchison I walked up the Matiri Valley to Lake Matiri, which I'd never heard of before, much less been to. The walk was gentle, considering the earthquake-riven country all around it. It took me through beech forest to a lovely little hut on the edge of the lake, where I sat on the porch and contemplated the still water below and the mountains and the peace and earnestly wished I never had to go anywhere else. The spectacular scenery was courtesy of the Alpine Fault. All around were the scars of rock falls and slips and landslides, one of which had created the lake itself. Yet it didn't seem so much earthquake-riven land as a singular art form, a huge, sculptured rockscape.

High above lay two remarkable plateaus, said to be extremely rare in this country, tussock-covered benches named, respectively, Thousand Acres and Hundred Acres, curious names given that neither of them measured up in terms of size. But they were not as curious as the Devil's Dining Table, which locals told me was the nickname for the smaller plateau. It hinted at a calamitous past, or future.

No one needed any convincing about earthquakes in Murchison. On 17 June, 2019, the town remembered the magnitude 7.8 earthquake that had struck at 10.17 a.m. exactly ninety years before. Seventeen people died, fourteen of them killed by landslides. It was New Zealand's third worst earthquake tragedy, after Napier and Christchurch. Roads and telephone lines were wiped out and it was almost a day before anyone outside Murchison knew it had been all but destroyed and most of the town's 300 people made homeless. A local man, Bert Spiers, waded through flooded rivers and hiked over landslides and through bush for forty-one kilometres to Glenhope (now just an old railway station and some farmhouses) to send out word of the tragedy. Some of Spiers's family still live in Murchison.

On the earthquake's ninetieth anniversary, three survivors were still alive, for Murchison is a seriously stable small New Zealand town, comforting in its endurance, reliant on dairy farming, passing traffic and, to a degree, earthquake damage — quakes created the falls and rapids and white water beloved of kayakers, many of whom acclaim the town as the white-water capital of New Zealand.

Fewer than 500 people live in Murchison now. To me, after more than half a century's passing acquaintance with the town, it didn't seem to have changed much. The old Hampden Hotel (Hampden was the original name of the town when it was founded following a gold rush) still stood on its corner, its splendid verandas as close to pristine as old pubs could get. The old stables, St Paul's Church, the picture theatre, the council chambers and the post office still existed, even if their uses had changed a bit. The town still possessed the best junk shop in the South Island and its general store, Hodgsons', might have been a museum piece if it wasn't so … useful. The butcher's shop was closed, but a sign on the door promised that home kill was still available. The French pastry shop hinted at another life. So did the courthouse, which once presided over New Zealand's and possibly the world's first suicide bombing.

On 14 July 1905, two local farmers had taken a very old dispute to court, the one claiming the other had stolen two heifers from his property. The defendant, one Joseph Sewell, entered an unusual plea: he'd strapped sticks of gelignite to his body, and, in the middle of the sitting, shouted, 'I'll blow the devil to hell, and I have enough dynamite to do just that.' This being contempt of court at its most egregious, he was persuaded to leave the building. Sewell detonated the charge when a policeman tried to arrest him on the street, and blew himself to pieces; no one else died in the explosion.

At the resulting inquest his daughter Alice Sewell, according to the *Grey River Argus*, testified that her father's mind had been affected by the friction with his neighbour, one Mr Neame, to the extent that he hadn't worked at all the previous day, 'a very unusual thing'. He'd kept explosives for the purpose of blowing up stumps. She'd seen her father outside the court and heard him say he'd blow everyone up if they said two more words. Someone must have uttered the fatal phrase, for next thing, she said, 'the explosion occurred'. A local constable, Ed Scott, testified that Sewell was 'literally blown to atoms'. The jury decided the deceased had been in a state of temporary insanity.

A plaque still recorded this event in quiet Murchison's history, but larger monuments to the greater tragedy, the 1929 earthquake, were everywhere: slips, rocks, lakes, mountains hammered to pieces, landscapes battered into bits. I walked up a track in the Matakitaki River valley near the town. It led up a creek, through bush, then got steeper and emerged at the bottom of a huge slip triggered by the earthquake. As I went higher, the terrain became more sculptured: giant blocks of rock as smooth and straight as if they'd been cut by some celestial stonemason and fashioned into arches, rectangular ashlars, capitals, flagstones, pillars, blocks, orderly forms in disorder, a ruined city of rock in perfect shapes lying beside cliffs that seemed to have been carved from the landscape.

Murchison at least survived its earthquake, and even prospered from another, the Kaikoura quake, which made it the only watering-hole in a very long stretch of road. When you travelled west of Murchison you drove past cliffs spitting rocks that were contained by wire fences. The country around here was cleft, as if someone had taken a very big axe to it. I resolved never to be near that spot during an earthquake, which, I suppose, only shows what a waste of time resolutions are.

Continuing on from Murchison, I came to a fork and took the road west across the Maruia River, past the old town of Lyell, once the site of one of the country's biggest goldfields, twisting along the Buller River to Inangahua Junction. It's called a junction because the railway line from the north, the fabled Nelson line, was supposed to meet the western Stillwater to Westport line right here. That did not happen because the Nelson line was never finished, a controversial subject to this day. But trains still ran through the junction on their way to Westport, and the town slumbered on happily until one day its fifteen minutes of fame truly arrived, to its great dismay.

On 24 May 1968, at 5.24 in the morning, an earthquake struck the area. It was rated X on the Mercalli scale, which meant it was very destructive; the 2011 Christchurch earthquake was only VI. At Whitecliffs, down the Westport road from Inangahua Junction, Mrs Rona Jackson was killed when adjacent cliffs collapsed and crushed her house. Her husband was milking cows in the nearby shed. Her mother, Mrs Fanny Blackmore, who was also in the house, was pulled out alive but later died in Reefton hospital. Someone was building another house on the section now, which I suppose showed that hope really did spring eternal, or possibly that planners have short memories.

Elsewhere a taxi driver died when the approach to a bridge subsided just as he was driving over it. A few days later repair gangs assembled at the Murchison rugby ground to be flown into Buller Gorge. One young man begged for a ride; he'd never been in a helicopter before. An older man gave up his seat and the helicopter took off with the pilot and two passengers. The rest of the gang travelled by truck and as they made their way into the gorge they saw the burning helicopter beside the road, the two workmen still strapped into their seats. In low fog the helicopter had flown into power lines over the Buller River. The pilot had apparently tried to jump clear. His body was found on the riverbed.

Inangahua then was three areas: the township of Inangahua, Inangahua Junction, and Inangahua Landing beside the river. The junction was worst hit. The town's old hotel was destroyed by a slip which also pushed houses off their foundations and crushed buildings. People had to walk over rocks and slips to Reefton to get food and medical help, and Reefton had suffered too, scarcely a house with a chimney still standing in days when everyone heated their homes with coal. A vast landslip blocked the mighty Buller River, creating such a lake the authorities feared it would burst and flood both Inangahua and Westport. Both towns were evacuated and many never returned to Inangahua, although the moment passed without further tragedy. About 300 people lived in Inangahua then. It wasn't a big place, but it got a lot smaller.

When I visited, nothing was moving in Inangahua. Of the 144 people reputed to be still living here, there was no sign. The café was closed. The 'Historic Lyell' display in the museum, the old town hall, was closed. The abandoned church was for sale. Clearly some people still lived there, for gardens were tended and (some) houses painted, but of the gardeners or any kind of citizenry there was no sign.

The landing is no more than a sign, and a cemetery marks the Junction, where I walked between mossy memorials. A cross recorded the death of a woman and her nine-month-old son, who were killed in the Buller Gorge in 1929. Life could still be dangerous here, apparently. 'Stay in car,' a sign advised, 'you are entering a 1080 zone' — 1080 being a poison used for pest control. I took the sign writer's advice, although not through fear; there just did not seem any good reason for staying there. Earthquakes had effectively cleared the land.

Instead, I drove back to the fork near Murchison and took the road south along the Shenandoah River valley and over the Shenandoah to Springs Junction. From here roads lead west to Reefton, and south to Christchurch, as well as north to Murchison. Not far from the Junction is a place called Calf Paddock, near Marble Hill. It's a popular spot, a place where you can park your motorhome, have a picnic, pitch your tent or walk the bush track to the lovely Lake Daniells. It also neatly straddles the main fault line, so it's popular with seismologists and scientists too. They dig trenches and map past earthquakes and try to predict the Big One. It seemed to be a happy equilibrium between hope and disaster. Here was to be found some relief from the relentless hand-wringing.

The Alpine Fault turns here, veering towards south from its previous southwesterly course. Scientists call this turn the Big Bend. Here they were digging into the rock layers and studying evidence that there had been fewer quakes to the north of the bend. In other words, the bend might be a protective buffer between earthquakes in the fault line to the south, and points north. So the northern parts of the South Island, and Wellington, might not be as endangered as previously thought. As much as seismologists ever became popular public figures, these fellows would be cheered on every centimetre of their rocky, muddy, uncomfortable way.

South of Springs Junction lies Lake Christabel. It takes seven hours to walk to the lake and I haven't been there, but people who have say it is very beautiful, a little lake lying diamond-like in the mountains, surrounded by deep bush and, of course, lonely. Lake Christabel was formed by a prehistoric earthquake-created landslide that dammed the river, and the lakebed entombs an earthquake history, a seismological archive containing more evidence of the fault line's machinations. I have two things to say about this. The first is a heart-felt 'Go for it!', for the need to know our fate is pressing, to say the least. The second is the observation that this particular branch of earth sciences certainly takes its people into the most lonely, remote and absolutely magnificent parts of this great nation.

So many places in the South Island are wonderful because of earthquakes. Quakes hoisted the Southern Alps into the sky, then the Alps ambushed the weather patterns flying over the Tasman Sea and created the rainforests of the West Coast and the fiery nor'westers of the Canterbury Plains. The fault line was responsible for the escarpments, cliffs, intricate landforms and superb patterns that place the South Island of Aotearoa among the most beautiful places on Earth. Yet the fact remains that, even after dozens of studies, some with international researchers and costing millions of dollars, nothing has changed: nobody can predict when, exactly, the Alpine Fault will once again rip the land asunder.

*

I drove through Reefton to Greymouth then took the road south, stopping at Whataroa. I wanted to go to a spot called Gaunt Creek. This place is unique, for there you can actually see the fault line, see the two tectonic plates pressing together, the Australian Plate nudging the Pacific Plate.

The Australian Plate was once part of the southern continent of Gondwana, which included the landmasses that are now Australia, Antarctica, India, Africa and South America. Gondwana began to break up about 185 million years ago, with India drifting north around 100 million years ago and Antarctica going its own way about 55 million years later. Today the Australian Plate includes not just the continent of Australia but also parts of New Zealand and New Guinea and a bit of the Indian Ocean basin. The Pacific Plate is an even bigger affair, with most of it lying beneath the Pacific Ocean.

Imagine the tremendous forces at work, shifting the earth's crust. Their encounter was never going to lead to a gentle coexistence.

They didn't just meet and greet. They were two colossal bodies springing against each other. Ructions were involved. To make things more interesting, parts of one plate dive under parts of the other. In the North Island the Pacific Plate ducks under the Australian. In the South Island, the Australian Plate slides under the Pacific Plate. Either way, it's a war of the worlds.

Although you can see the fault line from space, tracking it on the ground is often more difficult. Gaunt Creek's contribution to the geological trove is the fact that, there and nowhere else, a slip has exposed the fault. At Gaunt Creek you can stand with a foot on each tectonic plate so that you straddle the two worlds, hoping, of course, that the Big One will not choose that exact moment to strike lest your stance became a little wider than physically desirable.

The site is on a farm whose owner saw the potential for a wider audience than the teams of seismologists who drill and probe this phenomenon. So, on this chilly day, I went into Whataroa, hopped onto a little green and cream bus with the driver, Elisabeth, and her two children, Victoria and Archer, drove past a curiously named feature, Ralfes Knob, and headed up the beautifully named Waitangitaona Valley. We drove along the tawny valley floor, the dense West Coast bush pressing down the mountainsides, then sidled off along Gaunt Creek, which wasn't gaunt at all, really, just a stream cutting through the layers of glacial gravel.

The world's seismologists had beaten this shingle track and made their own mark on the landscape with a seismic observatory, aka a shipping container. Here, they had the privilege of studying the only naturally exposed major fault in the entire world, and of drilling straight into an active fault line. Here, open to public view, was the manifestation of the forces that had literally moved mountains, sucking rock from deep in the ground, thrusting up the Southern Alps and lengthening the South Island.

I studied it from the opposite side of the creek, which overnight rain had made a little high that day. It was a gash of minty green cataclasite, or fault rock, against a sharp line of brown glacial gravels in a grey landscape, the kind of thing that, had you not known of its significance, you might have looked at, wondered about for a moment or two and moved on.

All around, slips and shakes had carved the landscape into faces, grooves, cuts, spikes. I could scarcely believe I was standing there, exactly at the collision point between two vast plates, where anybody, not just a geologist, or a scientist of any kind, but any simple Joe could actually see what all the fuss was about, even sense the forces.

Heaven and a few geoscientists only knew what this place would be like in a decent shake. This spot focussed all of our fears, worries and expectations regarding the huge disaster the Big One would inevitably create. Nothing could prevent it. Gaunt Creek had been like this, more or less, since the last huge shake in 1717. It was time for another bang, and the probes here at Gaunt Creek might at least give notice and, come the calamity, offer the opportunity to study the mechanics of an earthquake from the inside, learn how the fault worked and about the arrival of the beast, rather than simply measuring the aftermath.

In 2011 scientists began drilling into the rock here and mined the first samples of the Alpine Fault. They found a narrow zone, less than half a metre wide, of a kind of earthquake grease: a very fine mixture of clay and rock. Beyond this was a rocky mush, and beyond that, fractured rock. This structure held back vast amounts of water on one side: an earthquake on the fault, scientists feared, could be hydraulically supercharged.

This was one of the most exciting places in the world for a seismologist. I walked through gorse while far below my feet millions of years of intercontinental drift were at work. Yet up here it was silent and all seemed so peaceful, so innocent. We drove out over the fault line, which, I now knew, was diving below us at a forty-five-degree angle.

*

The Alpine Fault line runs south past Franz Josef Glacier and Fox Glacier. As if, anyone familiar with the West Coast might say, south Westland didn't have enough problems already.

In the last few years, cyclones and floods had washed away bridges and roads, cutting off towns and services, trapping tourists and bringing the Coast to a standstill.

So what would a sizeable earthquake do? What would it cost? Billions, of course. When seismologists and earthquake authorities called meetings on the West Coast, they were very well attended.

There was no getting away from the fault line down here. A little south of Whataroa it runs through the central business district of Franz Josef. The town was quiet the day I visited. No thumping helicopters, just one tourist coach parked on a side road, a few visitors puddle-jumping along the street, others hunkered under umbrellas, restaurant owners looking hopeful. Wisps of chimney smoke hung low in the air, almost indistinguishable from low cloud.

When the Alpine Fault throws its fit, Franz Josef will be torn apart, all right. The fault lies below the town's main street, crosses the service station's forecourt. Geoscientists predict that in a serious fault rupture the town would be hoisted two metres in the air and shoved sideways by nine metres, which by my own rough estimates would put it within spray distance of the troublesome Waiho River, a rampant beast that was filling with sediment and getting ready to flood the town again.

The risk is so great that the geoscientists have suggested the entire town be moved to a nice new lakeside location, perhaps beside Lake Mapourika, ten kilometres north. The townspeople weren't keen on that idea, but then, they aren't keen on anything else either, and even staying put is risky.

Some 330 people live in the town, whose tourist industry brings in $350 million a year, or more than a million for every man, woman and child. Many visitors are glacier tourists, and the town's main asset is melting. You might forgive a few locals, especially those whose income is linked to tourism in whatever way, for being a little edgy. They are being assailed both above and below ground.

I pulled into the service station for petrol and asked the attendant what it was like to have a fault line running through the pumps.

He looked foxy. 'I can't say.'

Yes, I said, I'd read it in a book (Geoff Chapple's *Terrain*).

It became apparent that while he'd said 'I can't say', he meant 'I won't say.'

'I know quite a bit about geology,' he said, which did not surprise me even a little bit, given where he lived.

'Sorry,' I said, 'I didn't realise it was a secret.'

'It's not a secret,' he said, 'it's a subject of confidentiality. Business confidentiality.'

'Well, good luck,' I said.

'Can't say when it'll happen though,' he said. 'Maybe fifty years, maybe 500.'

Perhaps he didn't go to the meetings. Or perhaps he did, for even the geoscientists could not say with any certainty what was going to happen, or when; their best guess was a 30 percent likelihood of a rupture in the next half-century. That might sound remote, but I'd been through thousands of earthquakes in Christchurch, a part of the country everyone thought so safe that the odds had been much, much longer. Fox Glacier village, further down State Highway 6, was equally vulnerable, although this is a competition that absolutely no one can win.

One thing the experts agreed on was that a main Alpine Fault rupture would be no mere shake, no shrinking violet. The earthquake would be huge, not just strong. It would be an all-out raucous, savage brawler.

Seismologists were expecting a quake of magnitude 8-plus, ripping up the coast from South Westland and roaring through the mountains into the east and to Marlborough and being felt right across the Tasman in Sydney. 'Significant' building damage, they said, but 'significant' to me sounded feeble. Try horrible.

Such a quake would tear into buildings not just on the West Coast, where property values are relatively low, but into Queenstown, where they are not. It would move mountains, rend plains, bury whole areas up and down its length, sometimes under many tens of millions of tonnes of rock. Rivers would flood, new rivers be created. Bridges would be wrecked, power cut, cellphones made useless, water and sewage systems ruined, businesses closed. Tsunamis would sweep across lakes and down rivers. The landscape would be wrenched, hammered, dismembered. Emergency and medical services would be overwhelmed. Then there'd be aftershocks ...

What they were describing was Armageddon. What were the chances? One in three of it happening in maybe fifty years? They were not odds I'd bet on.

The picture became more explicit as disaster planning advanced. A whole Coast-full of tourists, tens of thousands of them, would need to be evacuated from wherever they were trapped. The damage caused by Cyclone Gita was a peccadillo. A massive earthquake, in terms of severity, was on another planet. One authority calculated a rupture that could block 120 sections of road. Down in South Westland there was only one road. If it got blocked, you got trapped or, of course, worse.

Tourists were vulnerable. They travelled in cars and buses not designed for rough work. They wore clothes suited to bars and cafés and selfies. Watching their confusion during Cyclone Gita, I'd felt their biggest problem was that they didn't have a clue. They didn't know what to do, or where to go or even, sometimes, where they were. That was not their fault, that was just the nature of modern tourism.

Even in preliminary disaster planning, Otago and Southland were scrapping over who might take them. Or who might have to pay. For example, Stadium Southland wanted $680,000 to make their stadium ready to receive refugees. Environment Southland declined.

The 10,000 or so locals who, the experts calculated, might be cut off would fare better. They had the gear, they knew the country, they were resourceful and, probably most significantly, they were quite used to being isolated.

One statistic was missing from the forecasts: the death toll. One hundred and eighty-five people died in Christchurch, and 164 were seriously injured. Billions of dollars poured into Christchurch following the earthquakes. But nobody, nobody, ever suggested that the earthquake might have been worth those lives, or that in any way the books were balanced.

There was no pot of gold at the end of this rainbow, no silver lining. Earthquakes bring in billions of dollars, and are a renewable resource. But they are horrible, terrifying. They ruin lives and far too often end them. Nothing is ever the same again after an earthquake, not in any good way. No one who has lived through earthquakes could ever see gold in this fleece.

CHAPTER SIX

The Place in the Sun

I'd always thought of Mike Ward as Mr Nelson. The man is perfectly attuned to the city. He grew up there, went to school there, retired from teaching to become an artist there. He's an athlete. He cycles, runs, swims. He once entered the famed World of Wearable Art design competition and won the supreme award. He was the only person to finish every one of the first twenty-eight Coast to Coast races, and I first met him during that legendary race across the mountains and rivers of the central South Island. He was competing, I was writing, but just watching this man was exhausting.

He was a co-leader of the Values Party, and when it was succeeded by the Green Party he became a Member of Parliament for a term. He cycles everywhere on one of those deceptively reclining bikes. He's never had a driver's licence, although I read somewhere that if he could afford a Jaguar E-type he might break his duck. He's restored his heritage home near the city centre. His environmental and conservation values are so immaculate that he sparkles even in this gem of a city. He treads so lightly on the planet he needs a string to hold him down.

He expresses part of his philosophy like this: 'You spend your life working your arse off and you don't even enjoy yourself very much. You surround yourself with a heap of shit that will bring you limited pleasure but will deprive you of the things that most delight you.' Well, wasn't that just Nelson?

Mike makes jewellery in a studio above the Morrison Street Café, successor to the Chez Eelco tradition. Chez Eelco was started by the Dutch immigrant Eelco Bosweijk in 1961 and was acclaimed by many as not only Nelson's but New Zealand's first real café; Bosweijk gave Suzy Moncrieff money to start the World of Wearable Art.

Mike's finger is always on the pulse. This is a tight city. He sells his jewellery in the Nelson Market on Saturday mornings. One morning as I talked to him there he took some silver wire and worked it around a jeweller's spike with some fine pliers and when I said goodbye he presented me with a perfect ring.

He was a candidate in the local body elections, standing for mayor of his city among a plethora of candidates promising to put things right, even if hardly anything here was wrong. Mike's election hoardings were dotted around the town, his mass of white hair neatly done up to startling effect; he was usually more … windswept. Other candidates promised to be committed, to be active, to work tirelessly for the good of Nelson. Mike Ward's hoarding carried only his picture and two boxes, one for mayor, one for councillor, both ticked.

He argued that Nelson could become a role model for the nation. After all, he claimed, the city spent more time on its bikes than other cities, joined more libraries and took out more books, went to more movies, and loved its markets and cafés. If there was something to get involved in on the planet, he said, there would be a branch of it there in Nelson.

It's a place the rest of the world looks at and asks how the city did it. After all, he calculated, a quarter of the population at any time in this country are depressed and anxious, 50 percent over the course of a year. You have to say we are doing something wrong. The pursuit of stuff is insatiable and deeply unsatisfying. Mike has written a book, as yet unpublished, with the title 'How to Look after the Planet and One Another and Yourself and Have a Lovely Time Doing It.'

And he's had a lovely time. 'This city has been extraordinarily kind to me,' he said to me. 'There's a warmth to this town, an affection. I wonder what the golden fleece is. Perhaps it's contentment.' Later we went downstairs and sat in the café in the sun. A seagull perched on the roof, perfectly white against Nelson's blue sky. Mike wore a red polka-dot shirt with a matching handkerchief in the breast pocket of his grey linen jacket, and a finely worked French horn brooch on his lapel. Two excellent cheese scones arrived with triangles of golden butter in a glass dish. A flash of white feathers and a squawk and one of the butter triangles disappeared. Even the seagulls get a fair go here.

We chatted about this and that, constantly interrupted by well-wishers who wanted to talk to Mike, shake his hand. Mike's reclining bike rested at the kerb, ready for the off. He was, I thought, pure Nelson, everything the city was, stood for. He was a practical environmentalist, and if he wanted to save the world, well, the world certainly needed saving. He was Nelson to the core: smart, politically knowledgeable, environment friendly, artistic.

Yet the city disappointed us both. In the mayoral election a couple of months later, Mr Nelson won only 1634 votes, coming third to last.

*

This city is a beautiful place. You fly into it on propeller-driven aircraft, one of the most beautiful flights in New Zealand no matter which direction you come from. Aeroplanes flit back and forth from Wellington every half hour. They are more frequent than many bus services in either city.

Aucklanders have almost as many connections with Nelson, and they get one of the world's great flights thrown in too. They travel low along the west coast of the North Island, puzzling over its complexities. What is that estuary? That crooked headland? Then they cut across Cape Egmont, looking right down the barrel of Taranaki, the volcano, then they're over the sea, with the Marlborough Sounds and D'Urville Island appearing to the left. They zoom low over blue sea, golden beaches, estuaries and an archipelago of sandy islands and then they are over Monaco, a suburb as unlike the Mediterranean principality as can be, perhaps wondering for how much longer its relaxed houses will be safe from the sea. And finally they land in an airport so neat and clean they feel they should wipe their feet before stepping onto the tarmac.

The new airport terminal was designed to handle 1.4 million passengers a year, at last count some thirteen times the native population. The city is very proud of it. The airport is a symbol, a recognition. Nelson people know they live in the best city in New Zealand. That might have made the city unattractively smug, but they see the new airport as proof. If so many people want to come here, well then.

The old terminal was a symbol of the past, one in which Nelson was just a small city at the top of the South Island. It kept out the rain, and that's about all that could be said for it. When the new terminal first opened, departing passengers were presented with cupcakes and gifts. One passenger said, 'It's very Nelson.' Lots of pine, appropriately, for pine plantations do well in Nelson's climate.

From the outside, the new terminal looks like a low mountain range, a series of peaks reminiscent of the architect Paul Pascoe's now demolished Christchurch Airport terminal. Inside it is timbered, great baulks of wood set at all angles looking like some giant bird's nest. Wildfires had recently stormed across the province, so thoroughly destroying the plantations that at one stage it appeared that the airport terminal might double as a monument.

My taxi driver explained to me the Jungian theory of synchronicity as we drove past the ornate stanchions and chains of Rocks Road running between cliffs and sea. This model city has escaped the urban diseases. It has the lowest unemployment in the land, little crime, no barren suburbs. People look puzzled when you ask about traffic jams, as if trying to remember the recipe. True, it is getting a little ... smaller? Rocks Road, always pride of the city, was to have been kitted out with a walking and cycling track until it was so bashed by high tides and strong winds that the plan was thrown away. The road was often closed for repairs, which was a shame, because it is one of the nicest routes in the country for through traffic.

Nelson, in fact, is being nibbled by climate change. Jackett Island, a long, low island fencing the estuaries between Motueka and Nelson, is not being chewed so much as gobbled. Residents of Monaco, that tiny half-island with only low-tide road access, are engaged in a war with the sea, which vandalised their walls, steps and even foundations. Older walls lie where they fell, chunks of stone and concrete like headstones to island dreams. Residents here must pray for salvation to God and Fulton Hogan equally — when I visited, the latter was engaged in propping up one side of their enclave.

I'd once admired the relaxed houses on this sandbar, with their fine sea views, but now they made me nervous. Signs warned traffic of the dangers of high-tide driving. Even so, I was entranced by the road. It passes one of the city's more unusual success stories, the Monaco village inn, with a medieval hotel beside it, standing in a copy of an imagined English village. A Mediterranean city-state cheek by jowl with ye olde English architecture might have been a culture clash elsewhere, but here in the sun they rubbed along just fine.

*

The sun shines here more than anywhere else except, sometimes, Blenheim — that's an annual contest. Nelson's long summers are blue, its winters just cold enough to call themselves decent. Surrounding mountain ranges shelter the city and plains from prevailing winds.

This day in early spring was pure Nelson as advertised: pale blue, cold, beautiful, gentle. I found a motel, or half a motel, the other half given over to young tourists, cheerful and noisy, then a good Turkish restaurant, its tiny tables all packed. The cold city streets were deserted but the bars and restaurants were not.

I walked to the city centre (who needs taxis here?), passing Nelson's medley of houses, some nicely restored early colonials and superb 1960s modernist homes sitting jowl by jowl with the new retirement colonies. The two outstanding characteristics of this city's people are that they are old, and they are white. Tasman sits high in the list of the ten most European regions in the land.

Nelson people are so content that the city's only visible social ill is smugness. And, perhaps, a tendency to go to bed early.

As Mike Ward told me, 'Most of us don't actually know why we come here. Perhaps it's because we think we'll find something — your golden fleece perhaps — without actually knowing what we're looking for.'

So, could Nelson itself be the golden fleece?

A century and a half ago this might have been the nation's capital and those Wellingtonians crossing Cook Strait to escape their cold and windy city would have thought that a jolly good thing too. Our fondness for endless argument was then in its infancy, if already a squalling child. Okiato, or Old Russell, in the Bay of Islands, had been our first pick for capital, from shortly after the Treaty of Waitangi was signed in 1840 until the following year, 1841. It was a short distance, seven kilometres, from Koroareka, the present Russell, then a little town with a fondness for mayhem.

But the nascent capital moved south to Auckland, all traces of this first attempt at a seat of government vanishing the following year, 1842, when the government house and offices in Okiato burned down. Auckland was an immature place but quite nicely located in the Hauraki Gulf. It offered two superb harbours, Waitemata and Manukau, lots of rivers and fertile land, and what were later to become million-dollar views, although Governor Hobson paid considerably less for them. He bought a large block of land cheaply from Ngati Whatua, on the Waitemata, or Tamaki-makau-rau. Hobson gave it a less pretty name: Auckland, named for his patron, Lord Auckland, governor-general of India and former first lord of the admiralty.

Hobson became governor and Auckland the colony's capital city. The new capital flourished. It established its credentials as the centre of New Zealand's embryonic civilisation by staging its first official execution, building a gallows and hanging a seventeen-year-old Maori called Maketu who'd murdered a family in the Bay of Islands. By 1900 it was the biggest city in the land.

Yet it suffered from a chant that was later to become its unofficial anthem: *Location, location, location.* Down south, Middle Islanders did not like their new capital. It was just too far away. If you lived in Otago, for example, it could (and did) take months to reach Auckland in time to take your seat in the General Assembly. Modern controversies over aircraft seats and the cost of Crown cars fade beside the expense of getting those early MPs to parliament. Whole ships were hired. Government records show that politicians might take two months to reach Auckland by sail, and even by steamer the voyage could last twelve days.

Once there, according to one account, 'the problems were not necessarily over. One ship anchored a mile offshore, and small boats ferried in the parliamentarians who were set down close to the beach and had to wade through mud and stones to reach land. Then they had to carry their bags for half a mile along the beach until they were met by carriages to take them to their accommodation, six miles away in town.'

New Zealand's first parliament started with a bang — twenty-one of them, in fact, as the guns at Fort Britomart gave the budding politicos a salute — and ended with a whimper, for all was not well within the new capital either. It found itself with embryonic issues which were later to become immoveable parts of the national legend. First, it was strapped for cash. Second, the settlers, or farmers, wanted to control what money there was, and they wanted more land too. That meant controlling the young government as well. Third, the new capital was resented from the outset, especially in the south. Not only was Auckland hard to reach, it was seen as an outpost.

Middle Island, as it was then, was well named, for at that time it was the true centre of New Zealand civilisation: it had the power, the money and most of the people. Not for the last time, a thought bubble hovered like the long white cloud over Te Wai Pounamu: Auckland be damned. The city took members of the new General Assembly away from their farms, pulled them out of their businesses, for long periods of time. That was a serious defect in the colony. What right did Auckland have to call itself the centre of power? Why should the new governor live there? Why should the south be subject to its laws and rulings?

Hobson did not survive the struggle. Already seriously ill, he was killed by a final stroke in 1842, just a year after he'd established the second capital. He was only forty-nine. His capital city outlived him by little more than a decade. By 1854, members of the young government were seriously fed up with their northern location. What was needed, everyone agreed, was somewhere more accessible. In 1856 it was decided that the General Assembly would not meet in Auckland, but 'in a more central position'. Politicians argued that the seat of government should be moved to 'somewhere upon the shores of Cook Strait', meaning, effectively, that the capital had to be either in Wellington or Nelson, although several other places were suggested. Both Picton and Havelock came into the reckoning.

Nelson's voice was strong. A fine city, most appropriate, most convenient, said its advocates. It was right in the centre of things, being in the geographical middle of New Zealand but also, significantly, on Middle Island, the dominant force in the New Zealand economy. The proposal was defeated, but then, so was the notion that the assembly might meet in Wellington instead. Geographically, the New Zealand parliament was in limbo.

Members of the assembly had another go at substituting Nelson for Wellington. The vote went nineteen to fourteen — against. Not for the last time, the peoples' representatives simply could not make up their minds. So they decided to pass the buck, not to someone within the country, but clear across the Tasman to Australia, thus beginning another great New Zealand institution: the Overseas Experts.

The experts on this first occasion, the Australians, were thought to be not just impartial, but highly capable: Francis Murphy, speaker of the Legislative Assembly of Victoria; Joseph Docker, a member of the Legislative Council of New South Wales; and Ronald C. Gunn, a former member of Tasmania's Legislative Council. They were charged with finding a central position for the new capital, somewhere on the shores of Cook Strait. The Australians took the job seriously or, at least, as seriously as anyone could when offered what later became known in media and political circles as a junket.

They travelled here, they journeyed there. They inspected Wellington. They sailed through Queen Charlotte Sound and had a good close look at Picton and Blenheim. They viewed Pelorus Sound and voyaged right up to Havelock, then scarcely a town at all, its glory days as home to space scientist William Pickering and Ernest Rutherford, father of nuclear physics, still ahead. They probably made the right decision there: at last count, Havelock's population was less than 500, and declining.

The Australians' two-page report on their extensive, expensive journey dismissed the southern options and summed up their view in a sentence: 'Having thus made themselves acquainted, as far as was practicable, with the character and capabilities of both shores of Cook's Strait, the Commissioners have arrived at the unanimous conclusion that Wellington, in Port Nicholson, is the site upon the shores of Cook's Straits which presents the greatest advantages for the administration of the Government of the Colony.'

A decision made for the convenience of lawmakers, but how woefully inconvenient it proved to be for them. Instead of

Nelson's sun, they got Wellington's dank. Instead of Nelson's warmth, they got Wellington's chill. Instead of Nelson's balmy breezes, they got the northerly and, when that wasn't blowing, the southerly. The Australians didn't have to live there, of course. They packed up, collected their cheques and went home, leaving New Zealand to adjust to its new political geography.

Auckland threatened to secede from the new nation, not for the last time. Empty as it may have been, that threat may have started yet another New Zealand tradition: no one south of it took Auckland seriously.

In 1865, the windy city became New Zealand's capital. Nelson missed out. Crown limousines did not sweep magisterially through its streets. Embassies did not line its avenues, nor did foreign dignitaries commit their arcane blunders here. Wellington took the prizes: parliament, Government House, King Dick statue and all.

Nelson merely contributed the Takaka marble façade of the parliament buildings, wiped its hands of the whole business, and got on with life. A rather pleasant one. No one wept then, or weeps now. Lamentations might have been heard at the time, but they were subdued. Nowadays, Nelsonians count their lucky stars.

What might have happened to them? The Wellington political scientist Stephen Levine glided through the question in his book *New Zealand As It Might Have Been* by looking at it through the eyes of the then prime minister, Helen Clark. She was gazing out of her Nelson office window on a superb day, awaiting the arrival of her deputy Michael Cullen and his splendid Nelson suntan. She pondered what might have been: they both might have been stuck in glum Wellington. Oh, the horror. The horror! Readers imagining a suntanned Michael Cullen might have thought much the same thing.

Which part of Nelson might have accommodated the parliament buildings? There could have been only one place for them, of course. Trafalgar Street is Nelson's main street, running up to Nelson Cathedral. The cathedral is important. It gives Nelson its city status and makes it both the oldest city in the South Island and the second oldest in New Zealand. It started out as a simple wooden building on a plot the Anglican Church bought at the top of that hill in 1848, looking directly over the city to the sea. Anglicans were always canny in real estate.

Maori had used the site for a fortified pa until it was grabbed by the New Zealand Land Company, whose main interest in Maori was how best to fleece them in the service of the mainly absentee speculators they represented. They had planned a settlement on 81,000 hectares of land, which they'd carve into a thousand allotments then sell them (for considerably higher prices than the land they'd sold in Wellington) and split the money between funding more immigration and their own bank accounts, for which they'd allocated a dividend of about 20 percent.

The profits depended, of course, on how much they'd pay the Maori owners. The Land Company's William and Arthur Wakefield claimed to have bought the land for axes, a gun and gunpowder, blankets, biscuits and pipes, or, in short, next to nothing. It was also agreed that the Maori vendors were to be given back a tenth of the total land 'bought' from them, more than 8000 hectares. That never happened. Maori were not allowed to live on their tenths, or cultivate them. Instead, the government leased that land to settlers, promising to invest the income in Maori. That never happened either, at least until the end of the century, and even then Maori got only half the income the land had earned. The so-called tenths were whittled down to less than twentieths. Worse, pa, cultivated ground, mahinga kai (natural resources) and urupa were all included in the areas taken by Pakeha. This injustice lasted for the next century and a half, until the Waitangi Tribunal gave the iwi involved some $200 million in cash, land and assets in compensation. Still, of the more than 8000 hectares promised as 'tenths', Maori were given back control of only 1400 hectares.

In the meantime they were, to say the least, irked. Settlers moved in despite their dubious hold on the land, though they were many fewer than the company expected. Worse, the company's rural land 'holdings' in Nelson fell well below target. The company needed more land and it looked to the Wairau Valley near Blenheim. Arthur Wakefield claimed to have acquired land there from the widow of a whaler who'd bought it from the Ngati Toa chief Te Rauparaha. The chief disagreed, and history now recognised Te Rauparaha as the wrong man to diddle. British and Maori clashed at Tuamarina, north of Blenheim. The British shot first. They killed Rongo, wife of Te Rauparaha's nephew Te Rangihaeata, another bad mistake. Four Maori and twenty-two British were killed in the subsequent confrontation, whose name was once the 'Wairau Massacre' but has since morphed into the 'Wairau Affray'. Some of the British were executed after surrendering. They included Arthur Wakefield. Governor Robert Fitzroy investigated and blamed the British.

On the other side of the ranges, Nelson took fright. Alarmed citizens sought refuge in the most likely spot, the top of the nearby hill, which had been chosen, of course, by Maori as the best spot for one of the pa whose sites had been so neatly stolen by the invading British. The newcomers returned the land to its former use: as a fortified village, with barracks, makeshift hospital, post office, courthouse, even a newspaper office. The Maori path was trampled smooth by frightened settlers seeking refuge each night.

The locals' fear slowly receded and eventually the Anglican Church was able to buy the site, for much the same reasons as its previous occupants wanted it: the hill commanded the land. They started out with a simple wooden building and enlarged it and in 1858 Queen Victoria by royal charter established Nelson as a bishop's see, thereby making Nelson a city. The old wooden place, added to here and there, lasted until an earthquake damaged its spire in the early twentieth century; it was condemned a few years later. A fine new cathedral was started in 1925 and, interrupted by the Great Depression and the Second World War, grew in fits and starts until, in the late 1950s, the church determined to finish it with a concrete tower.

Well, shades of the ruined Christchurch Cathedral post-earthquake. Howls of protest enveloped the hill. They might not use it much, for such was the fate of cathedrals everywhere, but Nelson people didn't want their cathedral mucked around with in such a manner. Despite all that, the tower was finished as planned. The trampled track up the hill was replaced first by wooden steps, which became greasy and started to rot. The Nelson philanthropist Thomas Cawthron, who paid for city fixtures ranging from the Rocks Road ornamental chains on the waterfront to the renowned Cawthron Institute, produced his cheque book. He footed the bill for new granite steps, which became as much a part of Nelson life as Tahunanui's beach.

They climbed in grand fashion from the top of Trafalgar Street to the cathedral in double and single flights with landings, stone walls and pillars, and decorative metal capping. The whole thing was as much a construction as the cathedral above, and, alas, rather more used. During the First World War, soldiers were farewelled from the steps, often forever, and those who returned were welcomed home and decorated there. Funds were raised on the steps for New Zealand's contribution to the war, which of course led to more farewells, wounded, decorations, etc, enlivened by annual flower festivals.

Two royal visits, in 1920 and 1927, brought crowds to the granite steps. In 1939, the Second World War broke out and the whole sad business did the rounds again on the cathedral steps. When Sergeant Alfred Hulme was awarded the Victoria Cross for leading counterattacks against the Germans in Crete and waging his own war against German snipers after the death of his brother on the island (he was thought to have killed more than thirty of them, sometimes disguised as a German himself, before being seriously wounded), his medal was presented on the cathedral steps. (Hulme's contribution to the New Zealand legend continued after the war; his son Denny became a Formula One world champion).

The end of the war in Europe and the later victory over Japan were celebrated by huge crowds on the cathedral steps, and they turned out again to cheer Field Marshall Bernard Montgomery during his victorious tour of New Zealand and Australia. Queen Elizabeth II and the Duke of Edinburgh walked all the way down the steps to Trafalgar Street in the 1950s. The royal visit attracted a huge crowd, even by the standards of a day when such visits whipped loyal crowds into frenzies of flag-waving.

Centennials and anniversaries also had their day on those steps. They'd been the gathering place for protests, notably the reaction to the government's decision to close the Nelson railway line. When the government abandoned its plans for a cotton mill at nearby Stoke in 1962, a distraught public gathered in their thousands on the cathedral steps. The 1981 Springbok tour brought nationwide protests and the cathedral steps became their focal point in Nelson. The steps were covered with protesters again the following year when the campaign to make Nelson nuclear-free was truly taking off; the city was declared nuclear weapon–free in 1983.

So it went. If you wanted to argue over society's evil du jour, condemn the government, vent your dismay over anything from dairy cows to global warming, the cathedral steps were the place to do it. When it was time to meet friends, mourn the dead or sing carols, you congregated on, yes, the cathedral steps. Far from reflecting a worried or an angry community, such events portrayed a concerned one.

In fact, the steps perform all the functions of a southern parliament right now. They are de facto parliament grounds, like Christchurch's Cathedral Square, Dunedin's Octagon, Auckland's Aotea Square, but with that special Nelson flavour: gentler, more decorous. They are also revered, preserved and protected by a high classification awarded by both Nelson City Council and New Zealand Heritage. And they are the city's best-known feature, not counting the sun.

Can a mere set of steps be all of these things? Well, yes. And more. They sum up this city: both argumentative and complacent, socially aware, smug, politically savvy, rooted, secure, beautiful, a version of the capital, in fact, without its acerbity.

*

Nelson might once have seen itself as isolated. Perhaps some in the city still did see it that way, and revelled in it. A friend who lived there for many years finally moved away because, he said, 'When so many people say to you, "They'll have to carry me out of here in a box," you know it's time to go.' Yet Nelson is much more about the people who stayed rather than those who left.

In his book Stephen Levine had Helen Clark welcoming the more balanced national development brought by the choice of Nelson as capital. Might that have been true? Whatever the case, with the possible exception of a few overblown egos in local government, Nelson does not regret missing out, not one bit. They are doing all right as they are, thank you.

Nelson is a city by name and a town by nature and, some claim, by ambition. When the regular (modest) population projections are published, there are various reactions. The first comes from local councillors who, like politicians everywhere, pat themselves on the back for their own perspicacity while fending off critics by wringing their hands over what should be happening but is not. The public meanwhile complain that the councillors are not planning properly. What of stormwater? New roads? Public transport? Housing? Dazzling new developments such as floating villages? One side argues the place was being constrained by what some in the city called the 'horse and cart brigade', another that too many people mean the place is going to the dogs, that it would be a new Queenstown if local people did not awake to the danger.

Nelson still owns the sun. National Institute of Water and Atmospheric Research (NIWA) figures put it at the top of the sunshine league, usually followed by Blenheim. Auckland and other main centres lag far behind, the capital city Wellington almost invisible in the gloomy distance.

Those figures might one day be turned on their heads, of course. Climate change has the NIWA temperature tables steadily rising: 'the hottest year on record' is becoming a cliché. Being at the top of the league might one day be less desirable than being at the bottom, but, in the meantime, Nelson simply sits prettily in the sunshine.

Some say that the city is too isolated ever to have been a capital city. They say Nelson is cut off, with just one road in and one out. That when you get in there you can get stuck. In fact, Nelson sits at the junction of three routes, or more accurately, three and a half. One trickles towards the west, reaching Golden Bay and halting at the base of Farewell Spit. It's an uneasy thoroughfare, for it traverses Takaka Hill and, even in good form, is slow and windy. And it's often not at its best, especially in the heavy rain becoming more common as the weather changes. Slips on the steep faces sometimes cover the road, forcing traffic onto bulldozed tracks that drivers of the early bullock carts would have recognised instantly.

Another route runs off to the southwest, down to Murchison and on to either the West Coast or over the Lewis Pass into

Canterbury. The half-route is precarious, a largely forgotten route that still clings to maps. It runs over the Wairau Pass to the south of the city, once used by Maori then by early drovers moving stock between Nelson and Canterbury. Part of it is still quite a good road between Nelson and Tophouse, site of the first of the nineteenth-century accommodation houses that formed a line down the centre of the island on the old stock trail to Christchurch, each designed to be a day's stock drive from the next. Beyond Tophouse, the road dives into country that is as wild as it was one and a half centuries ago. It passes the Rainbow ski field and crosses Rainbow Station on a toll road open to the public for only a few months each summer, eventually arriving at Hanmer Springs.

The main route south, though, heads northeast, climbing over the Whangamoa Saddle, one of New Zealand's legendary hills, to Havelock and then Blenheim. From there it heads south to Kaikoura and down the coast to Christchurch. When the Kaikoura earthquakes severed State Highway 1 north and south of Kaikoura, the then prime minister John Key announced that the government was examining alternative routes before attempting the massive task of clearing the coastal road. The Rainbow route bounced back into play. Its proponents argued that it would cost a mere $4 billion, placing highway reconstruction squarely in the realm of the golden fleece. When the coast road was re-opened, they said, it could be used as a freight road, clearing trucks off State Highway 1 and perhaps connecting with yet another possibility, a Whanganui to Motueka ferry service. In the meantime it would knock about one hundred kilometres off the inland route to Nelson through Murchison.

It didn't happen, of course. Instead, most of the inland Christchurch-through-Murchison road was used as a detour around earthquake-stricken Kaikoura, seriously beating up the lesser-used parts of that route.

Did any of this make Nelson more isolated than Wellington, lying in the jaws of its dog's-head promontory at the dead-end of its own island, barking into the teeth of gales that gashed Cook Strait from one direction then another? Nelson boasts a good harbour, Nelson Haven, which has accounted for only one notable shipwreck. The New Zealand Company immigrant ship *Fifeshire* arrived on 1 February 1842, and the date became Nelson's Anniversary Day. The *Fifeshire* rather ignominiously drifted onto a rock at the harbour entrance as it left, and was wrecked. No one died.

The rock became the star of the affair. It had been named Arrow Rock after the first immigrant ship, which had negotiated the entrance successfully. After the *Fifeshire* affair, it became known as Fifeshire Rock. One celebrated a success, the other a disaster. The two names co-existed quite amicably until Nelson City Council was paying for a new stainless steel-and-aluminium information panel on the waterfront. Which name to use? It opted for Arrow Rock. But in in the public mind disaster usually trumps success, and Fifeshire Rock remains popularly used.

Nelson's big transport problem is the lack of a railway. Since the 1860s, Nelson people have wanted trains to link them to the rest of the South Island and at one time they had part of a line. That story still angers citizens with longer memories, for despite more than eighty years of effort it ended up being a railway to nowhere.

The line was intended to run from Nelson to Inangahua Junction, where it would meet the Main Trunk Line. The dream started well. Work began on the line in 1873 and by 1876 it ran for thirty kilometres to the southwest of the city, almost reaching a place called Foxhill. There it paused while the national economy took a breath. When work resumed, the line was extended to Kohatu, now a junction where the roads to Nelson and Motueka meet, marked by a solitary pub.

Then, onwards! A road and rail bridge took the line across the Motueka River to a tiny place called Tadmor, hidden in a valley squeezed between the Hope and Pinchback ranges. This was a slow train, quite possibly the world's slowest. It had taken thirty-three years to get to this point, and it was still only sixty-six kilometres from Nelson, a rate of two kilometres a year.

Still, the railway pushed on through places that are just names, even on my elderly atlas, and invisible on the ground — Kiwi, Tui, Kaka (the nation busily eliminating said species all the while) — to Glenhope, back on today's main road, still just visible as a settlement. Construction was then halted by what modern time-tablers would call 'technical difficulties', namely the First World War.

It was 1920 before work began again and this time a determined effort took the line through to Kawatiri, where the road forks today, the southern branch heading through the mountains towards Blenheim. The railway people built a tunnel, and bridges, and they were so close to joining the main line at Inangahua that they could smell the coal. The end was (quite literally given subsequent events) within spitting distance.

By then, preliminary formation work on the line was nearing Murchison, 136 kilometres from Nelson, and the first train was expected to reach the town in mid-1931. Trains were operating along the finished line to Glenhope, carrying passengers and freight, and everything looked rosy until the government (whose foresight, to give them some credit, was overshadowed by the Great Depression) suspended work. Workers went on their Christmas holidays in 1930 in high spirits, but Christmas set a pattern that was to become common in the twenty-first century: early in the following January the workers were all made redundant. The government canned the railroad.

The line struggled on. Rail traffic continued to use the existing track until the government announced it was to be abandoned altogether. Four hundred people packed the last train to Glenhope in 1954, which wasn't quite the last because it won a stay of execution until the following year, finally closing in September 1955.

Oh, the fuss! Nelson's people took to the cathedral steps in protests, which were to make a young socialist, Sonja Davies, famous: she was one of nine women arrested and fined for sitting on the railway at Kiwi (I challenge you to find it) and stopping a train. (She became a trade unionist and tireless peace campaigner then a Labour Member of Parliament and third winner of the newly created Order of New Zealand.) A 12,000-signature petition went the way of petitions generally, and disappeared.

For a long time afterwards you could trace the railway through Tapawera, down the valley to Tadmor and to Kawatiri, where visitors can still inspect a tunnel and public walkway and wander through the loneliest station outpost in the country and wonder about this epic project. Kawatiri has only a platform, but a lonely station building still stands in a paddock, once its station yard, at Glenhope. Ancient rolling stock, sections of line and old station buildings are preserved in Nelson's Founders Park. In 2016 the tunnel through the Spooner Range near Nelson, one of the first great projects of the railway builders, reopened to the public. But, except for periodic efforts to rebuild parts of the old line, that was that. Railway-wise, Nelson remains out on its own.

*

Nelson basks in the admiration of visitors, but to me one of the mysterious things about the place is how few people live there. Actually live there, as opposed to wanting to.

The most comfortable city in the land has the best weather too, yet the population stands at around 130,000, divided almost equally between the city and the surrounding Tasman District, which includes the towns and settlements out on the plains and over Takaka Hill in Golden Bay. People are hardly packed into this golden land. In the first half of the twenty-first century, the population is predicted to grow by around 30 percent, but that still leaves plenty of room for locals.

People live longer here, and this isn't just local councillors boasting, it's official. Statistics New Zealand has declared that longevity-wise, Nelson is tops. Its citizens have the longest lifespan in the country. In fact, if you want to live longer, it's worth considering moving to the South Island (if you're not already there), for Canterbury, Marlborough and Otago are also near the top of the list. The only North Island region among the five leaders is Taranaki.

It's not Nelson's climate that promotes longevity so much as good housing, health and education. Health, wealth and happiness are the keys to a long life, and being Pakeha helps too. It's evident that Nelson does well in all departments.

Richmond, which looks like an outlying suburb of Nelson but is in fact the capital of the Tasman District, counts 21 percent of its population over sixty-five; the national average is around 14 percent. The population of the Nelson-Tasman region is considerably older than the New Zealand average, with fewer younger people.

The word 'golden' is used a lot around Nelson: golden years, golden times. Which made me wonder whether an aging nation could be Nelson's golden fleece. After all, 'capital' is heard often in this town, as in 'craft beer capital', or 'berry capital'. Could it also be the retirement capital, the golden age being the golden fleece?

The elderly are not just a renewable resource but a steadily growing one as the population ages and people live longer. Here they live in their own enclaves, the retirement villages whose immaculate houses and perfect little gardens spread tidily over the land.

I ventured into one of them and was immediately lost in its curly streets. The place had character, of a sort. It was porticoed and pillared and there was lots and lots of brick with, outside each home, a rather beautiful front garden. Yet if you multiplied each by 100, or by 200 (someone must keep count, but the place to me seemed endless), its character was a little, well, strained. How did people find their way around? Find their own home amidst the many? I once knew the mother of apparently identical triplets who when asked how she could tell them apart insisted that it was no trouble at all, because each was completely different. Residents here would probably have said the same thing had I been rude enough to ask them. But to me every bit of it was the same as the next, all set among apparently interminable curves and sweeping streets, driveways of identical homes filled with identical cars, Fits and Jazzes and Aquas and Corollas, and I was well and truly lost.

Like most male drivers, I was reluctant to ask for directions. But after winding this way and that, heading in the right direction and finding it was the wrong one, driving in circles for an aeon or two, I could see I was going to grow considerably older here unless I found a way out.

I asked a woman who looked as if she knew where she was. She did, she said, and advised I should stay on this street and drive on (I felt that with a little prodding she might have added 'without further ado') so I obeyed and found myself at exactly the same point I'd entered at. It was a lesson, but I wasn't sure in what. This was only one village in a region full of them.

Retirement villages lay in colonies. Nelson was not only a great place to live, it seemed a fine place to die also, although the city did its best to stave off the day of reckoning: signs on busy streets warned traffic to beware of the elderly (possibly because in my own experience the aged could get ratty when roused). The enclaves looked prosperous, and well kept, and inviting, even if some of them resembled the fortified settlements of Nelson's colonial past and seemed a tad barren: you were free to enter but you felt under scrutiny and what life there was appeared to take place behind the linen drapes.

THE PLACE IN THE SUN

National surveys always establish Nelson as the best place in the land to retire to: lovely climate, good health services, efficient public transport, nice communities, even if high property prices could bring on a heart attack in the unprepared. The only place that might be better, according to the experts (I am taking no responsibility for this) was Marlborough. Blenheim lacked the seascapes, the history, the grace and the charm, but apart from that was probably quite all right too.

That evening was fine, and warm, and quiet. I went back to my motel, put the beer firmly back into the fridge, did a few press-ups and went for a lively walk, staving off my own retreat to a retirement village for, oh, I don't know, an hour or two. Then I sat on the cathedral steps with rich cream masonry all around me, stones which seemed to have been smoothed by their history, and thought that, golden fleece or not, growing old in Nelson would be rather nice.

*

One summer morning long ago, I woke up in a tree. It seemed to be part of an enchanted forest. A shimmery mist lifted off the grass. The early morning light squeezed through in soft grey, like the set of an old film.

A woman stood below my tree. She seemed unsurprised, and called up to me. I said hello back, and asked had she seen a Scotsman? He was asleep under the hedge, she said. I climbed out of the tree, stiffly, for, like most adventures, sleeping in trees was uncomfortable.

A figure rose from under the hedge, studied as an actor. 'Oo-ah,' it said, not just an opening line, but a closing one too, for Alex the Scotsman was never loquacious. He hadn't said more than three words at a time in the six days I'd known him. 'What's for dinner?' Or, 'Want a beer?'

I'd been wandering along Motueka's main street. A car had pulled alongside and the driver had leaned over to call through the window, 'Know any jobs?'

A job was just what I was looking for. The Motueka Town Clerk himself had told me there was plenty of work around during that long-ago summer. I'd written to him, along with the town clerks of other South Island towns: Ashburton, Geraldine, Mosgiel, Kaikoura, Murchison, Hokitika. I'd decided that small towns were the real New Zealand. I'd seen the movies: *To Kill a Mockingbird*, *The Chase*, *In the Heat of the Night*. Small towns were friendly, intimate places, usually sunny. They held the secret of life, unlike the metropolis I lived in, Christchurch.

What were the chances of a job that summer? I asked them all. Kindly town clerks in Ashburton, Geraldine and Motueka replied that the chances were very good. The Ashburton man even suggested that I call in and see him and he'd sort something out. Motueka appealed most, with Geraldine a close second. New Zealand's passion for beer and cigarettes was being cultivated in Nelson. Hops and tobacco were then mainstays of the regional economy. They needed pickers.

The cool verandas of the town were inviting. They suggested an oasis, a sanctuary. It was said never to rain there. The sun shone all day, and possibly all night too. So Motueka it was, that summer. I threw a sleeping bag and a change of clothes into my old Ford coupé and drove out of Christchurch on the Main North Road, through Woodend, and Kaiapoi, and Amberley, where a traffic cop on a motorbike stopped me, peered at the warrant-of-fitness I'd borrowed from a friend with a moped, and told me I'd need to get a real one, which I promised to do, just as soon as I could get my front mudguards welded up — they were in the back, see? He knew a decent young fellow when he saw one, and waved me on.

I turned off State Highway 1 at Waipara, stopping at Frog Rock, which was compulsory, drove through Waikari, past the beautiful old pub in Hurunui, over the Lewis Pass, stopped at Maruia Springs for a hot dip, continued on to Murchison, branched off at the Kohatu Hotel and followed the winding road along the Motueka River valley.

And now here was Alex, an ally.

'Hop in,' he said, and in I hopped. We drove around for a while, then Alex said we'd never find a job that way, and he turned into the next driveway we passed.

A woman answered his knock on the door. She invited us in, or Alex at least, for he was a man in his mid-twenties, tall, well built, good-looking, with that beguiling Scots accent. She seemed a little surprised when I crept in after him.

She gave us tea and scones, and told Alex about her sister-in-law up the road.

'Is that right?' he said, and, 'Oh, it happens,' and, 'What a shame.'

Then she said that the surrounding farmers were always looking for workers at this time of year and she'd telephone around, and she got us a job first call.

'Thanks very much,' said Alex.

It was a tobacco farm owned by a South African called Graeme Hogg. He showed us our hut — two rooms, a little kitchen and a bathroom — and told us we'd start at eight o'clock next morning.

So we did. Our job was to hoe the rows of tiny tobacco plants. The work was boring, and we'd hop off to the pub on the stroke of five, Alex buying because I was only eighteen and looked twelve. In the evenings we worked in the tobacco factory for extra money.

Young persons at that time agreed that New Zealand tobacco was not nearly as good as imported stuff, especially Marlboros, or the fancy gold and black Sobranie Black Russians favoured by the cognoscenti. But the government then required manufacturers to include 30 percent local tobacco in their products. So Motueka boomed, until in the 1980s everyone agreed that tobacco was an extremely dodgy product that could do users serious damage. The last commercial crop was planted there in 1995. Tobacco farmers disappeared from the landscape and their pickers' huts and kilns slowly rotted.

We cared nothing for health problems then, and our hopes and dreams were much more local in nature.

One night Alex had news, great news, making him unusually extravagant. 'There's this place called Tadmor,' he said. 'Six hundred women. No men. Dance, Saturday night. We're going.'

We knocked off hoeing that Saturday, washed, changed, climbed into his Vauxhall (he liked the Ford coupé but we agreed we'd need the extra room for all those women) and set off, eyeing the swathes of tobacco with professional eyes, waving at the tobacco workers sitting outside their huts in the late afternoon sun.

THE PLACE IN THE SUN

We drove back along the valley, over the pass at Stanley Brook, and turned off the road onto a smaller one that soon became shingle and seemed set on taking us into the mountains. Just when we were lost on this fools' errand, we came across a tiny hall, on its own, with a sign announcing that this was Tadmor. The hall was the loneliest building in the world. It seemed deserted. Recriminations filled the car. Six hundred women, our combined arses.

Then we noticed a light. Inside, a few people were moving chairs, organising a stage. Yes, there was a dance on that night, they said. We should come back in a couple of hours and things would be different.

We drove along the road, went to sleep in the car, and returned without much hope.

What a change! The hall was full and, yes, full of women. And hardly any blokes, who anyway were hanging around their cars with long brown bottles of beer. Against all odds, contrary to my life experience then and since, the story was true.

'Quick,' said Alex, eyeing the competition, 'let's go.'

In we went, and we needed every bit of room in Alex's Vauxhall that night.

The women were university students, and nurses, and anyone with a summer to spare. They were picking raspberries, and they lived in huts very like our own, except much cleaner.

It was the summer of my content. We started work on the tobacco earlier and earlier, until it was scarcely light when we went out with our hoes, and knocked off in the early afternoon so we could wash and change and take the two-hour drive and arrive in Tadmor when the women had finished work, made dinner and had some to spare.

One weekend Alex's car gave out. We took the Ford instead. We went to the dance and afterwards roared along the road with passengers filling the space behind the seat and sitting all over Alex, whose eyes flashed so brightly I scarcely needed lights, and such was the distraction that I took a bend badly and shot off the road, down a steep bank, and finished with the front wheels in a stream.

'Well, fuck me,' said Alex, uselessly, for when the screaming died down our guests took off into the night. We could see that the car was going to stay there for a while. So we walked back along the road to Tadmor, intending to bludge a bed in a hut, until Alex decided a hedge was a better bet, and I spotted a nearby tree and fell asleep beneath it. Night noises awoke me, rustlings, footsteps, phantoms on the march, and I climbed onto a friendly branch. In the morning cattle grazed and the woman appeared below.

The car was towed back onto the road a couple of days later by a tractor, and I went home for Christmas, and got a real ticket from the same cop, who didn't have enough room on the front of it to list all the ways the car broke the road code so wrote on the back as well, and when I returned those tiny tobacco plants we'd been hoeing were as high as our heads and we spent our days picking their leaves and our nights working in the factory, and the women finished the raspberries and left Tadmor, and when the season was finished I went to university and Alex disappeared, never to be seen again.

The tobacco itself never made much of an impression on me. Apart from some youthful huffing and puffing, compulsory for a young man of the world, I'd never smoked.

When I went back recently, things had changed a little. You used to smoke tobacco in the pubs and buy cannabis in their car parks. Now it was vice versa, more or less. Cannabis was de facto legal, but growing tobacco commercially was not, although you could still grow your own.

The tobacco farms which once covered the district in lush green all summer were gone. I went looking for my old farm, but it seemed to have disappeared under the local airport. The weatherboard house might have survived, but our huts had not. They had in fact been dire, and I didn't miss them.

There was no trace of the kilns where women had hung bunches of tobacco leaves on long staves and we'd climbed high into the interiors to put them on racks, gushing sweat in their heat. These structures were never built to last. They were made of wood and corrugated iron, and filled with hot air from heaters which sometimes ran amok and reduced them to a few charred sticks.

I drove south along the Motueka Valley Highway and — my God, that was the old tobacco factory, surely? It stood beside the road looking derelict (although it may not have been; small town New Zealand retains a traditional dislike of throwing things away). Was it ever filled with light and noise and, unbelievably now, laughter? Once a temple to the holy smoke, it looked like those photographs of smokers' lungs: grey, decrepit.

I went on up the valley. It was a blue day with a little mist and the valley seemed filled with apples and hops, the good old mixture of something healthy and something possibly not but appealing anyway. I looked for those old pickers' huts where people once sat on verandas on fine evenings and waved at passing cars. I saw one of them, on a bank, where a solitary man once sat in a wicker chair and we honked and waved because we felt the world was in good shape and he rose to his feet in a welcoming way and sank down disappointedly as we passed. Now his hut was a ruin, and not much of one.

Old kilns and packing sheds stood in paddocks like lonely sentinels of an unfortunate past. The baches where legions of pickers lived and made merry for much of every summer had become sleepouts, garages, garden sheds.

I drove through Ngatimoti, where there was an art display in a hall at one time packed with dancers on Saturday nights. This was once a thriving town and you could still see where it had been.

A local band was loading strange, giant instruments into vans, a wooden xylophone into a car boot, on their way to somewhere else. Here was the old store, there the garage. The Ngatimoti school now boasted ninety-nine pupils. Only one more and it would hit its ton.

I wanted to go to the St James Church, in a little valley above the settlement. It stood on a rise, sparkly white, its war memorial flanked by two examples of the German *minenwerfer*, a type of mortar that was among the most feared of weapons in the First World War, the name coming from the wobbly moan of the shells as they spread destruction in the trenches. On this sunny day, on the green, green grass, they looked like discarded kitchen appliances.

War memorials stand in small towns all around the country, sometimes the only survivors of the town, their long lists of names testament to a tragedy that stripped the countryside of its young men and decimated families and communities. The memorial in that neat little church in Ngatimoti was especially poignant, for among the names inscribed on it was Private Willie Ham, the first New Zealander killed in the First World War.

This was strange country. Even its names were odd. A couple of years before, with several friends, I had crossed the Orinoco bridge at Ngatimoti and travelled up a valley once farmed by families whose sons' names were engraved on that memorial. One of them, Hec Guy, wrote a postcard home before he was killed at Passchendaele, in October 1917, still New Zealand's blackest day. The card was never posted. But it resurfaced a century later, intact, and found its way home.

Further up that valley the road became a track overhung with huge rocks. We abandoned our cars and spent three hours crossing and recrossing the river until we stopped before a huge pool. This was the resurgence of the Pearse River. It welled up from beneath the mountains forming an immense bowl of deadly stillness before it spilled over the outer edge and reassumed the shape of a river. I'd never seen such a thing before and stood like a child before the immensity of it, the power.

Strange country, strange people. Not far from here lived the country's last tobacco farmer. More accurately, former tobacco farmer, although Lawry Jury was contesting the title. When almost everyone else had abandoned the trade, Lawry had hung on, stubbornly. He lived on a sheltered stretch of valley road at a place called Pangatotara near Ngatimoti, where the fat, juicy tobacco leaves rose high in the warmth. Most of the other tobacco farms had disappeared into apples, kiwifruit and hops, which I thought was to the good.

I met him in his home in the valley, in a tiny community made up of people who had stayed. It was a nice place in red and black brick, quite modest, the kind of New Zealand home you saw everywhere and felt at ease with. Everything had that patina of use and care, rugs and tassels, of a house lived in for a long time. Lawry was a man of a certain age, a little brittle, which was understandable given the topic, and a grey goatee that jerked as he grew indignant, which was quite often.

We sat at a round table with a glass top. Lawry's grandson sat quietly beside us, reading. Under the glass were family photographs interspersed with newspaper accounts of Lawry's travails. The boy had heard the story before, and besides, he'd lived through part of it. The tale was a long one, for Lawry bore a grudge.

His wife's family had been tobacco growers in the days when I drove up and down the valley. Lawry had lived in Hastings. When he and she visited the family home, Lawry fell in love with this quiet, green place beside the river. Apart from anything else, he said, he didn't have to lock anything. Long drop toilets. Different now.

The tobacco had disappeared from the valley but he stubbornly continued growing a patch of it on his six-hectare block. The odd thing, to an outsider, was that he was allowed to grow it. However, he wasn't able to 'manufacture' it; that is, make it into tobacco for, say, cigarettes. He could dry it for himself or sell it in leaf form, but if he went any further he was 'manufacturing', which was against the law.

Customs clearly suspected Lawry wasn't playing the game by the rules. They had put him under surveillance. Lawry knew this.

He said they had a camera on a nearby hill, which was discovered by a hunter mate of his. But, he said, he didn't care, because he was doing nothing wrong.

He claimed to be selling his leaf to people who didn't want to smoke it, for example the woman up the road who made a poultice out of the dry leaf and used it as a dressing for horse injuries. Others used it as an insecticide. 'You soak the leaf, the water goes brown, you spray it on the roses,' he said (earnestly).

He'd thought of tourism too: People stopped and looked at his tobacco. Who'd have thought it? He was happy to show them around. He thought of 'manufacturing' it; paying the duty and selling it to his visitors.

Meanwhile Customs was watching him. They alleged he had sold a forty-kilogram bale of tobacco to a man in March 2010. They'd followed the man to Auckland, where they'd uncovered an illegal tobacco operation. Lawry insisted that he didn't know why the man wanted his tobacco. Customs equally firmly insisted that he did know.

To put this into perspective, there is big money in black market tobacco. It was estimated that the quantity of tobacco involved here, sold legally, would have generated some $3.3 million in duty. That was Customs' stake in the business. As far as I could see, the question of public health did not arise.

One dark night the police and excise people came calling in strength. The family's golden Labrador heard them first and let off a fit of barking. Lawry leaped out with a spotlight. At that point, the telephone rang. It was a police sergeant from Nelson saying the people outside the house were police, Armed Offenders Squad included. (Lawry had a rifle, he admitted, for shooting rabbits and so on, and it was unregistered.) A helicopter chattered about.

Lawry's daughter-in-law and her six-year-old child lived in a cottage on the property, and they were taken in the dark to the main house perhaps a hundred metres away. I imagined the fear of that. Police everywhere in the night, police dogs, armed officers. They'd loaded his tobacco on a truck, almost five tonnes of it, and carted it off.

That was in 2010. They took him to court for the first time but not the last. The District Court convicted him. His tobacco was seized and a $6000 fine imposed. He appealed to the High Court. His conviction was quashed and the court ordered the seized tobacco to be returned to him.

All the same, Lawry was annoyed or, as he put it, 'really stuffed off. I hadn't done anything wrong. If I had, I'd take the smack on the hand or the boot up the arse. They were telling the judge I was the main supplier to the black market. Bullshit.'

But Customs was clearly aggrieved also. They appealed to the Court of Appeal, which now ruled that Customs was right, Lawry wrong. Customs kept the tobacco.

His voice rose and fell as he related his tale, like a ship on a stormy sea. His grandson read on. 'They kept it,' Lawry said. 'It went rotten anyway.'

Now, here was the most remarkable part of Lawry's story. He just would not let go. Why should they pinch his tobacco, he reasoned, without compensation? So he went to the Supreme Court, asking for a hearing. They turned him down. That should have been an end to it, but I suspected that if there'd been another course, any legal avenue, Lawry would have taken it.

I looked around me again. A comparatively small block of land. He grew maize here, apples on the other side of the road. A modest house. Nothing so much as hinted at the fortune he was spending on his legal fees. By now, he reckoned, they were more than $100,000 — he wasn't sure of the exact amount, he said. He'd wanted to fight on, he said, but his lawyer had advised against it, firmly. Possibly the expression 'good money after bad' had come up.

I'd thought I'd find him both chastened and poor, but he was neither. He *was* poorer, but unchastened. I said that if I'd been in his shoes, I couldn't have gone through all of that, even if I'd had the money. He said the money had kind of sneaked up on him. But he was an innocent man, and an aggrieved one, for by his account he'd done nothing wrong.

He could have pleaded guilty and paid a fine. He told me that even his lawyer had urged him to quit. Just pay the fine, his lawyer pleaded, it would be cheaper. If he'd called a halt much earlier, his legal fees then, his lawyer had estimated, would have been between $35,000 and $40,000. Even that sum would belt most people between the eyes, but now his goatee took on a stubborn slant. 'Once you've kicked the ball,' he said, and it's started rolling ... 'well, it just keeps climbing.' He was lucky, he guessed, his wife had a good job and he had an income and they'd paid off their two mortgages ...

Even so, that was a lot of money to raise?

'I sort of borrowed from friends and family,' he replied.

I wondered first whether a guilty man would spend all of that money for no result; and second, how the world had changed. The authorities once went after cannabis growers with guns and dogs and lots and lots of police. Now cannabis was all but a non-issue, and tobacco was the culprit.

But one thing was clear. Whether you smoked it, sprayed it or applied it to sick horses, tobacco would never again be this region's golden fleece.

I was in a sombre mood driving away from the house. The valley had always been a pretty, peaceful place in my heart, and on that level I didn't want to know what went on behind the curtains. Now I did know, and couldn't unknow.

Tapawera lay further down the road. It was a contented little town once, with a golden fleece of its own: forestry. The huge Golden Downs state forest had spread over surrounding hills and the government-owned Forest Service effectively ran the town. It owned half the houses and almost everyone in Tapawera depended on it for a living. Even if they didn't work directly for the Forest Service, their businesses relied on those who did. Tapawera became a well-equipped small town with all the proper amenities: a school, swimming pool, playgrounds, parks, halls. Its inhabitants lived in well-built, comfortable state houses. If Tapawera seemed a little bland, only visitors seemed to care. For those inside the town boundaries, life was pretty good.

Too good, as it proved. The reforming Labour government of the 1980s decided the forests would be better run by private enterprise, and sold them. Too bad about the redundant workers, and the town. Those who wanted to stay could buy their houses cheaply. Otherwise, the workers took their redundancy cheques and left.

People who worked in the privatised forests lived mainly in towns around Nelson and Motueka, and that was where the logs went too. Tapawera settled into the quiet life of a leftover town, a residue of fittings and fixtures nicely in place so that you came into it as you might a show home, all set to go but with nobody in residence.

Three decades or so on, it appeared to be a comfortable New Zealand small town, without pretension but with all amenities. You emerge from the tight roads of the Motueka Valley in one direction and brace yourself for the bush and the mountains in the other. The public toilets here are especially popular.

But today I was taking the route from those old days of the tobacco fields. I crossed the Motueka River and there, on the other side, intact, was the old headquarters of the Golden Downs State Forests. It was a lovely building with an alpine look that would have been entirely at home in, say, Mount Cook village, with a long peaky roof and even a peaky veranda.

The steps and the double doors looked inviting, although I wasn't sure who might be invited, for it appeared to be deserted. It was a monument to a New Zealand that once was, a well-designed, well-made, publicly owned building that was equally reminiscent of the New Zealand that replaced it: redundant.

The road ran past it and along to Tadmor, once my heart's delight, named by a character called John Stanley, who left his name on Stanley Brook just over the hill. He was a Bible scholar, and Solomon built Tadmor in the wilderness.

I found the bend my car had once failed to negotiate and the lovely green countryside looked much the same except there was no tobacco and ... I couldn't see any raspberries either. I passed the old Tadmor hall, but wait a minute ... where had it gone?

The store that stood beside it was there or, at least, its sign was, with no building attached. I drove past it again, looked this way and that. I was quite used to revisiting places and finding that this building, or that feature, had disappeared, often into some sort of black hole in my memory. But the hall wasn't fanciful. It had definitely been there, beside the old store where I'd bought pies, and now, like the store, it wasn't.

I went through an adjoining gate warning of dogs. In a large garden a beardie and a retriever romped. Neither seemed dangerous. A woman welcomed me inside her home and I asked her about the hall. It had been torn down, she said, such a shame. No one had looked after it (hard to believe of the close community I remembered) and it had simply deteriorated, died of neglect. Only the hardwood floor had been saved, and that had been sold.

All the community's effort had gone into the church and it was pristine, I should look at it, she said, and I did and it was. The church had no minister, for the Anglicans had abandoned it and rather than see the century-old church and its land sold as a lifestyle block locals had banded together, bought and restored it. The town's church society looked after it. Local people were still buried in the cemetery, with the emphasis on local, for people here did not want an influx of bodies from outside the district. Tadmor was now a thinner community, but at least it was still there.

The woman's name was Janet Moffitt. Her husband, Bruce, came down the road on his quad bike and took off his boots and came inside too. They talked of a town people had once lived in, with a railway station and a post office and a blacksmith's shop and a school over there behind those pine trees and the hall in the paddock by the big oak tree. Now people passed through on their way to the Wangapeka Track in Kahurangi National Park, which humped into the sky on the far horizon.

We sat in the sunny living room of their comfy old house with that feeling of lives lived, looking at photographs of family, of Bruce's mother who'd died at the age of 102, and ate the sultana cake Janet had made. She offered lunch and seemed genuinely disappointed when I declined, foolishly, because the cake was very good.

These people had been at Tadmor for a very long time and originally owned a big block. Their fortunes were tied to farming history: in the downturn that had followed the new deal of the late 1980s they'd sold their hill country for forestry and looked around for more flat land, only to find it priced out of their reach by the dairy boom. So they'd decided they'd be better off doing casual work and living off what they could earn from their remaining land, and that's what they did.

A few raspberry farms survived, but the pickers and their huts had vanished. What work remained was done by machines. Dairy farms covered the land now. Hop gardens were doing well, though; the demand for craft beer was seeing to that. It seemed to me that farming, usually a chancy business anyway, was made ever trickier by its need to follow urban fashion or, as it might otherwise be known, whim.

The Moffitts were not complaining. Where else could they go? They'd have to find a house between Tadmor and Tapawera, for a start, because no one in their right mind would want to leave the district. They didn't even have curtains on their windows because they didn't need them. When they went to town they couldn't wait to get home again.

And she gave me a jar of medlar jam, old-fashioned fruit from an old tree in the garden.

*

Many a wonder crop had flourished under the Nelson sun: blackberries and black raspberries, apples and almonds and apricots, cherries and Chilean guavas, gooseberries and green tea and grapes, feijoas and figs, kiwifruit and kiwiberries, passionfruit and peaches, quinces and kumquats. Hemp would do well too, given the success of its illicit cousin cannabis in this region. This place was a cornucopia.

But hops were truly Nelson. The huge expanse of them. The leaning post-and-wire structures supporting long strings of hops reaching skywards but looking as if they were growing upside-down and dripping into the ground.

German and English settlers planted the first hops here almost simultaneously with European settlement: they could travel halfway round the world, but by God, they weren't going to live in a dry country. They wanted something to ease their passage into the new land, and beer was always pretty good at that.

Hop gardens (a nice homely touch, that 'gardens') spread through Nelson, whose latitude was just right for hop-growing, with high sunshine hours, access to water and irrigation, not much wind, good-quality soils and enough frost in winter to set the plants.

Nelson beer was rated both best and worst by young men of a certain era. In those days there was a choice, a popularity contest wavering between the products of Dominion Breweries and New Zealand Breweries. Some liked Wards XXXX, others DB Bitter, the difference being negligible but always good for an argument.

But on Nelson's own beer there was a rare unanimity. We all gagged over Harleys. The beer was named after an early Nelson brewer whose remains were generally believed to lie somewhere in the vats. It was worth going to Nelson just to have a glass of it and join the discourse knowledgably. I don't know now whether it was genuinely awful or just one of the victims of pub talk.

The first real alternative that I could remember, at least, came from Nelson's McCashin's Brewery, Macs. Terry McCashin, former All Black, was credited with beginning the craft beer revolution. His brewery, like so many others, was taken over by the big boys, but the original, in Stoke, was reopened by the McCashin family in 2009 and Nelson's foaming reputation for craft beer was then firmly established. No one now would complain about Nelson beer.

Small breweries have spread throughout Nelson and over Takaka Hill into Golden Bay. Nelson is now said to have more craft breweries per capita than anywhere else in the country and you'd have to say the golden brew is also the region's golden fleece if, that is, you can stand the mixed metaphor.

It certainly looked that way from the road. I drove out through those splendidly named suburbs, Hope and Brightwater, to Spring Grove, and on through the little houses and retirement suburbs of your everyday Nelsonian and out into the green, green land beyond.

Here, for some 160 years, the Ealam family has farmed sheep and beef, grown tobacco and stone fruit, and even, a century before, some hops. More recently, they were dairy farmers and, as was well known, dairy farming was making a lot of money.

The sixth generation of the family arrived in the form of Cameron Ealam: dark, intense, young, about as far from the popular image of a cocky as you could imagine. The scion of the family was also involved in farming, but obliquely. He had been the agribusiness manager of a bank in Ashburton. He'd worn suits to work rather than gumboots and did not have to get up before dawn. Then he'd worked things out on his computer and some of them did not add up. Why would the family go on farming cows when a thirty-five hectare hop garden could make much more money than 110 hectares of dairying — fifteen times more in fact? Well, the answer to that one is that every farming family should have a banker son.

'I wasn't that excited about dairy cows,' he said. He convinced his family, and anyone knowing how firmly three generations of a farming family would be glued to their notions would understand what a feat that was.

Cameron was an unusual case, a numbers man who knew his number eight wire, literally. They'd keep some cows, build up a breeding herd so no one had to milk them. Maybe they'd run some sheep, for grazing came in handy on a hop garden.

He knew about craft beers. He liked them, for a start. The industry was booming or, as he said, going through its kick-up. Hops had what he called an excitement factor. He also knew that the more he spent on the conversion the longer the money would take to repay, so he chucked his job and, along with his family, did a great deal of the conversion work himself. He sank the posts, wired them up.

We talked in the barren interior of his smoko shed. He looked at home there (after all, he was at home). The new age of farming fitted him well, like one of those tight suits bankers wore. Outside, the wires of his new hop farm glinted in the sun. The wires ran along the tops of high wooden poles and they looked like some giant musical instrument, a celestial harp perhaps. The hop vines were just emerging from the earth, each a few centimetres tall. The family had not attached strings to the wires yet: that would come later, four people taking a couple of weeks to do the job. Then the vines would grow to the top.

Cameron's great achievement was what you'd only loosely call a kiln. It was nothing like those old, shapely affairs still crumbling in the landscape, looking like pyramids atop a slender box. This one was a massive green steel shed housing machinery that seemed perfectly capable of producing a rocket-ship: vast cogs, a web of pipes and vats and handles and controls, huge vents, conveyors to carry the vines, machinery to strip off the flowers, or cones.

He explained them all to me. I was, of course, instantly lost, although one of his calculations made an impression: the kiln had cost millions of dollars and was used only three or four weeks a year, during the hop harvest window.

Essentially, you loaded the hops into one end and they came out the other, separated from the dross, cleaned, dried, packed into something roughly the size of wool bales. The drying, machinery or not, remained an art form. Cameron was still working on that one, had done all right last year, he said.

I said my image of craft beers involved people in straw hats carefully picking hops under the blue, blue sky. He said that was all very well, but his was a highly commercial operation.

Oh yes, there'd be a downturn — every industry had cycles and, despite New Zealand's unique advantages, it was a niche product and the big growers in the United States and Germany could flood the market — but his confidence in his industry was clear enough. He liked his company's fine product. In fact, he was quite a connoisseur of craft beer. He recommended a bar in the city. In the interests of research, I spent the evening there.

*

The Waimea Plains are the region's fruit bowl. Not for them the standard New Zealand farming country, bare green paddocks specked with sheep and cattle. They are covered in fruit and berries and hops, fragrant with blossom in spring, verdant all year. They are the boysenberry capital of the world. If something grows, it will grow in Nelson.

The golden fleece is no abstract concept in this cornucopia. It has roots and leaves and bears fruit. The sun doesn't just shine on the crops, it graces them, fills them with life and style.

Too much sun perhaps. In an arid summer, and there seems to be a rising number of those, the rivers dry up, and the aquifers, and the plains take on a dangerously golden tint. Lack of water costs growers dearly.

They found an answer. In the hills behind Brightwater, the Lee River wound its way down the Richmond Range to the plains below. Why not build a dam high in the Lee Valley to store river water in a big lake for irrigation, and to replenish the aquifers?

The growers and the orchardists loved the idea. They even managed to convince an initially reluctant local council, the

Tasman District Council, to chip in around 40 percent of the cost on the basis of *Catch 22*'s Milo Minderbinder principle: 'What's good for M&M Enterprises will be good for the country.'

Who would carry the baby if it all went wrong? Ignore your experience, various spokespeople urged the public, and trust us.

They called their project the Waimea Dam. Not just public money would go into the project, but public property too: some of the territory the project needed was conservation land. But benefits would flow like the river water once did. Aquifers and rivers would be recharged, even if local environmentalists argued that they had been plundered because too much water had already been allocated to growers by, yes, the same public authorities that were now backing the dam.

The irrigators in turn argued that the project was essential to the local economy, that their objective was not just to deliver water to themselves but to secure the needs of the community. And climate change was having its way with the countryside.

Well, dams have been a controversial subject in this country ever since the nation stopped seeing the great dam-builders of the south as benefactors and started viewing them as desecrators instead. The Waimea Dam was no different. Broadly, business interests liked it and the public did not, especially not the damage to the environment and the bit about them paying for it. As far as they were concerned, those who saw the golden fleece arising from properly watered ground could take a jump.

Nelson was not short of environmentalists, even less concerned citizens, and they took to the streets waving good old-fashioned placards. Meanwhile costs were rising, as often happens, from around $70 million in 2014 when the idea first took root to well into nine figures and lifting gently into the stratosphere. Not only locals were making a large contribution: government or taxpayer money was yet to come.

Somewhere along the line the project was rebranded as the Waimea Community Dam, a nice public relations touch, if a little cynical. Sometimes I wondered whether I was searching for the golden fleece and finding the golden fleeced.

Well, I had to go and look at the site of this marvel, or perhaps disaster. The valley road was not well marked, nor did it look well used. It was narrow and shingly, and winding too, the hills first pressing, then squeezing. A few homes were spaced along the way, well apart and becoming fewer as the road climbed. People here seem to like solitude. The hillsides lower down had been cleared and replanted in pines.

I turned into a long driveway creeping along the hillside to a house, relaxed, with lots of verandas and decks, and outbuildings. It looked as if it had been designed especially for this spot, for people who liked living this way, and it snuggled into the landscape. Bikes and various objects lay around, a bag of bones hanging from a hook outside a little freezer, hi-viz jackets, lots of pottery.

There was a vege garden and a flower garden with a woman working in it. No, the dam didn't worry her, nor did she know much about it. Perhaps ask Jack Ford, a little further up the road?

The road narrowed, skirted a few rockfalls. Serpentine was quarried up here, crushed for fertiliser. There didn't seem much room. I worried about what might happen if a truck came round one of the myriad bends. Just when I thought the road could get no thinner, it did.

I turned off to a cluster of buildings: a house, a shed, a big garage with two classic cars inside, both 1950s Chevrolets, and one of them restored, splendid in red and white. Jack Ford proved to be a long, thin gent with a goatee beard and a wry sense of humour. Perhaps he needed it to live up here, although I'd found the lonely valley road, seemingly empty, was in fact full of life.

He didn't have much of a problem with the dam either, except for its cost, which was the more interesting because he was the project's nearest resident. Perhaps he had lots to do; the second Chevrolet was a work in progress.

His place was very neat and fenced off, everything in its place, the home of a man alone. Jack had been a gold-miner in the hills behind Golden Bay, working in freezing water and pumping gravel collecting below the rocks in the stream beds and sifting it for gold. His pump also directed warm air into his rubber suit. My brother had been a gold-miner in the same place doing the same thing, but he hadn't heard of the warm-air business and instead froze half to death.

Jack just wished the council had told him more about the dam, which would not have been difficult, he said, because so far they'd told him nothing at all.

I went down to the river. It was more a stream really, a pleasant little thing that ran through bush and over rocks with a proper rustle. Oh Cromwell, oh Clyde. Oh, those splendid drowned gorges. What would all of those people have thought of this?

Jack was a perfectly good fellow. He even offered to sell me one of his Chevs, the unrestored one, and I even contemplated it, briefly.

Sometimes I think the big problem with New Zealand's backcountry is that we have too much of it. If someone wants to duff it up a little, we scarcely notice.

CHAPTER SEVEN

The Bay at the End of the Rainbow

My parents loved camping. Every Christmas at our house in New Brighton, Christchurch, we'd pack the trailer, a huge wooden construction fitted with a canopy so that a couple of kids could sleep in it, then, usually, unpack it again, for something had always been forgotten. Or was it in there after all?

That was an easy mistake to make, because at least half the possessions in the universe went into that trailer: pots, pans, Tilley lamps, meths, kerosene, cooker, collapsible bunks (they usually collapsed in the middle of the night, turfing their contents onto the ground), folding furniture (likewise), a giant canvas groundsheet, bedding, clothes, sinks, water barrels, food, toys, books and whatever new things my parents, usually Hec, my father, had dreamed up during the year. It might be a boat (always homemade, usually not lasting very long until, oh happy day, Hec finally bought a new fibreglass one), or a crafty new piece of tent furniture, or a cunning little refrigerator, or the latest camp stove which worked only after much deliberation from my father and anxiety from my mother.

Then the six kids would be shoved into the Ford Zephyr, a packing feat that far surpassed the trailer, and the entire arrangement would trundle up the coast over ranges that read like an incantation: the Hundalees, the Whangamoas, through Nelson and over Takaka Hill into Golden Bay, then over a final hill to Totaranui. The last part was the worst, then: little more than a muddy track, always slipping, and bends so tight the trailer sometimes had to be manoeuvred back and forth to get around them. It took us back into Tasman Bay, technically, rather than Golden Bay, but we weren't picky.

The journey took twelve hours on a good day, and at the end of it six kids were released into the wild and ran screaming into the cold sea while Mum and Dad set about getting the tent up, a job that seemed to us best left to Merlin the Magician. There we stayed for three weeks or so before the whole process was reversed, which took longer because Mum and Dad sorrowed over leaving their favourite place in all the world and the kids were disgruntled about the long trip home with no green sea or golden sand or glorious bush or anything else worth living for at the end of it.

We grew up with Golden Bay imprinted on our souls. It seemed apart from the rest of the country, separated not only by the fearsome Takaka Hill and twelve hours of stolid driving but also by a leap of fantasy, a short in the magic circuit. Golden Bay was the axis of all things wonderful.

When I was married myself, and before we had any children, I wanted to show Sally this place. Except for a lovely old house used by groups, Totaranui, thank God, had no accommodation. Everyone else had to bring their own roof, caravan, or tent, or sleeper. So we stayed in a motel at Pohara beach at the edge of Golden Bay, and went over the hill to Totaranui, and swam in the green sea and sat on the golden sand and fell in love with the place all over again.

We passed a row of little cottages on the way. We thought them as wonderful a collection of traditional New Zealand baches as could be found anywhere in the land. They were perfect, each one eccentric, pretty, given entirely to a life on the beach. We poked around those baches and for Sally it was love at first sight. She stopped a passing jogger to ask about them, and the jogger turned out to own one of them, and even to have met Sally, fleetingly, in Christchurch (this was the South Island, after all). She also knew that her neighbour was considering selling his.

I've thought about that day often. Why did Sally stop that particular woman, who alone could have pointed us in the right direction? And at that exact moment find a perfect coincidence of circumstances? For, over the next twenty years, no other bach of the ten would be sold. They stayed in the hands of their owners and usually passed from generation to generation.

We contacted the owner, who lived in Christchurch, and, yes, he was indeed thinking of selling, and, yes, we were welcome to have a look at his house. So we did, and loved its eccentricities, its colour, its life — for we recognised immediately that this place was a living creature, adapting to its inhabitants and changing their lives in turn.

It sat beside Ligar Bay, whose ribbon of sand expanded to a plain at low tide, dotted with pools, threaded with rivulets. The sand warmed the cold sea as the tide swept in, and in the still, warm summer nights you could hear fish jumping from the water and descending with a small, comfortable 'plop'.

Very soon we understood one truth about true Kiwi baches: you don't really own anything. Usually they sit on land that is in public ownership, beside rivers or beaches, places where long ago (for they are always old) people came to swim, or fish, or just to laze somewhere beautiful. Slowly, whatever those people stayed in— a barrel or a water tank or a packing case or a hut — grew into something more permanent.

They grew with the people who lived in them and their lineage gave them their character. Their occupiers of the moment might think that a wall needed a window. So they took a hammer and a saw and, hey presto, a window appeared. Or a door. Or a porch or a bedroom or, oh, wonderful luxury, a bathroom. Long before recycling transformed from a word into a philosophy, baches were always made of something from somewhere else, never something new. And they were simple structures, for who wanted to spend their holidays building, or painting, or mowing lawns, or trimming hedges, or pouring concrete or staining decks or fixing things that didn't really matter?

All of this resulted in homes that were unique to their owners, as fitting and comfortable as old clothes. The baches had a simple beauty that architects tried to copy, usually unsuccessfully, because they did not submit to computer-aided design or even worse, planning regulations. They reflected not one life, but a collection of lives.

Ours had been built a half-century before we bought it by an artist who had lived there for the rest of her life. According to folklore, when frailty forced her out of her house she pulled the curtains in her nursing home and died.

She'd created an enchanted garden. To get to her bach, you crossed a little bridge over a stream that crooned over stones tuned by centuries of water. You walked through the trees she'd planted: palms, pongas, pukas, ti-trees, feijoas, avocados. Her path, paved with white shells, led to a wide veranda with a clear roof where you could lounge in an old wooden chaise longue warmed by the sun or charmed by the rhythm of rain or soothed by the conversation of water. The doors were yellow in green walls.

In its front a creaky set of French doors led to a tiny garden where the artist owner had collected rocks and grown trees and hardy plants as a living buttress against the sea, which hissed and rustled and pounded, a constant accompaniment to our lives.

Inside were long, cool rooms and smooth wooden floors that caressed bare feet. Every room had its own style and character, for the house had simply grown into something perfectly suited for living at the beach. A little room without windows led from a hallway, so mysterious it was always a surprise to open the door and rediscover it. Years after buying the house we were still finding hidden cupboards.

The windows came from other houses: a stolid suburban house from the 1930s here, a rather grand Victorian bay there. Sawn driftwood made shelves, preserving jars with their bottoms cut off made lampshades, oyster shells made lightswitch pulls. Shells were everywhere they could be: set in cement, stuck on tiles, glued to walls. A mirror in the bathroom had once been the rear-vision mirror on a truck. A stand of bamboo in the garden gifted the shower curtain rail, and racks, and handles.

Best of all were the treasures under the house or stacked in the garage: great glass flasks, vintage saws, fishing nets, wood carvings, boxes of photographs, old paintings. The most enthralling was a huge box of buttons with one particular prize, a little enamelled forget-me-not. It was a happy place, redolent of past lives and lending its grace and style to present ones.

Baches bring out the inner soul, the alter ego, what you hope is the real you. Ours had strange pictures and wooden seagulls and varnished storks and china fish and not a single plate, knife, fork, spoon, pot or lid matched anything else.

Life here seemed to have gone on forever, and we were quite certain it would continue forevermore: we were just part of a continuum.

*

One dark night just before Christmas 1642, in a place not far from our bay or even possibly right in it, Abel Tasman and his crew of Dutchmen had nosed into an encirclement of signal fires as the Ngati Tumatakokiri warned each other of the encroachment. That first contact between Maori and Pakeha ended badly: four dead Dutchmen and an unknown number of Maori killed. The first European name for Golden Bay was Murderers Bay. Captain Cook called it Blind Bay and the French explorer Dumont D'Urville named it Massacre Bay. When coal was discovered, it became Coal Bay, then, fortunately for posterity, someone struck gold.

When Abel Tasman visited, villages dotted the shores, where food was easily found, with pa on its headlands and strongpoints. I climbed over Taupo Point at the bay's entrance and thought of the generations who must have lived here in the bush, their whare clinging to the rocks that formed natural terraces and trenches. People in this pa must have watched Tasman's ship sail into the bay, wondered about the way of life it was about to spring upon them, and thought, hand me my taiaha!

When the local council decided to widen the road, a team of archaeologists in the vanguard dug four holes outside our cottage and discovered adzes in three of them. As a New Zealand bloke I recognised a kinship with those Maori: where the hell did I leave my adze?

Tasman left his mark in the form of an elegant white column overlooking Ligar Bay, designed by the émigré architect Ernst Plischke and built in 1942 on the third centenary of Tasman's visit. Three of the dead sailors were named, but the fourth remained anonymous, like every one of the Maori casualties. According to the monument the sailors were 'killed by the natives of this country', whose side of the story was still unknown.

Life in Golden Bay quietened down after that.

We swam, and lay on the sand, and walked in the deep green bush, and climbed over Gibbs Hill into Totaranui, or around the coast to Mutton Cove or Anapai, where years before my mother had been transfixed by the ancient newspapers lining a pioneer cottage; she'd stay there for hours, marvelling over the stories, the way they were written, and most of all the fact that she could come out of raw bush into this remote archive.

Our universe was defined by Farewell Spit on one side and Separation Point, the marker between Golden Bay and Tasman Bay, on the other. Near Farewell Spit, Puponga, the northernmost settlement on the South Island, still showed traces of the coal mines that had only closed in 1974. On the tidal flats behind them countless whales had died, for whale strandings were common here. Across the flats Farewell Spit embraced the bay.

We'd walk to Wharariki, the wild, grand beach once one of New Zealand's best-kept secrets, now full of young tourists taking selfies with the baby seals in nurseries amid the rock pools and streams, the islets and cliffs sculpted by their holes and havens.

Golden Bay was easily cut off and quite often was. There was only one road in, and it ran over Takaka Hill, a notoriously high, steep and windy road with 365 bends; one, as everyone in the bay knew, for each day of the year. It was a rocky hill, known sometimes as the Marble Mountain for the stone quarried there and used, most famously, for the parliament buildings in Wellington. Great caves, pits, sumps and squeezes hollowed its insides.

Any decent storm over Takaka Hill would send rocks and rubble tumbling down the hillsides, sometimes sweeping away the road itself. The last section of this fragile link to be built was a hairpin known as the Eureka Bend, 'eureka' being not so much a cry of joy as astonishment that anyone could traverse a sharp slope of sheer, unstable rock. Not surprisingly, the Eureka Bend was usually first to go but alas, not the last. The road could be blocked in a dozen places, and often was. Then the only way in or out was by sea, around Separation Point to Nelson or Motueka as the bay's forefathers had done, or by flying into the little airfield, or, for the truly desperate wanting to avoid either sea- or air-sickness, by walking over the Heaphy Track to the West Coast, a journey of four to six days. Charles Heaphy is thought to have been the first European to walk over Takaka Hill into Golden Bay.

The result of all this was the rather pioneer outlook of the people who lived in the bay. They had to fend for themselves, and they did. They were a delicate mix of conservative and liberal, farmers and merchants rubbing along with environmentalists and escapists, their shared qualities being independence and love of place.

We lived happily among them, so joyously I often wondered why we kept a house in more sober Christchurch. Perhaps we thought we should keep a grip on reality, however tenuous. Or thought our life in Golden Bay too good to be true, which eventually it proved to be.

*

At one end of our own bay lay an estuary separated by a rock breakwater forming a tidal harbour. Jack Cropp, who with Peter Mander won New Zealand's first yachting gold medal at the 1956 Olympics, had a boatyard there. He and his wife, Judith, lived in a point above it, on the site of an old Maori pa. The rickety piles where I kept my ageing wooden boat had been part of his boatyard. His old slip was marked out by rusting wire cable and railway lines. His workshop straddled the track above the harbour, and Jack held court there amid a wild collection of tools and huge pieces of equipment whose functions you might only guess at. Jack would tell you if you asked, but you could then write off the morning or even, sometimes, the rest of the day.

Jack loved talking. We'd sit among cabins and hulls and experimental bits of sailing boats and he'd talk about his life in Redcliffs, Christchurch, and people he'd known, and how he'd come to win a gold medal at the Olympics.

He'd raced dinghies with Peter Mander then, often in boats he built himself. Mander, blind in one eye, was already one of New Zealand's best dinghy sailors, and the pair had fought their way to the top. Photographs show Mander, tall and handsome; Cropp, smaller, bashful.

When the two decided to have a crack at the 1956 Olympics in Melbourne, yachting was hardly on New Zealand's sporting calendar. The nation had never had a team of sailors in the Olympic Games. And these two weren't even from Auckland. Jack's face would shake and his rather large nose wobble when he remembered the consternation.

There was no money, of course. They'd have to do it themselves. Jack heard of a wool store being pulled down in the city. He went along, bought a huge kauri beam for £10, took it home and built two boats from it. He and Mander took one of them to the Melbourne Olympics, and they won. It was New Zealand's first-ever sailing medal.

Jack's gold medal was huge, and around his neck it seemed to bend its fragile-looking owner. But he wasn't slight, just wiry. His medal was stolen once and later found pushed under the door of the Nelson courthouse. Perhaps the thief was remorseful, or stricken by the enormity of his crime.

One of the boats was still in his shed when I first met him, as it had been since 1956. He'd raffled the other, the winning boat, to raise money for a young sailors' training programme. It was then being restored over the hill in Mapua and the restorer had called to ask if he might perhaps have a sail plan so that he could remake the mast and sails.

Certainly, said Jack. When the man arrived at the bay, Jack said, 'I can do better than a plan.' He pointed to the rafters where two masts were stored, complete with booms and rigging. 'We took both of them to Melbourne,' he said. 'I can't remember which one we used, but they're identical.' The happy man went home with the original gear.

The big shed scarcely noticed the difference. Jack kept everything. His shed was a museum, and Jack was an artefact too, a living example of passing values, and we loved his decency, his humanity.

*

Our immediate neighbours in Ligar Bay were Garth, a teacher, and Lesley, a social worker, and their three sons, who we watched grow from children into young men whose characters were so well formed by their free lives in the bay I trusted them all completely. I could not think of the bay without thinking of them. They were part of the sunshine.

Yet they lived an insecure life, and so did we. It was the place we loved most in the world, but the house was always on the edge. Storms and high tides threatened. One westerly gale blew all day as if every force in the heavens had been loosed; the winds blew so hard they wouldn't let the tide go out and the lagoon remained half full. In the evening a shag took refuge on our front steps, tucking its beak under its wing as if hiding from the storm. We thought the bird would die, but in the morning the wind dropped and it woke up and hopped off.

Like all Kiwi baches, our tenure was precarious. We lived on a strip of waterfront land which, in the 1920s, had been carved off a farm and gifted to the local council by its public-spirited owner, who later asked the council for permission to build a bach on it. His was the first. Then a row of sections was created, and one by one the baches were built, loved, and grew old. In the late 1940s and early 50s another four baches were built with the council's approval. Proper leases were then drawn up (with an annual rental of £5). Some people lived in their baches permanently, some lived there part of the time. They were always concerned about making their tenure more secure. They talked to the council about land swaps, licences, leases, even outright ownership. In the end twenty-five-year licences were issued, expiring in 2014, which seemed a very long time away when we bought ours, but went by in a flash.

We always believed those licences would be renewed. We loved our bach, and as things turned out, we loved it to pieces. For most of a decade we swivelled between hope and despair.

Things were changing in our bay. The farmland over the road was bought by a developer and carved up for holiday-home sections. A real estate agent was promising unrestricted sea views and telling buyers that the baches would soon be gone. Little grey-green and brown houses began to pop up, of that boxy, fibrous kind of design New Zealanders seem to think suits beachfront and bays. They pushed up against each other on their tiny sections, forming a slab of drab in that bright blue-and-golden place. We thought them graceless, compared with our charming Kiwi baches, which even then were becoming national icons. They thought our baches primitive and shabby. Their owners were of the tidy kind and the weekends rang to the merry sounds of chainsaws and line trimmers.

A new ethic was taking root in the bay. The supermarket, which previously had posted a set of rules for the buskers outside its doors (not too loud and so on), had put up a new sign: 'Because of health and safety issues, no buskers allowed.'

Some young tourists had their campervan bashed and set on fire. A local woman said, loudly, that the freedom campers had got what they deserved. A man was taken into custody, facing attempted murder charges.

Pressure began to build on the council from our new neighbours: end their tenure, get rid of them. Three polls, however, showed that most people both in Ligar Bay in Golden Bay generally wanted the baches to stay. The local community board agonised over the question, heard all sides, produced a report. It took an Official Information Act request to wring it out of the council. They supported us and we almost cried with relief. But community boards were little more than a nod to local democracy.

The real power lay over the hill in the council's sprawling offices near Nelson. There they were creatures of permits and plans and zoning. They ignored the community board's report. They called for a hearing.

They booked a hall and we all trooped along. Inside a circle of jolly councillors exchanged banter with a trio of well-fed bureaucrats while we huddled on hard seats at the end of the room and I knew we were fucked.

And so we were. All of the bach-owners were there, even one seldom seen who, despite being terrified by the prospect of losing his house, had thought he'd probably have to stay home and milk his goat instead.

Our opposition was out in force too. We eyed them with interest. Until now they'd been anonymous. My God, wasn't that …? And that man over there, wasn't he …? But he'd always told us he was right behind us. With a knife, evidently.

And over there, why, there was a local councillor, a candidate for a political office who'd assured us that she'd vote against the move to oust us and had made much of bringing fellow councillors over the hill so they could find out what they were voting for, an attitude which slowly became diluted in her emails and disappeared on the day. She voted against us.

As the contingent from the 400-square-metre lots in the new subdivision over the road from the baches trotted out their stuff while by stern decree from the chair we were ordered to remain silent, I studied the councillors and their assembly and wondered if democracy really had come down to this: a day out, a facsimile meeting, a free lunch and a day's pay with allowances.

One of the officers read a roll-call of all the remaining baches in the Tasman District, a short list but poignant, and it became clear what they were saying: in three years' time there would not be a Kiwi bach left in the district. Then someone moved the motion and we were lost.

Sally sobbed beside me. We went home to our bach and walked hand in hand on the beach and watched the young karoro making their squeaky-wheel calls and we knew that these walks had numbers attached to them and we were counting down.

Our lawyer believed we had justice on our side and waived his fee. He was working in what he believed to be the public interest. He was indignant. He thought there were grounds for a judicial review. The council heard of his advice. It threatened us with hefty costs should we lose.

We were angry, in no mood for threats. We would fight on. Then something happened. Unforeseeable circumstances. Irresistible strength. Let's call it a force majeure. The 22 February 2011 earthquake ripped Christchurch apart. We filled our car with petrol and drove for fifteen hours to Golden Bay. Our bach was quiet, as it always was. But it had been raining heavily all day. Torrentially.

The stream began to rise. Night crept in. We heard rocks rumbling like marbles in the stream beside us and we assured each other that things always seemed much worse than they were, in the dark. Late in the evening I went outside once more, just to check. Water was bursting out of the culvert carrying the stream under the road, blasting away its banks. It was already lapping close to the house.

By the time we'd grabbed a few things, we had to wade out of the house through waist-deep water thick with mud. Our faithful Subaru, which had already rescued us from two earthquakes and taken a terrible pounding, had been parked on a terrace above the stream. But the stream was now a river and the terrace was sliding into it, along with the car. Hopeless, we knew, but we slid down too and climbed into it. The engine started. I turned the wheel, pressed the accelerator and to my amazement the car began to climb. Slowly, slipping half a metre backwards for every metre it gained, its four-wheel drive dragged us to safety. The road was disappearing too, but enough of it was left for us to drive around the headland where Abel's plinth stood tall and white against the storm.

We drove to a friend's house, hosed ourselves down, changed, poured a drink. Safe. For half an hour. The neighbours warned us. The cliff above was collapsing. We had to get out of that house. Right now.

We were evacuated a third time that awful night, from the local community hall where we'd taken refuge with our friends. It too was threatened. The civil defence people found us a motel. In the early hours I heard water. I got out of bed, walked onto the veranda. Water was lapping over it. The motels looked as if they were floating. Our friends came out of the unit next door. We shrugged. Enough was enough, we agreed, went back to bed and, surprisingly, fell asleep.

We awoke to a gaunt new world. Floodwaters were receding, but roads were blocked everywhere. Our bach was cut off by road, but we found a way round the back on foot. We arrived at what was, only a day before, the bridge over the stream. The bridge had gone. The bach had survived, but the section it stood on had disappeared and the house stood like a castle on a pinnacle.

It was a disaster too far. We wept, and drove out of the bay.

We couldn't get back into our bach. The land was too damaged. We could repair the site, and the house, and live there for the two remaining years of our licence. Barring judicial reviews, etc. Or we could relinquish the licence and leave.

I wrote to the council. You win, I said. We were angry, and bitter, but we'd had enough. We were going.

*

One bright morning a few years later the telephone rang. Garth had died. We hadn't seen him since we'd left; we were all too raw to revisit that part of our past. Now it seemed like a little part of our world had died with him.

We wept. Lovely Garth. A good man, and a decent one, who'd lived his life as well as he could, taking care of his corner, his marks on the earth being happy children, both his own and those he'd taught, and all things bright and beautiful in his gardens. He'd found a place he loved, and he'd wanted no other.

He and Lesley had found another house beside another estuary in the bay, for Golden Bay was full of intricate waterways and private places. The three boys were living overseas.

From Auckland, where we had moved, we flew south, landing in the soothing charm of Nelson. We drove through Motueka. There'd been trouble at the hill, of course. A cyclone had cut off Golden Bay completely. Food, milk, fuel and medical supplies were being shipped in by barge. People and cars could travel the same way, if they were prepared for a five-hour journey. People queued for seats on the local airline's little planes.

Golden Bay was used to being isolated, and hunkered down for the blast. Fuel was rationed, shopkeepers were reporting panic-buying. Tourists queued for information. The Hill slowly re-opened to traffic, but rebuilding the road had reduced it to a single lane. We edged past the slips, the full weight and rubble of the Marble Mountain above us, the abyss below. Neither of us had been back to the site of our lovely house. It was too painful, even years later. But this time, we had to.

There wasn't much left of our place. The council had promised that landscaping, and trees, and an idyllic foreshore would replace the baches, as well as a picnic area and a path. All that was there was a desiccated strip of ground. It looked like a rundown car park. A few rocks, some clumps of grass. The only trees were those we'd planted ourselves, or a few of them. The rest had been rooted out, evidently to give beachgoers a little more mud to spread themselves on. Of Garth's beautiful garden, only a couple of refugee trees remained, shivering.

Something far worse stood in their place. A plaque on a rock said that along this foreshore for over forty-five years there had existed 'nine private dwellings known as baches'. The baches had been removed 'after years of legal wrangling'. The council seemed to have had nothing to do with it, and was even grieving alongside us, for some bureaucrat had then composed a paean. It said, 'With the removal of these baches another slice of New Zealand culture in Golden Bay history will have gone.'

Gone? Wasted. Blasted. Kicked in the guts and left for dead. The flood's scars had grown over and there was no trace of me or my family, nor of anyone else who'd lived there. They'd taken away everything human and replaced it with … what? Over the road, the subdivision had grown into a standard modern holiday-home settlement in dull shades — ordinary, mundane. It showed no sign of life. The house owned by one of our most righteous critics was now partly hidden by an equally ordinary dwelling: he'd sold off the view he'd alleged we were blocking.

Garth and Lesley were the people who'd lost most in the scourge and their patience and kindliness had put me to shame. They'd been heartbroken, but they'd lost none of their humanity, their faith in the community, their goodness.

Now the family gathered in the little cemetery beside the old white East Takaka church. It was full, of people who'd loved Garth, neighbours and friends, and people whose lives had been woven into this place.

They'd wrapped Garth in a sail from the old Idle-Along yacht he'd sailed so often and lowered him into the grave. We covered him with flowers and seashells.

I stood there in the sunshine, looking at these people we'd known for so many years, and I thought of the bay, and the life, and the beauty, and all the anger that had darkened my soul seemed to evaporate in the blue sky.

We wept for Garth, and for Lesley, and I thought of my own long, lucky life so entwined with this place, so much a part of the south, and knew then that my search for the golden fleece was over. I'd found it, here.

ACKNOWLEDGEMENTS

Thank you to the many people who helped me with this book, in particular Madge Snow, Richard Bailey, Richard Herdman, Nicky Anderson, Mike Ward, Lawry Jury, Janet and Bruce Moffitt, Cameron Ealam, Tony Kokshoorn, Evan Birchfield, Elisabeth Frankish (and Victoria and Archer), the Brays and my lifetime partner, support and love, Sally. I'm grateful to my publisher, Alex Hedley, and editor, Scott Forbes, for their encouragement, support and care.